Thomas Brown

Selected Philosophical Writings

Edited and Introduced
by Thomas Dixon

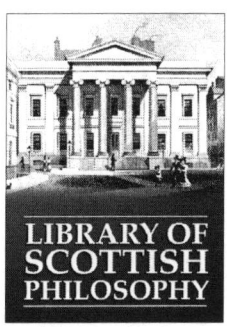

IMPRINT ACADEMIC

Copyright © Thomas Dixon, 2010

The moral rights of the author have been asserted
No part of any contribution may be reproduced in any form
without permission, except for the quotation of brief passages
in criticism and discussion.

Published in the UK by Imprint Academic
PO Box 200, Exeter EX5 5YX, UK

Published in the USA by Imprint Academic
Philosophy Documentation Center
PO Box 7147, Charlottesville, VA 22906-7147, USA

ISBN 978 1845401627
A CIP catalogue record for this book is available from the
British Library and US Library of Congress

Full series details:

www.imprint-academic.com/losp

Contents

Series Editor's Note v

I Introduction 1

II Observations
Selection 1. Preface 31
Selection 2. On Instinct 37
Selection 3. On Generation 39

III Inquiry
Selection 4. Preface 43
Selection 5. The Real Import of the Relation
              of Cause and Effect 46
Selection 6. Mr Hume's Definition of a Cause 49
Selection 7. Physical and Efficient Causes
              and the Will of the Deity 52
Selection 8. Mr Hume's Essay on Miracles 59
Selection 9. Mr Hume on Customary Conjunction 65
Selection 10. Mr Hume and Dr Reid on the Idea of Power 73
Selection 11. Scepticism, Atheism, and the Existence of God . . 83

IV Sketch
Selection 12. Mental Phenomena 89
Selection 13. Philosophy of the Human Mind
              Comprehensive of Many Sciences 90
Selection 14. Analysis of Mind and Matter 93
Selection 15. Of the Sensations Commonly Ascribed to Touch . 98
Selection 16. Classification of Mental Phenomena:
              Condillac and Reid 123

V Lectures

Selection 17. Consciousness 127
Selection 18. Classification of the Phenomena of Mind 134
Selection 19. Emotions 147
Selection 20. Sympathy 153
Selection 21. Ethics 161
Selection 22. Virtue and Moral Emotion 165
Selection 23. William Paley and Adam Smith 171
Selection 24. Moral Sense and Moral Emotion 179

Index 189

Series Editor's Note

The principal purpose of volumes in this series is not to provide scholars with accurate editions, but to make the writings of Scottish philosophers accessible to a new generation of modern readers in an attractively produced and competitively priced format. In accordance with this purpose, certain changes have been made to the original texts:

- Spelling and punctuation have been modernized.
- In some cases, the selected passages have been given new titles.
- Some original footnotes and references have not been included.
- Some extracts have been shortened from their original length.
- Quotations from Greek have been transliterated, and passages in foreign languages translated, or omitted altogether.

Care has been taken to ensure that in no instance do these amendments truncate the argument or alter the meaning intended by the original author. For readers who want to consult the original texts, full bibliographical details are provided for each extract.

The Library of Scottish Philosophy was originally an initiative of the Centre for the Study of Scottish Philosophy at the University of Aberdeen and the first six volumes were commissioned with financial support from the Carnegie Trust for the Universities of Scotland. In 2006 the CSSP became one of three research centers within the Special Collections of Princeton Theological Seminary, and subsequent volumes have received financial support from the Seminary. The selections in this volume were prepared for publication by Mr James Foster, Editorial Assistant to the CSSP at Princeton.

Acknowledgements

The CSSP gratefully acknowledges the financial support of the Carnegie Trust and Princeton Seminary, the enthusiasm and excellent service of the publisher Imprint Academic, and the permission of the University of Aberdeen Special Collections and Libraries to use the engraving of the *Faculty of Advocates* (1829) as the logo for the series.

Gordon Graham,
Princeton, May 2010

I
Introduction

Thomas Brown's Place in Nineteenth-Century Philosophy

Thomas Brown was one of the most influential and widely read British philosophers of the first half of the nineteenth century. As Professor of Moral Philosophy in Edinburgh from 1810 until his early death in 1820, Brown delivered a series of lectures on the philosophy of the human mind which, in their published form, went through numerous editions, winning him a reputation for metaphysical brilliance on both sides of the Atlantic. His thought provided a bridge between the Scottish school of "Common Sense" associated with Thomas Reid, and the later positivism of John Stuart Mill and others.[1] Brown shared with his Common Sense predecessors the view that certain beliefs, such as the belief in an external world and in causation, were primary and irresistible intuitions. In other ways, however, Brown's thought had more in common with eighteenth-century sceptics and empiricists, including such figures as David Hume and Etienne de Condillac. As James Mackintosh put it, much of Brown's philosophy constituted "an open revolt against the authority of Reid."[2] Writing in 1900, Leslie Stephen suggested that Brown was "the last in the genuine line of Scottish common-sense philosophers" and that his thought illustrated the gravitation of that school towards "pure empiricism."[3]

Thomas Brown made significant contributions to several areas of philosophy. In the philosophy of perception he emphasised the importance of the "muscle sense" in bringing about beliefs in external objects. In the philosophy of the human mind, Brown rejected the

---

[1] For useful general characterisations of Brown's philosophy, see Welsh 1825; Mackintosh 1837, pp. 335-52; McCosh 1875, pp. 317-37; Stephen 1900, pp. 267-87; Harris 2002b; Copleston 2003, pp. 383-92; Stewart-Robertson 2004; Paoletti 2006. On the Scottish Common Sense school, see McCosh 1875; Grave 1960; Martin 1961; Davie 2000.
[2] Mackintosh 1837, p. 345.
[3] Leslie 1900, p. 285.

traditional faculty psychology, which posited such entities as the will and the intellect, and reduced all mental phenomena instead to a series of associated "states" or "affections." These he divided into three categories: sensations, thoughts, and emotions. His was one of the first and most sustained treatments of the "emotions" as a coherent psychological category, which would come to subsume and supersede established categories such as the "passions," "affections," or "active powers" of the mind.[4] In the philosophy of science, Brown was rigorously phenomenalist, rejecting all metaphysical entities, whether subtle fluids, mental faculties, or causal powers. His *Inquiry into the Relation of Cause and Effect* (1818) provided a perceptive and influential commentary on the views of David Hume, and also gave the first unambiguous defence of what has become known as the "uniformity" or "regularity" view of causation.[5] Although many expressed concerns over Brown's apparent lack of Christian orthodoxy, and over his reduction of moral judgements to the experience of a particular kind of emotions, his *Lectures* and his *Inquiry* both included reasoned arguments in favour of theistic belief.

Brown's reputation was at its height during the two decades after the posthumous publication of his *Lectures* in 1820. These were widely acknowledged to be the most successful and popular work of their kind ever to have appeared. Henry Cockburn described the book as one of the most "delightful books in the English language," which had enjoyed "unexampled success."[6] The historian of Scottish Common Sense philosophy, James McCosh, painted a vivid picture of the impact of Brown's lectures:

> A course so eminently popular among students had not, I rather think, been delivered in any previous age in the University of Edinburgh, and has not, in a later age, been surpassed… In the last age you would have met, in Edinburgh and all over Scotland, with ministers and lawyers who fell into raptures when they spoke of his lectures.

The published version of the lectures enjoyed "a popularity in the British dominions and in the United States greater than any philosophical work ever enjoyed before." "The writer of this article,"

---

[4] Selections 18 and 19. I have written about Brown's role as the "inventor of the emotions' in Dixon 2003, pp. 109-34, 2006, pp. 27-31.
[5] Psillos 2010, forthcoming.
[6] Cockburn 1909, p. 347.

McCosh added, "would give much to have revived within him the enthusiasm which he felt when he first read them."[7] Writing at the end of the nineteenth century, the British philosopher Robert Adamson wrote of the *Lectures*: "It is no exaggeration to say that never before or since has a work on metaphysics been so popular."[8]

Several former Edinburgh students later wrote about the experience of hearing Thomas Brown lecture in person. The historian and philosopher J. D. Morell recalled:

> The style was so captivating, the views so comprehensive, the arguments so acute, the whole thing so complete, that I was almost insensibly borne along upon the stream of his reasoning and eloquence. Naturally enough I became a zealous disciple; I accepted his mental analysis as almost perfect; I defended his doctrine of causation; with him I stood in astonishment at the alleged obtuseness of Reid.[9]

Sir Walter Scott's son-in-law John Gibson Lockhart included an account of a lecture by Brown in his fictionalised portrait of Edinburgh society, *Peter's Letters to his Kinsfolk* (1819). The students in the lecture room awaiting Brown's appearance, in Lockhart's version of the scene, include "a Pyrrhonist from Inverness-shire" alongside an "embryo clergyman" hoping for enlightenment about cause and effect and "feeling rather qualmish after having read that morning Hume's Sceptical Solution of Sceptical Doubts." Nearer the professor's table sits "a crack member of some crack debating-club." At last the dandyish Professor himself arrives "with a pleasant smile upon his face, arrayed in a black Geneva cloak, over a snuff-coloured coat and a buff waistcoat" with a "physiognomy very expressive of mildness and quiet contemplativeness." Brown's elocution is "distinct and elegant" and his metaphysics enlivened by quotations from the poets.[10]

Brown's fastidious manner and poetical style were not, however, to everyone's taste, and the positive appraisals of his work could seem embarrassingly overdone. The poet Edwin Atherstone's exuberant praise of Brown in 1831 was a case in point. "For myself," Atherstone wrote, "I know not a writer, with the exception of Shakespeare, Milton, Homer, and Scott, from whom I have derived such

---

[7] McCosh 1875, pp. 322-4.
[8] Quoted in Trotter 1901, p. 431. On the Lectures see also Welsh 1825; Harris 2002b.
[9] Morell 1846, pp. vi-vii.
[10] Morris 1819, vol. 1, pp. 173-8.

high delight as from Dr Brown."[11] This was too much for one reviewer. "Was ever such a category put on paper before?" he asked. "It is as if a man should say his favourite musical instruments were the organ, the harp, the trumpet, the violin, and the sewing-machine."[12] Thomas Carlyle might have agreed, recalling Brown as "an eloquent acute little gentleman, full of enthusiasm about simple suggestions, relative, etc." which he found utterly dry and uninteresting.[13] Carlyle described the "immaculate Dr Brown" as "a really pure, high, if rather shrill and wire-drawing kind of a man"; and is reported to have referred to him as "Miss Brown" and "that little man who spouted poetry."[14] Another contemporary commentator, Mrs Anne Macvicar Grant, wrote from Edinburgh to a friend in Glasgow of Brown's "great fertility of mind" and "delightful variety of intelligence and playfulness in conversation, which, in the long run, conquers the prejudice resulting from a manner so affected and so odd, that there is no describing it."[15]

Brown's influence was felt well beyond the lecture halls of Edinburgh. His readers included not only British and American university students who read his *Lectures* as a textbook, and the educated public at large, but also many of the most distinguished thinkers of the nineteenth century. John Stuart Mill was influenced by Brown and defended him against a ferocious attack by the Kantian metaphysician William Hamilton.[16] Another of Mill's philosophical antagonists, William Whewell, had also been engaged by Brown's philosophy as a young man, writing to a friend in 1822: "Have you read Brown's books? They are dashing, and on some material points strongly wrong, but about cause and effect he has an admirable clearness of view and happiness of illustration."[17] In the United States, Brown's works were widely reviewed in the periodical press and were particularly championed by Samuel Gilman and Francis March.[18] The American philosopher Noah Porter wrote in 1874 that "The influence of Brown's terminology and of his methods and conclusions has been potent in the formation and consolidation of the

---

[11] Napier 1879, p. 107.
[12] Browne 1879, p. 447.
[13] Froude 1882, vol. 1, p. 25.
[14] Shepherd 1881, pp. 16-17; Jessop 2004.
[15] Grant 1845, pp. 99-100.
[16] [Hamilton] 1830 repr. in. Hamilton 1853, pp. 39-99; Mill 1865b, pp. 153-89.
[17] Quoted in Snyder 2006, p. 47n.
[18] [Gilman] 1821, 1824, 1825; [March] 1860.

Associational Psychology – represented by J. Mill, J. S. Mill, Alexander Bain and Herbert Spencer."[19] William James would later recall, when delivering his Gifford Lectures in Edinburgh, that he had spent his youth "immersed in Dugald Stewart and Thomas Brown," whose works had inspired "juvenile emotions of reverence" that he had not yet outgrown.[20] Brown could count among his nineteenth-century admirers positivists, empiricists and pragmatists. But another of his most enthusiastic followers was the leader of the evangelical revival that culminated in the 1843 Disruption in the Scottish church, Thomas Chalmers. And it was one of Chalmers" deputies in the evangelical movement, the church historian David Welsh, who was to become Brown's biographer.[21]

Brown's reputation did not diminish considerably before 1850, and after that primarily through the influence of William Hamilton and his circle (of which Thomas Carlyle was also a member). The reprinting of Hamilton's 1830 *Edinburgh Review* article, "Philosophy of Perception: Reid and Brown" in his *Discussions* in 1852 made available to a much wider audience in Britain and America a savage attack on Brown's philosophical competence and probity. Hamilton accused Brown of silently appropriating his ideas from French sources and of completely misunderstanding the philosophy of Thomas Reid. Several significant discussions of the philosophy of perception, with particular reference to Brown and Hamilton, were subsequently published. Two of these (by John Stuart Mill and by Francis March) staunchly defended Brown and accused Hamilton, in turn, of misrepresentation and intellectual dishonesty.[22] Even Hamilton seems to have had at least some second thoughts about his assault on Brown. In the republished version of the 1830 article, after a section describing Brown's interpretation of Reid's philosophy as "not a simple misconception, but an absolute reversal of its real and even unambiguous import," Hamilton added the terse parenthetical observation: "This is too strong."[23]

In France, where Brown's lectures made less of an impact (and were never translated), the reception was, again, mixed. François Réthoré, Professor of Logic in Tours and the principal French com-

---

[19]   Porter 1874, p. 410.
[20]   James 1902, p. 2.
[21]   On Welsh's life and thought see Dunlop 1846; Harris 2002a.
[22]   Alison 1853; [March] 1860; Maguire 1860; Mill 1865b, pp. 153-89.
[23]   Hamilton 1853, p. 60.

mentator on Brown, described him as the greatest metaphysician Scotland had ever produced.[24] Victor Cousin, on the other hand, thought Brown a very mediocre philosopher, and one who had been responsible for giving Hume's theory of cause and effect a "deplorable popularity" in both Britain and America. He also considered Brown to be an "infidel."[25] In 1834, having recently received a copy of the seventh edition of Brown's *Lectures*, Cousin wrote to William Hamilton to encourage him to keep up the fight against Brown's influence: "Mon Dieu! Luttez, mon cher Monsieur, luttez sans cesse contre cette funeste popularité." Hamilton wrote back that he was "delighted to find you estimating Brown at his proper value."[26]

Education and Early Life: Physician, Philosopher, Poet

Thomas Brown was born on 9 January 1778, the thirteenth and youngest child of Reverend Samuel Brown, Minister of Kirkmabreck, Galloway, and his wife Margaret. Reverend Brown died in Thomas's infancy. Having been tutored at home in Edinburgh by his mother, and schooled in England under the care of his uncle, Brown enrolled in the University of Edinburgh in the winter of 1792-3, just before his fifteenth birthday. He followed a wide variety of courses, including logic (with Professor James Finlayson) and moral philosophy (with Professor Dugald Stewart), before embarking on legal studies. He did not persist in this course, however, turning instead to medicine, and eventually taking his MD in 1803. Brown practised as a physician from 1803 onwards, entering into partnership in 1806 with Dr James Gregory, Professor of the Practice of Physic in the university. Brown only ceased medical practice when he was appointed to the chair of moral philosophy in 1810.

During Brown's years of study, he made friends with a group who were to become enormously influential through their founding of the *Edinburgh Review*. The three most important events during these years were Brown's involvement in the founding of a new natural-philosophical student society, the Academy of Physics in 1797; his publication, in 1798, of a substantial critique of Erasmus Darwin's *Zoonomia* (1794-6); and his contributions to the early numbers of the *Edinburgh Review*. This fertile formative period, from

---

[24] Réthoré 1863, p. 247.
[25] Maine de Biran 1834, pp. xxv-xxvi.
[26] Veitch 1869, pp. 153-4.

1797-1803, was the source of all the key ideas that he would develop further in his mature philosophical works.

On 7 January 1797, two days before his nineteenth birthday, Brown was one of a group of Edinburgh students who met to found a philosophical club called the Academy of Physics. The driving force behind the society was Henry Brougham, who would go on to become Lord Chancellor. Other founder members included Brown's good friends John Leyden, William Erskine and James Reddie. Francis Horner and Francis Jeffrey (later the first editor of the *Edinburgh Review*) subsequently joined too. Five to ten students would be present at each meeting to hear and discuss a paper on a subject in physics, chemistry, philosophy or history. Brown gave a few papers himself, including one on the philosophy of heat, and was acting as secretary to the Academy at the time of its dissolution, to be superseded by a new Chemical Society, in May 1800. Brown's attendance at the Academy provided an opportunity for him to discuss the views on natural philosophy and metaphysics that became central to his responses to Erasmus Darwin. The Academy had agreed on a philosophical manifesto including the statements that mind existed and matter existed, but that nothing could be known of their essences, and that "Every change indicates a cause but of the Nature of necessary connection we are entirely ignorant." These principles embodied the same sparse metaphysics, and phenomenalist epistemology, which Brown would espouse in all his later published works. [27]

The young Brown's first performance on the public stage as a writer and metaphysician came during this same student period. His *Observations on the Zoonomia of Erasmus Darwin* (1798) was described by James Mackintosh as "the perhaps unmatched work of a boy in the eighteenth year of his age."[28] The book gained Brown an early reputation for philosophical acumen as well as the nickname "Darwinian Brown."[29] Erasmus Darwin (grandfather of Charles) was, as Brown would later be, a poet, a physician, and a philosopher. He had, like Brown, studied medicine in Edinburgh, although almost half a century earlier. Alongside the posthumously published *Temple of Nature* (1803), and *The Botanic Garden* (1789-91), Dar-

---

[27] Academy of Physics Minute Book, National Library of Scotland, Acc. 10,073/1, pp. 41-4. See also Welsh 1825, pp. 77-9, 498-506; Cantor 1975.
[28] Mackintosh 1837, p. 336.
[29] Bain 1882, p. 48.

win's *Zoonomia, or, The Laws of Organic Life* (1794-6) was his most important published work.[30] *Zoonomia* was controversial for its suggestion that all living things had developed from a common ancestor, and for its materialistic account of mind.

Prior to publishing his *Observations*, Brown had sent a manuscript version of his criticisms to Darwin, which led to a somewhat heated correspondence. This correspondence started in October 1796, when Brown was indeed only eighteen years old, and continued into the following year, during the period of the founding of the Academy of Physics. It may have been the realisation that he was dealing with a mere student that contributed to the irritation evident in some of Darwin's responses to Brown. One of these was omitted by Welsh from his account of Brown's life on the grounds that it cannot possibly have been intended for future publication. In his response to this particular letter Brown refers to Darwin's "angry feelings" and to "the contemptible light in which you view the manuscript." On the envelope of one of his letters to Brown, Darwin scribbled: "I wrote the inclosed [sic] at a public house when I was much fatigued, and I fear you will not be able to decipher it. … I do not recollect any other of your objections, but I thought them all easily answered."[31]

In the *Zoonomia*, Darwin had constructed a Romantic metaphysics, opposing mechanistic accounts of life with his own brand of vitalism. Naturally, in the 1790s, in the immediate aftermath of the French Revolution, political anxieties about the implications of materialism and atheism were intense. Although, at the beginning of the work, Darwin endorsed the standard metaphysics of the day — including the separation between two substances, spirit and matter — as the work progressed it would have become clear to his readers that Darwin was not using the word "spirit" in a conventional sense. Darwin rather used the terms "spirit," "spirit of animation" and "living principle" to refer to a subtle fluid, "which resides throughout the body," but especially in the brain and nerves; which may be "matter of a finer kind," and which causes contraction of animal fibres. This "spirit of animation," Darwin argued, even if it may be, in some ambiguous sense, immaterial, must be able to assume the

---

[30] On Darwin, see Stirling 1894, Ch's 2 and 3; King-Hele 1963, Ch. 4; Primer 1964; King-Hele 1977, Ch. 12, 1986, p. 14; McNeil 1987, pp. 100-5; Porter 1989.
[31] Welsh 1825, pp. 44-66; King-Hele 1981, pp. 298-303.

property of solidity in order to interact causally with the muscles and limbs.[32]

Brown's response in his *Observations* undertook a sometimes wearyingly detailed unpicking of the arguments of *Zoonomia*, focusing especially on the appeal to subtle fluids and on the associated, apparently materialistic, account of mind. In the course of this critique can be found the seeds of many of Brown's later philosophical positions. It is here, for example, that we find the first indication of certain views, later described as "positivist" by John Stuart Mill and others:

> To philosophize is nothing more, than to register the appearances of nature, and to mark those, which each is accustomed to succeed; and, though we have words, which seem to express, causation, we shall find, if we examine the ideas signified, that they merely state the existence of a change.

Philosophy should be, Brown argued, "nothing more than the statement of a series of phenomena." It was for these reasons that Darwin's appeal to unobservable subtle fluids was unphilosophical. If natural philosophy was in the business of describing mere regularities in phenomena, nothing was added to the account by appealing to the action of unseen substances supposedly intervening between the observed causes (such as stimulation of the bodily senses) and observed effects (such as mental sensations).

This rejection of the interposition of an ethereal fluid between mental and physical events would be extended in Brown's later writing on cause and effect to a rejection of any intervening item at all, whether an ethereal "fluid" or a mysterious "power," between causes and effects. In the *Observations*, this minimalist account of causation was also used to attack Darwin's alleged materialism. "The systems of materialism," Brown wrote, "owe their rise to the groundless belief that we are acquainted with the nature of causation." The difference between the materialist and the "mentalist," as Brown termed himself, was that the latter was prepared to admit ignorance of the manner in which material changes caused mental changes, whereas the former claimed to know that ideas were constituted by the movements of an unobserved subtle fluid.[33]

---

[32] Darwin 1794-6, vol. 1, pp. 10-12, 23-30, 109-16.
[33] Selection 1. Brown 1798, Preface.

The selections from the *Observations* included below illustrate Brown's opposition to materialism and subtle fluids; his stance on philosophical method and the nature of causation; and also his scepticism about Darwin's controversial view that the "various species of animal, and vegetable life" had proceeded "from a single living filament, susceptible of modification, by the accretion of parts, and by its own exertions."[34]

Opposition to materialism also set the tone for several articles written by Brown for the *Edinburgh Review* in 1802-3. The core members of the Academy of Physics and the founders of the *Edinburgh Review* were in large measure the same people. They had attended Dugald Stewart's moral philosophy lectures, were Whigs rather than Tories, tended more towards rational and natural religion than full-blown Christianity, and were also united by a worldview based on reverence for inductive natural philosophy. The names of Bacon and Newton had almost saintly status for these individuals.[35] Brown contributed six articles in the first year of the review's existence, including one criticising Thomas Belsham's materialistic philosophy of mind, and another casting a sceptical eye at the new science of phrenology.[36] Brown also contributed an article on the philosophy of Immanuel Kant, one of the first on this subject to be published in Britain. The article reviewed a summary of Kant by the French philosopher Charles Villers.[37] The fact that Brown based his account on a secondary French source rather than on the original German has, understandably, been a cause for criticism. René Wellek's judgment on Brown's review, in his 1931 study on *Immanuel Kant in England, 1793-1838*, was that Brown had succeeded only in destroying a philosophical idol who bore the faintest of similarities to the real Kant, and that he thus misled and deterred many potential readers of Kant unnecessarily.[38] James McCosh wrote of Brown's article simply that "the whole review is a blunder."[39]

Brown's main criticism of the Kantian system as he understood it was that it failed, despite its claims, to establish a third way between dogmatism and scepticism. He added that there was an unnecessary

---

[34] Selection 3. Brown 1798, p. 463.
[35] Clive 1957; Cantor 1975, pp. 131-4.
[36] [Brown] 1803b, 1803c.
[37] Villers 1801.
[38] Wellek 1931, pp. 32-8.
[39] McCosh 1875, p. 320.

"minuteness of nomenclature" in the system, which did not correspond to the discovery of a comparable number of new facts or relations.[40] He would later make the same criticism of Reid and the Common Sense school.[41] It was perhaps fitting that Brown's influence and reputation would be seriously damaged later in the century by the efforts of William Hamilton, who was both a Kantian and the leading nineteenth-century proponent of the Scottish Common Sense philosophy. Through Hamilton, the Kantians ultimately had their revenge for Brown's youthful dismissal of their system.[42]

The following year, 1804, saw the publication of Brown's first volume of poetry. Sir Walter Scott wrote to a friend: "Tom Brown is well, but having published a collection of poems which were rather too metaphysical for the public taste, he has become shyer than ever."[43] Brown seems to have been alone in thinking his time and talents equally well used in composing poetry as in writing and teaching metaphysics. Cockburn recalled that "His friend Dr Gregory described his poetry as too philosophical, and his philosophy as too poetical."[44] Welsh recorded, similarly, that there was increasing consternation during the later years of Brown's life about the frequency with which he published new poetical works and the amount of time he spent on these at the expense of philosophy.[45] The most successful of Brown's poetical works was *The Paradise of Coquettes* (1814), which was published anonymously, and reviewed favourably by Jeffrey in the *Edinburgh Review*.[46] His collected poetical works were published in four volumes posthumously in 1820. There was never any demand for a second edition.[47]

The Leslie Affair: Cause and Effect

The "Leslie Affair" of 1805-6 provided the occasion for Brown's first mature philosophical work, his treatise on cause and effect. The idea

---

[40] [Brown] 1803a, pp. 263-4.
[41] Brown 1828, Lecture 32, p. 207.
[42] McCosh 1875, pp. 319-20 makes the same point. On Hamilton's philosophy see Tropea 2001.
[43] Grierson 1932, p. 309.
[44] Cockburn 1909, p. 347.
[45] Welsh 1825, pp. 393-4.
[46] [Jeffrey] 1814.
[47] On the relationship between Brown's metaphysics and his poetry, see Rands 1970, 1974.

behind all three editions of this work was simple. There was nothing more to causation than uniform succession:

> It is this mere relation of uniform antecedence, so important and so universally believed, which appears to me to constitute *all* that can be philosophically meant, in the words *power* or *causation*, to whatever objects, material or spiritual, the words may be applied.[48]

Brown gave an even more succinct formulation in his *Lectures*:

> To express, shortly, what appears to me to be the only intelligible meaning of the three most important words in physics, immediate invariable antecedence is power; the immediate invariable antecedent, in any sequence, is a cause; the immediate invariable consequent is the correlative effect.[49]

Brown's treatment of causation was widely praised from the outset, first as a controversial pamphlet in 1805, through its development into a more substantial second edition the following year, and then into its fullest and final form, the weighty *Inquiry into the Relation of Cause and Effect* of 1818, from which several selections are given below. Brown's friend Erskine described the *Inquiry* as "the first perfect work on a metaphysical subject" and "the crown of modern metaphysics."[50] A possibly more impartial judge, Henry Buckle, considered the book to be "one of the greatest which the century has produced."[51] The Scottish philosopher Alexander Campbell Fraser later referred to it as a book which had exercised "so considerable an influence in my early education."[52]

The controversy that gave rise to Brown's treatise concerned the proposed appointment of John Leslie to the Edinburgh chair of natural philosophy. Leslie, the favoured candidate of the evangelical wing of the church, had enthusiastically endorsed Hume's account of causation. Opponents of his appointment, wishing to see a local clergyman appointed, now claimed that this endorsement of Hume by Leslie implied religious heterodoxy.[53] Brown and Dugald Stewart were both prominent among those who sprang to Leslie's

---

[48] Selection 5. Brown 1818, p. 15.
[49] Brown 1828, Lecture 7, p. 38.
[50] Quoted in Welsh 1825, pp. 154, 454.
[51] Quoted in Burke 1970, pp. 342-3.
[52] Fraser 1904, pp. 83-4.
[53] On the details of the Leslie case see Clark 1962; Morrell 1975.

defence.[54] The incident serves as a useful illustration both of the complexity of religious and political alliances in the university (in this case Christian evangelicals and religious rationalists found themselves allied against the moderate wing of the church), and also of the way that local political circumstances can provide both the motive and the occasion for the production of new philosophical works. In this case, Brown's desire to see the Edinburgh Town Council abandon its custom of appointing only ordained ministers to chairs was the motive, and the furore surrounding Leslie's candidature, and his endorsement of Hume, was the occasion.

The product was the 1805 pamphlet, in which Brown argued that Hume's doctrine in no way tended towards infidelity. In fact, Brown argued, the reverse was the case. It was those who believed in the reality of a third item — some causal power intervening between cause and effect — who were demeaning the Deity. On his theory, Brown concluded, the glory of the Creator was increased, "by destroying that supposed connecting link between the antecedent will of the Deity and the consequent rise of the World, which, if it be not greater than the Creating Will, must at least seem to divide with it the grandeur and the glory of the Magnificent Effect."[55] Despite the ingenuity of the argument, and the successful appointment of Leslie to the chair, the allegation that this view of causation undermined causal arguments for the existence of God persisted, notably in Lady Mary Shepherd's 1824 *Essay Upon the Relation of Cause and Effect*.[56]

Brown's ideas about causation continue to be invoked in contemporary philosophical discussions. Stathis Psillos has made a particular study of Brown's view, which he describes as "intricate, deep and interesting" and as a partially successful attempt to "carve a conceptual space between Reid and Hume and to combine the thought that causation as it is in the world is invariable sequence with the thought that belief in causality need not require observations of invariable successions." In light of this, Psillos suggests, Brown's place in the history of thought about causation "needs to be favourably

---

[54] Wright 2005.
[55] Selection 4. Brown 1818, pp. xiii-xiv. See also Selections 7, 8 and 11 for Brown's account of the role of the Deity.
[56] [Shepherd] 1824, pp. 136-51; Blakey 1848, vol. 4, pp. 39-46. Wright 2005, pp. 338-40 provides an excellent summary of the theological issues at stake.

re-assessed."[57] Such a reassessment of Brown's *Inquiry* might examine three particular aspects of its importance: first as an extended critique of David Hume's theory of causation; secondly as the first substantial defence of the "uniformity" or "regularity" view of cause and effect; and finally as a source of later positivist ideas.

Bernard Rollin has written that the *Inquiry* "probably contains more careful, detailed, textually documented criticisms of Hume's theories than any work which preceded it."[58] Brown disagreed with Hume about the source of our unshakeable belief in the necessity of causal connections. Hume argued that it came from habit or custom; that the many times we had observed B follow A in the past led us, on seeing A the next time, automatically to expect that B must again follow. Brown argued, on the other hand, that the notion of a causal connection between A and B was a simple intuition, not an idea that was a copy of any impression or series of impressions, nor the product of a rational inference: "it is intuition, only, that passes over the darkness that is impenetrable to our vision, and speaks to us, as from another world, of the things which are beyond."[59] Brown emphasised that, as Hume had himself recognised, it did not follow any more from our seeing a stone fall a thousand times than it did from our seeing it fall once that it would always fall in the future:

> [T]he propositions *B has once succeeded A*, and *B will for ever succeed A*, are not more different, nor less comprehensive the one of the other, than the propositions *B has a thousand times succeeded A*, and *B will for ever succeed A*. Why should the future resemble the past? At every stage of observation, this question may be equally put; and, at every stage, it is equally unanswerable.[60]

In other words, although we cannot justify the practice, we cannot help projecting past regularities into the future. But, for Brown, we are addicted to such projection from birth, not addicted to it by repeated experience, as Hume would have us believe. In this case Brown displayed his affinity with the teachings of the Common Sense school, and dissented from the Humean account. [61]

---

[57] Psillos 2011.
[58] Rollin 1977, p. ix.
[59] Selection 9. Brown 1818, p. 356.
[60] Selection 9. Brown 1818, pp. 356-7. See also Brown 1828, Lecture 6, p. 35.
[61] For further discussions of Brown and Hume on causation see also Rollin 1969, 1977; Mills 1984; McRobert 2000; Fieser 2005, vol. 2, pp. 69-76; Harris 2005; Wright 2005; Psillos 2010, esp. pp. 136-9, 2011.

In other key respects, however, Brown definitively rejected the Common Sense school's analysis of the problem. Brown took Reid and his followers to task for alleging that Hume thought we lacked any meaningful notion of causal power. Brown explained that Reid and others had wrongly ascribed to Hume the following syllogism: "We have no idea which is not a copy of some impression; we have no impression of power; we therefore have no idea of power." When in fact what Hume argued was: "We have no idea which is not a copy of some impression; but we have an idea of power; there must therefore be some impression from which that idea is derived."[62] This then returned Brown to the question of the true source of the idea of causation, which, as we have seen, he held to be innate and which Hume had suggested was acquired.

Brown also struck out into new territory by providing the first substantial defence of the "uniformity" or "regularity" view of causation, and by countering Reid's famous objection that on this account night must be considered the cause of day.[63] The regularity view has sometimes been attributed to Hume. In fact the idea of causation, for Hume, involved not just an idea of uniform temporal succession but also one of necessary connection. There is much dispute over how to interpret Hume on this point.[64] But Norman Kemp Smith and others have denied that Hume was an exponent of the mere "uniformity" view. "Thomas Brown is the first and outstanding exponent of the uniformity view of causation," Kemp Smith wrote, "and has been eulogised by Mill precisely on this account."[65] Brown asserted that "cause" and "power" simply meant invariable antecedence; whereas Hume's point was that, however hard we looked for causal power, all we perceived was invariable antecedence.

Although Brown's philosophical writings on cause and effect preceded by three decades the creation of the *Philosophie Positive* by Auguste Comte, it was certainly the case that later British thinkers

---

[62] Selection 10. Brown 1818, pp. 442-3.
[63] For Brown's response to Reid's well-known objection that, on this view, night should be considered the cause of day, see Selection 9. Brown 1818, pp. 384-7.
[64] On the place of this issue of Humean interpretation within the broader "New Hume" debate, see Strawson 1989; Psillos 2002, Ch. 1; Beebee 2006; Craig 2007.
[65] Smith 1941, p. 91n. This is reiterated by Strawson 1989, p. 7n.; Psillos 2010, pp. 136-9.

sympathetic to positivism (including Buckle and Mill) saw in Brown an able thinker who could be posthumously recruited to their cause. Leslie Stephen, in his 1900 volume on James Mill, wrote that Brown followed Hume and anticipated Comte in his insistence that "cause" did not mean power, but merely invariable antecedence. Brown, Stephen concluded, was a man "clearly on the way to positivism."[66] Mill was influenced in his own thinking on causation by reading Brown's *Inquiry* in 1822. He, like Stephen, seems to have thought that Brown's and Hume's views on causation were identical, and that both were also largely identical with Comte's view:

> Among the direct successors of Hume, the writer who has best stated and defended Comte's fundamental doctrine is Dr Thomas Brown. The doctrine and spirit of Brown's philosophy are entirely Positivist, and no better introduction to Positivism than the early part of his *Lectures* has yet been produced.[67]

John P. Wright has demonstrated, furthermore, that later logical positivists, in adopting David Hume as a celebrated forerunner of their own views on science and causation, were in fact adopting Brown's views rather than Hume's.[68]

Revolting Against Reid: The Philosophy of the Human Mind

Like John Leslie and many others before him, Thomas Brown had to overcome local political and theological resistance before he could be elected to a chair at Edinburgh University. Doubts about Brown, a layman with Whig sympathies, had hampered his candidacy for the chairs of rhetoric and of logic. But the vigorous support of Dugald Stewart, the proviso that Brown should be appointed jointly with Stewart and not solely in his own right, and the support of some influential Tories, including Dr James Gregory, ensured that Brown was eventually appointed Professor of Moral Philosophy on 2 May 1810. In practice, he had already taken over from Stewart, whose health had prevented him from continuing to lecture. Francis Horner wrote to Brown a few days later to congratulate him that "the interests of philosophical opinion in Scotland" had been "rescued from the danger which seemed to threaten them with complete ruin, of the chair of Moral Philosophy being filled by one of those political

---

[66] Stephen 1900, p. 273.
[67] Mill 1865a, p. 8.
[68] Wright 2005, pp. 345-7.

priests who have already brought such disgrace upon the university."[69]

There is some evidence that Dugald Stewart later came to regret his enthusiastic support for Brown's candidature, and to moderate his high opinion of his talents.[70] His young colleague's lectures, while following a similar format to his own, covering the philosophy of physical inquiry, the philosophy of mind, ethics and natural theology, were, in terms of doctrine and emphasis, radically different. Brown's main passion was for the philosophy of the human mind (hence the title of the published *Lectures*), and the majority of the lectures were given over to developing his "physiology of the mind" or "mental chemistry," and elaborating upon his "laws of suggestion" (similar to the laws of "association" of ideas found in earlier writers such as David Hartley, David Hume and Erasmus Darwin). As a result of this, some of Stewart's favoured topics in moral philosophy, ethics and political economy were marginalised. More importantly though, the *Lectures*, in revolting openly against Reid were revolting tacitly against Stewart. This, indeed, was precisely how Brown himself saw it. In a letter to his friend Erskine, at the end of his first academic session as Professor of Moral Philosophy, he wrote "I was very much *constrained*, as you may believe, by the unpleasantness of differing so essentially from Mr Stewart on many of the principal points. But... *Dr Reid's* name fortunately served every purpose, when I had opinions to oppose in which Mr Stewart perhaps coincided."[71]

That first series of lectures in 1810-11, Thomas Chalmers later wrote, had been "gotten up with something like the speed and power of magic."[72] Brown made some further alterations to his series of a hundred lectures (over half a million words in length) in the succeeding academic sessions. He also continued to work during these years on his treatise on cause and effect, which reached its final form in 1818. But his career as Professor of Moral Philosophy was to be cut short by illness. Having collapsed while lecturing in December 1819, Brown was sent to London by his physician for a rest and change of air. He died there on 2 April 1820 at the age of forty-two.

---

[69] Welsh 1825, pp. 163-90; Cockburn 1909, p. 237. See also Bourne and Taylor 1994, p. 635.
[70] Stewart 1792-1827, vol. 3, Note C.
[71] Quoted in Welsh 1825, p. 195.
[72] Chalmers 1846, p. x.

Brown's *Lectures on the Philosophy of the Human Mind* was hurriedly posthumously prepared from his manuscripts and published before the year was out, reaching its twentieth British edition in 1860.[73] The *Lectures*, which were never intended for publication, preserve something of their author's poetical lecturing style, and reveal Brown's thoughts on emotions and ethics, which he did not write about elsewhere.[74] The selections from the *Lectures* offered below focus especially on these latter topics, as well as on Brown's denial that consciousness was a separate mental faculty, and his distinctive classification of the states of the human mind.[75]

The version of his philosophy of the human mind that Brown did intend for publication was a textbook, based on his lectures, which was published in unfinished form shortly before his death. The book's full title was *Sketch of a System of the Philosophy of the Human Mind, Part First, Comprehending the Physiology of the Mind*. Not even this first part had been completed, but Brown decided it better to publish this than nothing. In the preface, Brown emphasised that this was merely a sketch, rather than a full discussion of his "many original views of the general phenomena of the mind, and many new analyses of some of its most perplexing phenomena." He used the same preface to give a very forceful statement of his opposition to the faculty psychology of "a particular School of Metaphysics" that was "prevalent in the northern part of the Island."[76] The order and division of the material in the *Sketch* mirrors closely that followed in the first half of the *Lectures*, the principal difference between the two treatments being the brevity of argument, simplicity of prose, and relative lack of illustrative examples in the *Sketch* compared with the *Lectures*. The decisions Brown took about which aspects of the material to emphasise in his textbook give us some clue as to what he considered the most important topics. Around a quarter of the *Sketch*, for example, is taken up with a discussion of the muscular feeling of resistance and of Reid's and Hume's arguments regarding belief in an external world.[77] This emphasis is also reflected in the choice of selections from the *Sketch* below.

---

[73] The MS lectures are held by Edinburgh University Library, Dc.2.10-13.
[74] Selections 19-24.
[75] Selections 17 and 18.
[76] Selection 12. Brown 1820, pp. viii, x.
[77] Selection 15. Brown 1820, pp. 77-144.

One key aspect of Brown's revolt against Reid was on this question of belief in the external world, which had become a staple of eighteenth-century philosophical debate. Brown denied that Reid had, as had sometimes erroneously been claimed on his behalf, successfully refuted the sceptical arguments of Berkeley and Hume, and given a reasoned proof of the existence of an external world. It may be, however, that on this point Brown was closer to Reid's own position than he realised. We could not help believing in an outward material world, Brown taught, just as we could not help believing in the regularity of nature, but neither experience nor reasoning could provide an adequate basis for those beliefs; it was intuition that was their source. As we have seen, Brown's philosophy of cause and effect combined the emphasis on intuitive universal beliefs characteristic of the Common Sense school with an inherent sympathy for Humean scepticism. This combination was also apparent in the *Sketch* and the *Lectures*. Brown could, perhaps, be described as a "Common Sense sceptic." A quip of Brown's, asserting the similarity of the Reidian and Humean philosophies, suggests that he did indeed think it quite possible to combine the two:

> Reid bawled out that we must believe in an outward world; but added, in a whisper, we can give no reason for our belief. Hume cries out we can give no reason for such a notion; and whispers, I own we cannot get rid of it.[78]

Brown's aim was to assert each proposition with equal force.

Brown's analysis of the belief in an outward world was distinctive in the emphasis it put upon a sixth sense — the muscular sense of resistance. His Scottish and French predecessors alike (for example, Reid, Stewart and Condillac) had agreed that the five senses together, and especially the sense of touch, were sufficient to produce belief in the reality of an external world. Brown placed a great deal of emphasis on the feeling of resistance in the muscles and the bodily frame. This, he said, was the sensation that was most responsible for bringing about such belief. Several commentators, past and present, have cited this theory as one of Brown's most important and original contributions to the history of psychological thought.[79]

However, it was this very same doctrine that was at the heart of the accusations made by William Hamilton from 1830 onwards that

---

[78] Mackintosh 1837, p. 346. See also Selection 15; Brown 1820, pp. 142-4.
[79] McCosh 1875, p. 328; Boring 1950; Reed 1997, pp. 64-74.

Brown had, in addition to misunderstanding Reid, made countless "silent appropriations" from the French *Idéologues* in general, and from Antoine Destutt de Tracy in particular.[80] The accusation of disguised dependence, if not out and out plagiarism, was subsequently repeated in two works by French writers.[81] There was certainly a good deal of similarity between de Tracy's and Brown's accounts of the special role of muscular resistance in bringing about belief in external objects.[82] However, this might just as well be explained by common sources (including Condillac and Berkeley) as by Brown's dependence on de Tracy. [83] Another source for Brown's ideas on the muscle sense would have been Darwin's *Zoonomia*. Darwin had suggested that "the whole muscular system may be considered as one organ of sense," and that this organ was the primary source of our notions of solidity and extension.[84]

The connection between Brown's philosophy of the human mind and that of the French *Idéologues* was also made by three of the nineteenth-century's principal historians of philosophy. Robert Blakey, J. D. Morell and James McCosh all accused Brown of expounding a philosophy of mind that was at least allied with, if not identical to, French Sensationalism.[85] Brown himself was, in fact, very critical of Condillac and the sensationalists for their "excessive simplification" of Lockean mental philosophy, but he was equally opposed to the Reidian multiplication of powers and faculties. Over-simplification of the mind and the creation of redundant categories were both equally mistaken, and "the philosophy of Dr Reid, with its long catalogue of intellectual and active powers of the mind, may be considered as exemplifying one extreme, as the philosophy of Condillac exemplifies the other."[86] Brown differed from Condillac in that Condillac claimed that sensations were somehow transformed into more complex mental states whereas Brown preferred the statement that certain primary sensations caused more complex mental states;

---

[80] Hamilton 1852, p. 868n.; Hamilton 1853, p. 99n.; Halévy 1901-1904, vol. 3, p. 247.
[81] Réthoré 1863, pp. v-vi, 128-9, 238-51; Picavet 1891, pp. 494-7
[82] Compare Brown 1828, Lecture 24, esp. pp. 148-51 with Destutt de Tracy 1970, vol. 1, pp. 124-9.
[83] For further discussion see also Mills 1987; Stewart-Robertson 1988.
[84] Darwin 1794-6, vol. 1, p. 123.
[85] Morell 1846, vol. 2, pp. 27, 33; Blakey 1848, vol 4, p. 28; McCosh 1875, p. 10.
[86] Selection 16. Brown 1820, pp. 178-9.

he called Condillac's system a form of "intellectual alchemy," in contrast to his own "mental chemistry."[87]

The principal ways, then, in which both the *Lectures* and the *Sketch* constituted a revolt against the philosophy of Reid and Stewart can all be traced back to the same origin, namely Brown's refusal to believe in the reality of unobservable metaphysical entities. As we have seen, "power" was interpreted by Brown as shorthand for invariable antecedence and not as the name for any kind of entity. He was equally iconoclastic when it came to belief in physical qualities or properties; these were to be understood as shorthand for the fact that certain substances existed in particular causal relations with other substances. Again, when it came to the philosophy of the human mind, Brown rejected belief in the reality of psychological "powers" or "faculties." All that existed, on Brown's philosophy of mind, was the mind itself in different states.[88]

These ideas certainly had considerable influence within the fields of mental science and psychology during the middle decades of the nineteenth century. Several of Brown's teachings, including especially his version of the "mental science" methodology, and his new classification of mental states, were widely adopted.[89] Brown had divided mental-scientific methodology into two tasks: first, analysing mental states into their components ("mental chemistry" — an idea picked up on by both the Mills), and, secondly, discovering the laws of succession of mental states ("mental physics").[90] These were what Brown called his "laws of suggestion." The division of mental phenomena into "Sensations," "Thoughts" and "Emotions" was another characteristic feature of Brown's system that was adopted by several later psychologists; as was the classification of the emotions as "Retrospective," "Immediate" and "Prospective." Later writers who showed their indebtedness to Brown by adopting some or all of these positions included the Congregationalist divine George Payne, James and John Stuart Mill, evangelicals such as David Welsh, Thomas Chalmers and Thomas Upham, the Scottish philosophical writers John Abercrombie and George Ramsay, the Scottish-Canadian minister William Lyall, and later nineteenth-cen-

---

[87] Brown 1828, Lectures 32-33, pp. 207-13. On the similarity of Brown's and Condillac's systems, see Stephen 1900, pp. 282-4.
[88] Selection 18. Brown 1828, Lecture 16, pp. 97-103.
[89] Selections 12-14.
[90] Mill 1829; Mill 1843, vol. 2, pp. 502-5.

tury psychologists including Herbert Spencer, Alexander Bain and James McCosh.[91] It was through the works of writers such as these that Brown's presence continued to be felt in theology, philosophy and psychology through to the end of the nineteenth century.

Rational Religion and Ethical Emotions

Many of the later nineteenth-century philosophers and psychologists who were influenced by Thomas Brown were to be found at the secular end of the spectrum of thought. And accusations of religious heterodoxy, explicit or implicit, were a recurring feature of nineteenth-century responses to Brown's writings, especially in reviews written for Christian periodicals in Britain and America. Even Brown's friend and student David Welsh felt some anxiety about taking on the role of biographer to someone who was reputed to be indifferent to Christianity, and whose published works were indicative of a purely philosophical and natural religion, rather than the distinctively Christian faith of the evangelicals, with its emphasis on the Bible, sin, and salvation. Welsh's biographer wrote that "No one lamented more than Dr Welsh his distinguished friend's religious views. He, during Dr Brown's life, pressed on him the arguments in favour of the Christian faith," but apparently without success.[92]

The championing of Brown by another divine was a major factor in the continued attention devoted to his work during the 1830s and 1840s. The evangelical leader Thomas Chalmers has been described variously as "the second most influential Scotsman of his generation," as "possibly the most influential Scotsman of his generation," and, by James McCosh, as a thinker who "had greater influence in moulding the religious belief and character of his countrymen than any one since the greatest Scotchman, John Knox."[93] Chalmers led an ultimately unsuccessful campaign to have a monument erected to Brown in Edinburgh.[94] He did, however, succeed in keeping the

---

[91] Payne 1828; Mill 1829; Chalmers 1833; Lyall 1842, 1848, 1855; Mill 1843; Ramsay 1848, 1853, 1857; Upham 1856; Bain 1859; Spencer 1870-72; McCosh 1880, 1886, 1887. On Brown's impact on psychology see Stephen 1900, pp. 271-87; Page 1980; Flynn 1988; Richards 1992, pp. 332-9; Reed 1997, pp. 68-76; Dixon 2002a, 2002b, 2003, Ch's 4 and 5.
[92] Dunlop 1846, p. 24.
[93] McCosh 1875, p. 393; Hilton 1988, p. 55; Devine 1999, p. 364.
[94] On Chalmers' admiration for Brown, see Hanna 1878, vol. 1, pp. 490-4; vol. 2, pp. 4-5, 99, 104-5. Letters relating to the planned memorial are held in

memory of Brown's thought alive by writing the Preface to an 1846 reissue of the ethical portions of Brown's *Lectures*. The influence of Brown's ideas, especially his treatment of the emotions, had also been very evident in Chalmers's 1833 Bridgewater Treatise, *On the Power, Wisdom and Goodness of God as Manifested in the Adaptation of External Nature to the Moral and Intellectual Constitution of Man*.[95]

Chalmers held that the most important function of natural theology was "guiding the way to our Revealed Theology." He noted that Brown did "not expressly treat of revelation," and later that "Brown had very low and inadequate views of the character of God." But Chalmers reassured his readers that many of Brown's views "shed a pleasing and confirmatory light on what may be termed the moral dynamics of the gospel." What Chalmers' preface to the ethical portion of the *Lectures* sought to show was that Brown's views could be profitably used by Christians, even though they were not themselves inherently Christian. Chalmers recommended that Brown be read alongside Dugald Stewart and Bishop Butler, and that readers would then discover that Brown's philosophy could suggest "many accordances between the science of mind and the subject-matter of Christianity."[96] As is clear from several of the reviews of Brown's works in the periodical press, however, many were not convinced that his works could be thus baptised. The *Christian Spectator* in 1826, for example, complained that Brown's *Lectures* contained "scarcely the remotest reference to a single passage" of scripture, that his system was "essentially pagan," and that it could prove dangerously "seductive" to "inexperienced youths, fond of speculation," not yet settled in their Christian commitment.[97] In his lectures on natural theology, Brown, it was true, did not invoke the Bible. He confined his remarks instead to standard philosophical arguments for the existence, power, and goodness of the Author and Preserver of nature. His religion seemed more rational than revealed, which is what his evangelical critics would have meant by calling him "pagan."

Brown's ethical system seemed more pagan than Christian to such critics too. Here Brown's interest in the "emotions" was again prom-

---

New College Library, Edinburgh, CHA 4.54.42; 4.64.3-7; 4.101.1-2; 4.240.83. See also National Library of Scotland, MS 3704, ff. 84-6.

[95] Chalmers 1833. See Dixon 2003, pp. 127-34.
[96] Chalmers 1846, pp. xxii-xxiii; see also Hilton 1988, p. 179.
[97] Anon. 1826, pp. 153-5.

inent, as is evident in the selections from the ethical part of the *Lectures* included below. Brown's view of moral judgement was that it was in fact a kind of emotion. We might detect here an echo of Hume's famous dictum that "Reason is, and ought only to be the slave of the passions."[98] Brown distinguished his view from that of "moral sense" theorists such as Hutcheson, as well as from the utilitarian theory of William Paley.[99] For Brown, our moral approval of an action is identical to a particular kind of feeling. "To say that an action excites in us this feeling," Brown wrote, "and to say, that it appears us to us right, or virtuous, or conformable to duty, are to say precisely the same thing." Our moral capacities, Brown concluded, could be traced back to an "ultimate fact in the constitution of our nature," namely the "original tendency of the mind, by which, in certain circumstances, we are susceptible of moral emotions." The universality of morality was justified by the identical constitutions of all human minds, and this constitution revealed the intentions of the Deity.[100]

Jerome Schneewind has emphasised the originality of Brown in defending this ethical emotivism: "Brown, apparently alone among nineteenth-century moralists, denies that morality is a matter of reason, and claims that it rests solely on feeling."[101] Only in the twentieth century would it become more common for philosophers, notably logical positivists and existentialists, to interpret moral statements as expressions of emotion rather than as ascriptions of objective moral qualities. In ethics then, as well as in metaphysics and epistemology, Thomas Brown seems indeed to have been a man clearly on his way to positivism.

References

CW = included in Thomas Dixon (ed.) (2003), *Life and Collected Works of Thomas Brown (1778-1820)*. 8 vols. Bristol, Thoemmes Press.

Alison, William P. (1853). "Observations on the Speculations of Dr Brown and other recent Metaphysicians, regarding the Exercise of the Senses." *Transactions of the Royal Society of Edinburgh* 20: 513-40. CW vol. 8.

Anon. (1826). "Thomas Brown, *Lectures on the Philosophy of the Human Mind.*" *Christian Spectator* 8: 141-55. CW vol. 7.

Bain, Alexander (1859). *The Emotions and the Will.* London, Parker.

---

[98] Hume 1978, p. 415. See also Dixon 2003, pp. 104-9.
[99] Selections 23 and 24.
[100] Selection 22. Brown 1828, Lecture 74, pp. 493-4.
[101] Schneewind 1977, pp. 78-81, quotation at p. 78.

_____ (1882). *James Mill: A Biography*. London, Longmans, Green, and Co.

Beebee, Helen (2006). *Hume on Causation*. London and New York, Routledge.

Blakey, Robert (1848). *History of the Philosophy of the Mind: Embracing the Opinions of All Writers on Mental Science from the Earliest Period to the Present Time*. 4 vols. London, Saunders.

Boring, Edwin G. (1950). *A History of Experimental Psychology*. 2nd edition. New York, Appleton-Century-Crofts.

Bourne, Kenneth and William Banks Taylor, (eds) (1994). *The Horner Papers: Selections from the Letters and Miscellaneous Writings of Francis Horner MP, 1795-1817*. Edinburgh, Edinburgh University Press.

Brown, Thomas (1798). *Observations on the Zoonomia of Erasmus Darwin*. Edinburgh, Mundell. CW vol. 2.

_____ (1803a). "Villers' *Kant*." *Edinburgh Review* 1: 253-80. CW vol. 3.

_____ (1803b). "Belsham's *Philosophy of Mind*." *Edinburgh Review* 1: 475-85. CW vol. 3.

_____ (1803c). "Villers on Gall." *Edinburgh Review* 2: 147-60. CW vol. 3.

_____ (1818). *Inquiry into the Relation of Cause and Effect*. 3rd edition. Edinburgh, Constable. CW vol. 4.

_____ (1820). *Sketch of a System of the Philosophy of the Human Mind, Part First, Comprehending the Physiology of the Mind*. Edinburgh, Bell and Bradfute. CW vol. 5.

_____ (1828). *Lectures on the Philosophy of the Human Mind*. Edinburgh, Tait. Originally published, in four volumes, in 1820. CW vol. 6.

Browne, Matthew (1879). "Macvey Napier (ed), *Selection from the Correspondence of the Late Macvey Napier Esq., Edited by His Son* (1879)." *Appleton's Journal* 7: 445-451.

Burke, John G. (1970). "Kirk and Causality in Edinburgh, 1805." *Isis* 61: 340-354.

Cantor, Geoffrey (1975). "The Academy of Physics at Edinburgh 1797-1800." *Social Studies of Science* 5: 109-134.

Chalmers, Thomas (1833). *On the Power, Wisdom and Goodness of God as Manifested in the Adaptation of External Nature to the Moral and Intellectual Constitution of Man*. 2 vols. London, Pickering.

_____ (1846). "Preface", in Thomas Brown, *Lectures on Ethics With a Preface by Thomas Chalmers*. Edinburgh, W. Tait. CW vol. 8.

Clark, I. (1962). "The Leslie Controversy, 1805." *Records of the Scottish Church History Society* 14: 179-197.

Clive, John (1957). *Scotch Reviewers: The Edinburgh Review 1802-1815*. London, Faber and Faber.

Cockburn, Henry (1909). *Memorials of His Time*. New edition. Edinburgh, Foulis.

Copleston, Frederick (2003). *A History of Philosophy. Volume 5: British Philosophy Hobbes to Hume*. London and New York, Continuum.

Craig, Edward (2007). "Hume on Causality: Realist *and* Projectivist?", in R. Read and K. Richman (eds), *The New Hume Debate*. Revised edition. London, Routledge, pp. 113-21.

Darwin, Erasmus (1794-6). *Zoonomia, or The Laws of Organic Life*. 2 vols. London, Johnson.

Davie, George Elder (2000). *The Scotch Metaphysics: A Century of Enlightenment in Scotland*. London, Routledge.
Destutt de Tracy, Antoine Louis Claude de (1970). *Éléments d'Idéologie*. 2 vols. Paris, Vrin. Originally published, in four volumes, in 1801-15.
Devine, T. M. (1999). *The Scottish Nation 1700-2000*. London, Allen Lane.
Dixon, Thomas (2002a). "George Ramsay", in W. J. Mander and A. P. F. Sell (eds), *Dictionary of Nineteenth-Century British Philosophers*. 2 vols. Bristol, Thoemmes Press.
_____ (2002b). "William Lyall", in W. J. Mander and A. P. F. Sell (eds), *Dictionary of Nineteenth-Century British Philosophers*. 2 vols. Bristol, Thoemmes Press.
_____ (2003). *From Passions to Emotions: The Creation of a Secular Psychological Category*. Cambridge, Cambridge University Press.
_____ (2006). "Patients and Passions: Languages of Medicine and Emotion, 1789-1850", in F. Bound Alberti (ed.), *Medicine, Emotion and Disease, 1700-1950*. Basingstoke, Palgrave Macmillan, pp. 22-52.
Dunlop, Alexander. (1846). "Memoir of David Welsh", in David Welsh, *Sermons*. Edinburgh, Kennedy.
Fieser, James, (ed.) (2005). *Early Responses to Hume's Metaphysical and Epistemological Writings*. 2 vols. Bristol, Thoemmes Press.
Flynn, Philip (1988). "Scottish Philosophers, Scotch Reviewers, and the Science of Mind." *Dalhousie Review* 68: 259-83.
Fraser, Alexander Campbell (1904). *Biographia Philosophica: A Retrospect*. Edinburgh and London, W. Blackwood and Sons.
Froude, James (1882). *Thomas Carlyle: A History of the First Forty Years of his Life, 1795-1835*. 2 vols. London, Longmans, Green and Co.
[Gilman, Samuel] (1821). "Thomas Brown, *Inquiry into the Relation of Cause and Effect*." *North American Review* 3: 395-432. CW vol. 7.
_____ (1824). "Thomas Brown, *Sketch of a System of the Philosophy of the Human Mind* (1820)." *North American Review* 19: 1-41. CW vol. 7.
_____ (1825). "Thomas Brown, *Lectures on the Philosophy of the Human Mind*." *North American Review* 21: 19-51. CW vol. 7.
Grant, Anne MacVicar (1845). *Memoir and Correspondence of Mrs Grant of Laggan, Edited by her Son, J. P. Grant Esq.* 3 vols. Second edition. London, Longman, Brown, Green, and Longmans.
Grave, Selwyn (1960). *The Scottish Philosophy of Common Sense*. Oxford, Clarendon Press.
Grierson, Herbert, (ed.) (1932). *The Letters of Sir Walter Scott 1787-1807*. London, Constable.
Halévy, Elie (1901-1904). *La Formation du Radicalisme Philosophique*. 3 vols. Paris, Alcan.
[Hamilton, William] (1830). "Philosophy of Perception: Reid and Brown." *Edinburgh Review* 52: 158-207. CW vol. 7.
Hamilton, William (ed.) (1852). *The Works of Thomas Reid D.D. With Preface, Notes, and Supplementary Dissertations*. 3rd edition. Edinburgh, MacLachlan and Stewart.
_____ (1853). *Discussions on Philosophy and Literature, Education and University Reform*. 2nd edition. London, Longman, Brown, Green and Longmans.

Hanna, William (1878). *Memoirs of Thomas Chalmers*. 2 vols. New edition. Edinburgh, David Douglas.

Harris, James A. (2002a). "David Welsh", in W. J. Mander and A. P. F. Sell (eds), *Dictionary of Nineteenth-Century British Philosophers*. 2 vols. Bristol, Thoemmes Press.

―― (2002b). "Thomas Brown", in W. J. Mander and A. P. F. Sell (eds), *Dictionary of Nineteenth-Century British Philosophers*. 2 vols. Bristol, Thoemmes Press.

―― (2005). "The Reception of Hume in Nineteenth-Century British Philosophy", in P. Jones (ed.), *The Reception of David Hume in Europe*. London, Thoemmes Continuum, pp. 314-26.

Hilton, Boyd (1988). *The Age of Atonement: The Influence of Evangelicalism on Social and Economic Thought, 1785-1865*. Oxford, Clarendon.

Hume, David (1978). *A Treatise of Human Nature*, ed. L. Selby-Bigge and P. Nidditch. Oxford, Clarendon. Originally published in 1739-40.

James, William (1902). *The Varieties of Religious Experience: A Study in Human Nature. Being the Gifford Lectures on Natural Religion Delivered at Edinburgh in 1901-1902*. London, Longmans, Green, and Co.

[Jeffrey, Francis] (1814). "The Paradise of Coquettes." *Edinburgh Review* 24: 397-412.

Jessop, Ralph (2004). "Thomas Brown", in M. Cumming (ed.), *The Carlyle Encyclopedia*. Madison, NJ, Fairleigh Dickinson University Press.

King-Hele, Desmond (1963). *Erasmus Darwin*. London, Macmillan.

―― (1977). *Doctor of Revolution: The Life and Genius of Erasmus Darwin*. London, Faber.

――, (ed.) (1981). *The Letters of Erasmus Darwin*. Cambridge, Cambridge University Press.

―― (1986). *Erasmus Darwin and the Romantic Poets*. Basingstoke, Macmillan.

[Lyall, William] (1842). *Strictures on the Idea of Power; With Special Reference to the Views of Dr Brown in his "Inquiry into the Relation of Cause and Effect"*. Edinburgh, Johnstone. CW vol. 8.

Lyall, William (1848). *Sermons*. Edinburgh, Johnstone.

―― (1855). *Intellect, the Emotions, and the Moral Nature*. Edinburgh, Constable.

Mackintosh, James (1837). *Dissertation on the Progress of Ethical Philosophy*. 2nd edition. Edinburgh, Black. Extract included in CW vol. 8.

Maguire, Thomas (1860). *Sir William Hamilton and Dr Thomas Brown, A Paper Read Before the Dublin University Philosophical Society*. Dublin, McGee. CW vol. 8.

Maine de Biran, Pierre (1834). *Nouvelles Considérations sur les Rapports du Physique et du Morale de l'Homme*. Paris, Ladrange.

[March, Francis Andrew] (1860). "Sir William Hamilton's Theory of Perception." *Biblical Repertory (later the Princeton Review)* 32: 273-307. CW vol. 8.

Martin, Terence (1961). *The Instructed Vision: Scottish Common Sense Philosophy and the Origins of American Fiction*. Bloomington, Indiana University Press.

McCosh, James (1875). *The Scottish Philosophy from Hutcheson to Hamilton.* London, Macmillan. Extract included in CW vol. 8.
____ (1880). *The Emotions.* London, Macmillan.
____ (1886). *Psychology: The Cognitive Powers.* London, Macmillan.
____ (1887). *Psychology: The Motive Powers.* London, Macmillan.
McNeil, Maureen (1987). *Under the Banner of Science: Erasmus Darwin and His Age.* Manchester, Manchester University Press.
McRobert, Jennifer (2000). "Introduction", in J. McRobert (ed.), *Philosophical Works of Lady Mary Shepherd.* 2 vols. Bristol, Thoemmes Press. Vol. 1, pp. v-xxvi.
Mill, James (1829). *Analysis of the Phenomena of the Human Mind.* London, Baldwin and Craddock.
Mill, John Stuart (1843). *A System of Logic, Ratiocinative and Inductive, Being a Connected View of the Principles of Evidence, and the Methods of Scientific Investigation.* 2 vols. London, Parker.
____ (1865a). *Auguste Comte and Positivism.* London, Trübner.
____ (1865b). *An Examination of Sir William Hamilton's Philosophy and of the Principal Philosophical Questions Discussed in his Writings.* London, Longman Green Longman Roberts and Green. Extract included in CW vol. 8
Mills, John (1984). "Thomas Brown's Theory of Causation." *Journal of the History of Philosophy* 22: 207-27.
____ (1987). "Thomas Brown on the Philosophy and Psychology of Perception." *Journal of the History of the Behavioral Sciences* 23: 37-49.
Morell, J. D. (1846). *An Historical and Critical View of the Speculative Philosophy of Europe in the Nineteenth Century.* 2 vols. London, Pickering.
Morrell, Jack (1975). "The Leslie Affair: Careers, Kirk and Politics in Edinburgh in 1805." *Scottish Historical Review* 54: 63-82.
Morris, Peter [Pseudonym, J. G. Lockhart] (1819). *Peter's Letters to his Kinsfolk.* 3 vols. 2nd edition. Edinburgh, Blackwood.
Napier, Macvey, (ed.) (1879). *Selection from the Correspondence of the Late Macvey Napier Esq., Edited by His Son.* London, Macmillan.
Page, F. Hilton (1980). "William Lyall in his Setting." *Dalhousie Review* 60: 49-66.
Paoletti, Cristina (2006). *La Difesa dell'Errore: Senso Comune e Filosofia Positiva in Thomas Brown.* Bologna, Clueb.
Payne, George (1828). *Elements of Mental and Moral Science.* London, Holdsworth.
Picavet, François (1891). *Les Idèologues.* Paris, Alcan.
Porter, Noah (1874). "Philosophy in Great Britain and America: A Supplementary Sketch", in F. Ueberweg (ed.), *History of Philosophy from Thales to the Present Time. Vol. 2, History of Modern Philosophy.* London, Hodder and Stoughton, pp. 349-460.
Porter, Roy (1989). "Erasmus Darwin: Doctor of Evolution?", in J. R. Moore (ed.), *History, Humanity and Evolution: Essays for John C. Greene.* Cambridge, Cambridge University Press, pp. 39-69.
Primer, Irwin (1964). "Erasmus Darwin's Temple of Nature: Progress, Evolution, and the Eleusian Mysteries." *Journal of the History of Ideas* 25: 58-76.

Psillos, Stathis (2002). *Causation and Explanation*. Teddington, Acumen.
____ (2010). "Regularity Theories", in H. Beebee, C. Hitchcock and P. Menzies (eds), *The Oxford Handbook of Causation*. Oxford, Oxford University Press, pp. 131-57.
____ (2011) "Regularities all the way down: Thomas Brown's Philosophy of Causation", in Keith Allen and Tom Stoneham (eds), *Causation and Modern Philosophy*. London, Routledge.
Ramsay, George (1848). *Analysis and Theory of the Emotions*. London, Longman, Brown, Green and Longmans.
____ (1853). *An Introduction to Mental Philosophy*. Edinburgh, Black.
____ (1857). *Principles of Psychology*. London, Walton and Maberly.
Rands, Alma Clara (1970). "Thomas Brown's Theories of Association and Perception as they Relate to his Theories of Poetry." *Journal of Aesthetics and Art Criticism* 28: 473-84.
____ (1974). "The Metaphysics, Epistemology, and Poetry of Thomas Brown." University of California, Riverside, PhD Thesis.
Reed, Edward (1997). *From Soul to Mind: The Emergence of Psychology, From Erasmus Darwin to William James*. New Haven, Yale University Press.
Réthoré, François (1863). *Critique de la Philosophie de Thomas Brown*. Paris, Auguste Durand.
Richards, Graham (1992). *Mental Machinery: The Origins and Consequences of Psychological Ideas. Part I: 1600-1850*. London, Athlone Press.
Rollin, Bernard (1969). "Thomas Brown's Criticism of Hume on Causation." *Archiv für Geschichte der Philosophie* 51: 85-103.
____ (1977). "Introduction", in Thomas Brown, *Inquiry into the Relation of Cause and Effect*. Delmar, NY, Scholars Facsimiles and Reprints, pp. v-xvii.
Schneewind, J. B. (1977). *Sidgwick's Ethics and Victorian Moral Philosophy*. Oxford, Clarendon Press.
[Shepherd, Lady Mary] (1824). *An Essay Upon the Relation of Cause and Effect, Controverting the Doctrine of Mr Hume Concerning the Nature of That Relation; With Observations upon the Opinions of Dr Brown and Mr Lawrence Connected with the Same Subject*. London, Hookham. Extract included in CW vol. 7.
Shepherd, Richard Herne (1881). *Memoirs of the Life and Writings of Thomas Carlyle, with Personal Reminiscences and Selections from his Private Letters*. 2 vols. London, W. H. Allen and Co.
Smith, Norman Kemp (1941). *The Philosophy of David Hume*. London, Macmillan.
Snyder, Laura (2006). *Reforming Philosophy: A Victorian Debate on Science and Society*. Chicago, University of Chicago Press.
Spencer, Herbert (1870-72). *Principles of Psychology*. 2 vols. 2nd edition. London, Williams and Norgate.
Stephen, Leslie (1900). *The English Utilitarians. Vol. 2, James Mill*. London, Duckworth. Extract included in CW vol. 8.
Stewart-Robertson, Charles (1988). "A Scottish Horse-Tale: Ideology, Conspiracy and the Fall from Enlightenment." *Rivista di Storia della Filosofia* 3: 443-78.
Stewart-Robertson, J. C. (2004). "Brown, Thomas (1778-1820)", in *Oxford Dictionary of National Biography*. Oxford, Oxford University Press.

Stewart, Dugald (1792-1827). *Elements of the Philosophy of the Human Mind*. 3 vols. London, Strahan and Cadell.

Stirling, James Hutchison (1894). *Darwinianism: Workmen and Work*. Edinburgh, T. and T. Clark.

Strawson, Galen (1989). *The Secret Connexion*. Oxford, Clarendon Press.

Tropea, Savina (2001). "Introduction", in S. Tropea (ed.), *Works of William Hamilton*. 7 vols. Bristol, Thoemmes Press.

Trotter, Alexander (1901). *East Galloway Sketches: or Biographical, Historical, and Descriptive Notices of Kirkcudbrightshire, Chiefly in the Nineteenth Century*. Castle-Douglas, Adam Rae.

Upham, Thomas (1856). *Principles of the Interior or Hidden Life*. New edition. London, Sampson, Low, Son and Co.

Veitch, John (1869). *Memoir of Sir William Hamilton*. Edinburgh, Blackwood.

Villers, Charles (1801). *Philosophie de Kant, ou Principes Fondamentaux de la Philosophie Transcendentale*. Metz, Collignon.

Wellek, René (1931). *Immanuel Kant in England, 1793-1838*. Princeton, Princeton University Press.

Welsh, David (1825). *Account of the Life and Writings of Thomas Brown M.D.* Edinburgh, Tait. CW vol. 1.

Wright, John P. (2005). "The Scientific Reception of Hume's Theory of Causation: Establishing the Positivist Interpretation in Early Nineteeneth-Century Scotland", in P. Jones (ed.), *The Reception of David Hume in Europe*. London, Thoemmes Continuum, pp. 327-47.

II

Observations

SELECTION 1

Preface[1]

The system of life, which forms the groundwork of Zoonomia, is marked by the same bold originality of thought that distinguished the theoretical part of the Botanic Garden. The field of conjecture, and consequently, of error, appears to be less; as the changes of life are not distant, like those, which elevated our mountains, or gave motion to the planetary system. They continually take place, before us: and, together with those experiments, of which every one may himself be the subject, Dr Darwin has enjoyed the peculiar opportunities of observation, which long, and extensive medical practice affords. But it is the lot of theorists, to be satisfied with less evidence of their own opinions, than of those of others; and opportunities of observation, though they greatly aid us, in discovering the errors of any other system, are, therefore, in general, insufficient to show us the futility of our own. Some perceived relation must always precede opinion; but it is often founded on slight analogies, and induction is afterwards made, more to support, than to try its validity. The phenomena are viewed, in the light, in which we wish them to appear, rather than in that, in which nature presents them; and inconsistencies are thus unnoticed, which readily occur to him, who has no other interest in a work, than as it adds to his store of truths. Some of these inconsistencies, which the author of Zoonomia has not been able to avoid, in the leading principles of his theory, and in the explanations founded on them, it is the object of the following pages, to point out.

---

[1] [Extracted from *Observations on the Zoonomia of Erasmus Darwin, M.D.*, Edinburgh: Mundell & Son, 1798, pp. vii-xxii. N.B. in the Selections following, footnotes are the original auhtor's except where enclosed in square brackets, as here.]

Though to form a system be, in general, to incapacitate ourselves, for just observation, when well conducted, its evils are more, than counterbalanced, by its advantages. If phenomena were connected, in our mind, merely by the order of time, in which they occurred, few would be remembered, nor, though memory were tenacious, could much aid be derived from it; as the advantage of experience consists, not in suggesting indifferently a multitude of circumstances, but in suggesting those particular circumstances, which we have found, at different times, to produce effects, similar to those, we desire. We cannot observe the various appearances of nature, without remarking certain circumstances, in which they agree; and to remark these circumstances is to arrange the similar appearances. It is thus impossible, not to systematize; and, hence, the question should be, not whether systems be useful, but to what extent, and in what mode, they can be most usefully formed.

To philosophize is nothing more, than to register the appearances of nature, and to mark those, which each is accustomed to succeed; and, though we have words, which seem to express causation, we shall find, if we examine the ideas signified, that they merely state the existence of a change. We say, that a body is moved, by impulse, by gravity, by chemical affinity; but we only state the fact of motion, in different circumstances. While we confine ourselves to the order of succession of observed changes, no evil can result from systems; but, if, between observed changes, we suppose another, we do not render the production of the last change more explicable: we only add to it another inexplicable change. When Newton applied to planetary motion the principle, by which bodies fall to the ground, he did not form an hypothesis; because he did not attempt, to explain the cause of the motion, in either case. He merely stated a known fact, and placed out of view the hypothesis, that had obscured it. A body falls to the ground: to this we give the name of gravitation. The curvilinear direction of the planets shows them to be acted upon, by different forces, by one of which alone, they would fall to the sun. This effect being, in no respect, different from the fall of bodies, on our earth, the same name is given to it. In this, there is no hypothesis. We do not consider the fall of bodies, on the earth, as the cause, by which planets are retained, in their orbits: we are merely led by the one, to observe the other, and register them, as similar appearances.

Philosophy being nothing more, than the statement of a series of phenomena, a system is evidently liable to two errors: it may either omit parts of the series, or suppose parts, which do not exist.

From the former of these no system can be free, which is not framed, by an omniscient being. In our first attempts to philosophize, we suppose changes to be immediately successive, between which, we afterwards find a multitude of effects, to intervene; and the progress of knowledge conflicts, in the discovery of these intervening effects. Our inaccuracy of perception we endeavour to remedy, by patient analysis; and the defect of our senses thus becomes the source of our most refined pleasures. We have no reason, however, to censure a system, for a defect, which is unavoidable; nor does the omission lead to other errors. The unknown changes necessarily following that, which we know, we may safely infer from it the effects, which, in reality, follow them.

When we suppose parts of a train, which are not immediately observed, our conjecture may be right; but it is only a conjecture: and a mistake may be productive of evil, by leading us to infer phenomena, which do not take place, and thus unfitting us, for accurate observation.

In no instance, may we justly infer an intervening change, unless the phenomena, immediately preceding, and following, be precisely the same, as those, which we have always remarked, to precede, and follow that change. Nor is a single observation sufficient: for a difference may exist, unknown to us. It is necessary, that the preceding circumstances be frequently varied; and, if we uniformly observe a corresponding variation of the succeeding circumstances, the inference may be allowed. It is thus we suppose the existence of other animated beings. Bodies, similar to our own, exist: we observe, that the same circumstances, which excited us to certain motions, excite them to similar motions; and hence, we infer, in them, the same sentient change, as in ourselves. But, if, either the preceding, or the succeeding circumstances, were the reverse of those, observed in our own case, we should no longer be justified in inferring the intervening change.

If evil result, when the supposed parts of the series are phenomena, which we have really observed, in other circumstances, it greatly increases, when the supposed parts have never been observed; as the ethereal fluids, of various kinds, which have been introduced, to explain the actual changes of nature, by those, who forgot, that the changes of the ethereal fluids were themselves equally inexplicable. A system, of this kind, leads us from the true province of philosophy, by deluding us, with the belief, that we know the *causes* of phenomena; and attentive observation, and arrangement of similar appearances becomes laborious, when compared with the ease of conjecture.

In no instance, then, is the introduction of unknown substances allowable: for, though they correspond exactly, with the preceding, and succeeding phenomena, no advantage will result; as these are not rendered more explicable, nor are we, in any respect, wiser, than before the introduction: and, if they do not exactly correspond, the hypothesis is not merely unsupported, but evidently false, and must, if adopted, give rise to innumerable errors.

The motions of life are not more inexplicable, than that of bodies towards each other, as in the gravitation of the solar system: yet, in this case, we do not call in the aid of a fluid, to render the motion more complicated, but wisely confine ourselves, to a statement of the fact. We are conscious of certain feelings, and we have uniformly found some of these feelings, succeeded by muscular motion; but, though, by the future improvement of our optical instruments, a subtle fluid were shown to us, and its vibrations, or vibratiuncles, or direct motion pointed out, we should, indeed, have traced another link, in the series of changes, but we should not be justified, in regarding the motions of the fluid, as constituting our feelings. We might, with equal reason, before the discovery of an intervening fluid, consider the expansion of the skin, as the sensation of heat, or the motion of the muscular fibres, as the act of volition.

The systems of materialism chiefly owe their rise to the groundless belief, that we are acquainted with the nature of causation. In the external world, we merely know a change of position. Oxygen, hydrogen, and caloric exist: they change their place: water exists. When one of the ingredients of a compound substance is added to the others, we term it the cause of the compound; because, when it is added, the compound exists. Thus, evaporation, we say, is caused by heat; because, when a certain quantity of the matter of heat is added to water, vapour exists. In like manner, when one of the ingredients is withdrawn, we consider this privation, as the cause of the remaining compound. Thus, we say: rain is occasioned by cold. Whenever, therefore, we observe addition, or subtraction, we think, that we have discovered a cause; and, to observe addition, or subtraction, it is necessary, that we know, not merely a single change, but a series of changes. Thus, were it possible for us, to see oxygen, and hydrogen, alone, and water instantly formed, without knowing the existence of caloric, the change would appear inexplicable; but the mystery would vanish, if the addition of caloric, the intervening change, were pointed out. As the material phenomena attract our chief attention, and as, in them, we are able to trace a series of additions, or subtractions, which we are erroneously accustomed to consider, as a series of causes, we endeavour, in every change, to find something intervening. But, in perception, there is no addition, nor subtraction: light is not to be found, in the sensation of vision, nor air, in the sensation of sound: nothing intervenes. But causation means the intervention of something; and, therefore, as nature does not present a series of changes, we invent one. A subtle fluid is best adapted to quick changes; and we accordingly resolve perception, into vibrations, or vibratiuncles, or direct motion.

Had we been accustomed, to consider phenomena, as a series of *changes*, rather than of *effects*, it is probable, that no system of materialism would have been formed. We should then have known, that all changes are equally inexplicable, and that the philosopher, who traces a series, where we supposed a single change, only adds to the multitude of facts, of which human ability will never be able, to discover the connection. The mentalist[2] allows that he is ignorant of the mode, in which the sensation of vision is induced; but the rational materialist must, in like manner, allow, that he is ignorant of the mode, in which the first vibration of the vital fluid is excited by the action of light. What, then, have we gained from the labour, and ingenuity, he has employed, in constructing his hypothesis, and adapting it to all the phenomena of life? We think that we have gained much. The phenomena of life are not, indeed, rendered explicable: the number of inexplicable changes is, on the contrary,

---

[2] Terms, merely negative, as that of *immaterialist*, are often convenient in philosophy, being a shorter mode of expressing those, who, though of different opinions, in other respects, agree, in denying a particular proposition. On this, account, however, they sometimes lead to confusion; as the frequent use of the generic name prevents a specific one, from being adopted. Thus, the schools of Berkeley and Reid, agree, in denying the materiality of the sentient principle, but are not distinguished, by specific names. I use the term mentalist, to denote those, who believe the existence of a sentient principle, or mind, and of matter, or an external cause of certain changes of mind, but to which mind bears no other relation, than that of mutual susceptibility of affection.

increased. But, though the real mystery be the same, the apparent mystery is less, by being divided. It is in physics, as in moral sentiment. We think less of the crimes of Domitian; because there were a Nero, and a Caligula. For a solitary sufferer in an earthquake, our pity is strongly roused: but a whole city is laid waste by it; and, because innumerable tears are shed, our own do not fall. In like manner, in materialism, if there were only a single affection of the percipient fluid, we should feel ourselves, as ignorant of causation, as the mentalist. But there is a series of affections. The fluid vibrates, from side to side, or its particles move, in a straight line; and we think, that we know more, because there is more, of which we are ignorant.

That there exists a sentient principle, the materialist, and the mentalist agree: that our ideas, emotions, desires, are modes of this sentient principle, they also agree. In what, then, do they differ? Simply in this. The mentalist acknowledges, that he is ignorant of the nature of that, which causes his ideas, and that, hence, the proposition, which states the sentient principle to be the same, in nature, as that, which causes its changes, is to him unintelligible. The materialist, on the contrary, maintains, that he is conscious, not merely of ideas, but of the nature of that, which causes his ideas; in other words, that the sentient principle, affected, in a certain manner, is not still the sentient principle. If this does not imply a contradiction, it will, at least, be difficult, to state the mode, in which the knowledge of the nature of the cause of our ideas is acquired. All, that we can infer from them, is the existence of something, by which they are excited; but, that the sensation of sound resembles a vibration, or that any other of our sensations resembles that, which produces it, we have only the unsatisfactory evidence of conjecture. To the unknown cause of our sensations, whatever be its nature, we give the name of matter; and, though, in common language, we find it convenient, for the purposes of life, to speak of our sensations themselves, as existing externally, we must allow, that the *matter*, the real external cause of our sensations, may be different from them, in every respect. If, then, the materialist mean, that the sentient principle resembles our ideas, the proposition is nugatory; as it only states, that the sentient principle resembles itself: but, if he means, that the sentient principle resembles the cause of our ideas, he asserts, that what we know resembles that, which we do not know.

SELECTION 2

On Instinct[3]

On the subject of instinct, two questions have arisen.
1. It has been disputed, whether there be any principles of action, independent of experience; whether animal exertion necessarily imply an object, of which the mind is conscious, or be not sometimes the immediate effect of sensation.
2. It has been disputed by those, who admit the existence of original predispositions, whether man be distinguished from the other animals, as alone possessing higher principles of action.

It is by blending these questions that Dr Darwin has given to his section, on instinct, a conclusive air. A slight induction is sufficient to convince us, that the laws of exertion are not dissimilar, in different animals; but with a slight induction Dr Darwin has not been content. He has made us more intimately acquainted with the economy of our fellow "wanderers of the earth;" and, if a multitude of facts were necessary, has collected sufficient, to convince the most sceptical, that man, through possessing an organization, better adapted to higher attainments, is not guided by principles of action, essentially different from those of the brute. But, conceding this, we concede no more. To prove the similarity of the laws of animal exertion was not Dr Darwin's immediate object, but to prove, that instinct is not one of these laws. In this point of view, however, as a principal of action, common to us with the other animals, we are not justified by the evidence adduced, in rejecting its existence.

Those, who defend instinct, as "a divine something, a kind of inspiration," are, indeed, worthy of ridicule. But, if by the term instinct be meant a *predisposition to certain actions, when certain sensations exist*, the admission of it is so far from being ridiculous, that, without it, the phenomena of animation cannot possibly be explained. Instinctive actions, therefore, are not to be viewed, in the light of anomalous facts, and ascribed to a mysterious principle, uncaused, or to the continued interference of the Deity: they are to be considered, as the result of principles, original in the frame; so that, when the mind is affected, in a certain manner, a certain action, inde-

---

[3] [Extracted from *Observations on the Zoonomia of Erasmus Darwin, M.D.*, Edinburgh: Mundell & Son, 1798, pp. 263-269]

pendently of experience, necessarily ensues. In opposition to this opinion, Dr Darwin asserts, that all our actions, attended with consciousness, are acquired *by the repeated efforts of our muscles, under conduct of our sensations, or desires*, or, in the particular language of Zoonomia that there is no animal action, which is not immediately irritative, sensitive, voluntary, or associate. This point, therefore, is decisive of the question. If it be proved, that there exist fibrous motions, which have not been acquired by the repeated efforts of our muscles, or which have not originally been excited by irritation, Dr Darwin, however unwilling to consider an animal, as "little better than a machine," must have recourse to that instinct, which he characterizes, as *inexplicable*, but which is, in truth, inexplicable, only as being an ultimate fact, in animation, and not more mysterious than the mode, in which sensation is induced by irritation, or volition by sensation.

In his definition of actions, as opposed to instinct, Dr Darwin has himself admitted its existence. They are "acquired by the repeated efforts of our muscles, under the conduct of our sensations or desires." By advancing a few steps from the difficulty, he has thought, that it was completely obviated. The phenomenon, to be explained, without recourse to instinct, is not the repeated effort of the muscles, but their primary action. Of this sensation is the remote cause; and the only mode, in which the muscular contraction can be explained, is by supporting a necessary connection of the particular motive affection with the particular sensation. In these circumstances, no muscular action can be justly said to be acquired. Thus, to use one of the instances, adduced by Dr Darwin, the foetus cannot "learn to swallow by a few efforts:" for the volition, which excites the muscles of deglutition, will either be primarily induced by the sensation, or, if similar effects result from similar causes, will not be induced at all. The action, therefore, is not acquired by the repeated efforts of our muscles, but is original; or, in other words, when the mind is affected, in a certain manner, by the stimulus of food, the action of the muscles of deglutition necessarily ensues. The contraction is the effect of an essential principle of life; and experience, instead of adding to the stock of volitions, can do nothing more, than repeat the primary contractions. To consider repetition, or experience, as the cause of any muscular motion, implies a contradiction: for experience presupposes the motion and the effect must thus have existed, before its cause. When sensation has frequently succeeded the motion of a fibre, it is said, in its turn, to excite the motion. But, admitting this mutual convertibility, the sensation can have no influence on any other, than that particular fibre; and, in the original motion of the muscles of deglutition, the excited fibres are different. Sensation, indeed, precedes their motion; but there is no greater reason, that an affection of the sense of taste should be followed by an affection of the muscles of deglutition, than of any other muscles of the system. The principles of Zoonomia do not explain the connection; and it can only be traced to the original constitution of the mind, by which it is predisposed to exert itself, in producing a certain motion, in consequence of having been affected, in a certain manner. *Instinct* is the term, that denotes this predisposition; and we are thus obliged to recur to an *occult quality*,[4] to an inexplicable something, which connects with sensations actions, that have no apparent bond of union.

SELECTION 3

On Generation[5]

The various species of animal, and vegetable life, Dr Darwin believes to have proceeded, from a single living filament, susceptible of modification, by the accretion of parts, and by its own exertions.

This opinion may, perhaps, surprise us into a momentary assent, by its boldness, and the wonderful simplicity, which it seems to introduce; but, if we demand evidence, we obtain only a few loose analogies, which do not favour the supposition. Degrees of qualities, as of strength and swiftness, in the horse may, as Dr Darwin contents, be in some measure hereditary; but no new quality is superinduced, and, therefore, the species continues, the same. The winged butterfly, it will also be granted, bears little resemblance to the creeping caterpillar, or the respiring frog to the subnatant tadpole; but the wings, and the lungs are not communicated to their posterity. The butterfly and the frog produce again the caterpillar,

---

[4] I do not use the term, as peculiar to instinct: for the nature of every quality is, in truth, occult. We know, that agreeable food induces the action of swallowing, and that the magnet attracts iron; but, *a priori*, we might, with equal reason, suppose, that the iron would be repelled, and the sensation followed by the motion of my arm.

[5] [Extracted from *Observations on the Zoonomia of Erasmus Darwin, M.D.*, Edinburgh: Mundell & Son, 1798, pp. 463-467]

and the tadpole; and thus, instead of continued improvement, a circle of changes takes place.

The supposed original filament must have required nutriment, for its growth: yet no animal, nor vegetable matter, was in existence; so that, instead of giving rise to the various system of life, it must have perished, or continued to exist, unexpanded, and alone.

But, admitting it to have been capable of growth, and reproduction, as sexual generation was impossible, in a single individual it could multiply itself, only by the accretion of parts. Such a progeny, it is observed, "are always exact resemblances of their parent". To what then, if we suppose a single original filament, is the present difference of sex, and of species, to be ascribed?

Dr Darwin seems to consider the animals of former times, as possessing powers, much superior to those of their posterity. They reasoned on their wants: they wished: and it was done. The boar, which originally differed little from the other beasts of the forest, first obtained tusks, because he conceived them to be useful weapons, and then, by another process of reasoning, a thick shield-like shoulder, to defend himself from the tusks of his fellows. The stag, in like manner, formed to himself horns, at once sharp, and branched, for the different purposes of offence, and defence. Some animals obtained wings, others fins, and others swiftness of foot; while the vegetables exerted themselves, in inventing various modes of concealing, and defending their seeds, and honey. These are a few of many instances, adduced by Dr Darwin, which are all objectionable, on his own principles; as they require us to believe the various propensities, to have been the cause, rather than the effect, of the difference of configuration. The fish did not become a subnatant animal, by having received fins; as it must have been an inhabitant of the water, before it could have felt the want of them: and the hog must originally have had propensities, different from those of the sheep, or it would not have wished, nor attempted, the formation of its snout.

Of all modes of reasoning, that is the easiest, which contents itself, with simple supposition; but to this species of argument no bounds can be fixed. It will prove, as readily, that a single filament gave rise to the complicated system of the universe, as that it gave rise to all the tribes of animals, and vegetables, that inhabit our earth.

If we admit the supposed capacity of producing organs, by the mere feeling of a want, man must have greatly degenerated, or been originally inferior, in power. He may wish for wings, as the other bipeds are supposed to have done with success; but a century of wishes will not render him abler to take flight. It is not, however, to man, that the observation must be confined. No improvements of form have been observed in the other animals, since the first dawnings of zoology; and we must, therefore, believe them to have lost the power of production, rather than to have attained all the objects of their desire. If we may be allowed to judge, from their situation, the hare has still, in the chase, the same reason, as the birds of old, to wish for wings, and the dove for greater swiftness of flight, to escape from the pursuing hawk: yet the scale of inferiority still subsists; and such is the order of nature, that the strength of all is supported by the weakness of all.

III

Inquiry

SELECTION 4

Preface[1]

The Essay which follows is now presented to the lovers of Metaphysical Disquisition, in a form so much enlarged and altered, as to constitute almost a New Work. When originally written, with the view of giving some satisfaction to the public mind, on a subject of obscure and difficult controversy, to which peculiar circumstances had attracted a very general interest, it was limited, as much as possible, to an examination of the theory on which the controversy had taken place. In the Second Edition, I ventured to take a wider range, and to add such reasonings and reflections, as seemed necessary to elucidate some of the questions of greatest difficulty, in the philosophy of Cause and Effect. At the same time, however, many questions relating to that most comprehensive of subjects, were left wholly unexamined, and some others only briefly noticed, which deserved a much fuller discussion, both from their own importance, and from the light which they throw on Physical Inquiry in general.

In the present Edition, I have endeavoured to supply these deficiencies; and, with the hope of rendering more easily intelligible what has appeared intricate, as I conceive, chiefly because it has been long perplexed in the Schools, by a mysterious phraseology and the verbal inconsistencies of contending theorists, I have separated the view of the Philosophy of Causation, as a statement of simple philosophic truth, from the critical view of the doctrine of that bold and original Thinker, to whose ingenuity the abstract science of the connection of the sequences of events has been principally indebted; and to the examination of whose opinions on the subject, as partly

---

[1] [Extracted from *Inquiry into the Relation of Cause and Effect*, Edinburgh: Archibald Constable and Company, 1818, pp. v-xiv]

just and partly erroneous, the exposition of the abstract philosophy itself, which was treated before with constant reference to those opinions, might seem, in the former editions, to have been considered as subordinate.

If, in that last portion of my Work, which is now devoted to the review of Mr Hume's theory of our notion of Power, the criticism on his metaphysical style be less favourable, than the general opinion with respect to it, that has stamped it with a character of excellence, the justness of which it may now seem almost presumptuous in a single individual to question, I trust it will not be supposed to have arisen from any wish of detracting from the reputation of that eminent philosopher. The talents, which he undoubtedly possessed, were of so high a rank, that he may well bear to be estimated according to his real merit; and it would be as absurd to deny his acuteness and subtlety, and often, too, the easy graces of his composition, as it is unnecessary for his fame, to assert, that he is physically and logically faultless, in his mode of inquiring into the abstract truths of science, or of exhibiting to others with exactness the results of his inquiry. It is, indeed, scarcely possible to imagine a more convincing proof of that want of precision, which I have ventured to censure, in his method of analysis and in his metaphysical language, than the fact — if, on examination, it be found to be a fact — that from the first appearance of his Inquiries on this subject till now, he has been universally believed to maintain a negative theory of Power, which is not merely altogether different from the real doctrine of his work, but is in direct contradiction to the great argument which pervades it.

In the theory of our notion of the relation of Cause and Effect, which the following pages are intended to develop, I am aware, that to minds unaccustomed to philosophical analysis, and particularly to those who have been in the habit of attaching importance to some mysterious but insignificant phrases, the simple doctrine itself, and its equally simple phraseology, may appear an unwarrantable innovation on the received opinions and language. But I flatter myself, that, after reflecting on what is truly meant, in those received opinions, and in the general language on the subject, they will discover, that the innovations are rather on what has been unintelligible before, than on what has been truly understood; and that every thing which has been of any real value, in the ancient and well-accredited phrases, is retained in the few simple terms of the doctrine which is now submitted to their attentive review.

The very simplification of the language itself, in which we are accustomed to think of the abstract relations of things, is, as it appears to me, one of the most important contributions which metaphysical analysis is occasionally able to make to the Philosophy of Physical Inquiry—that highest and noblest logic, which, comprehending at once our intellectual nature and every thing which is known to exist, considers the mind in all its possible relations to the species of truths which it is capable of discovering. To remove a number of cumbrous words is, in many cases, all that is necessary to render distinctly visible, as it were to our very glance, truths which they, and they only, have been for ages hiding from our view. The distinction of Efficient and Physical Causes, for example, is one which has confused the notions of philosophers of every Age: and, if I succeed in making intelligible the illusion on which this distinction has been founded, though I should succeed in nothing more, I may still venture to flatter myself, that my Work will not be without influence on the progress of future inquiry.

It is no small part of science, to be well acquainted with its real boundaries; but it is necessary also to know, what it is which truly exists within these boundaries, and what it is which is only fabled to exist. As long as any mysterious connection is supposed between the phenomena, that are taking place at every moment before us, the mind must, from its very nature, be curious to investigate that ever-present though mysterious tie; nor will the simple assurance, that the discovery is impossible, be sufficient to destroy the curiosity, and thus to prevent the investigation that would vainly seek to gratify it. It is most satisfactory, therefore, to know, that the invariableness of antecedence and consequence, which is represented as only the sign of causation, is itself the only essential circumstance of causation; that in the sequences of events, we are not merely ignorant of any thing intermediate, but have in truth no reason to suppose it as really existing, or, if any thing intermediate exist, no reason to consider it but as itself another physical antecedent of the consequent which we knew before; and that this simple theory, far from being in opposition to the sublime doctrines of Religion, tends, on the contrary, to make those great doctrines at once more intelligible and more sublime—by simplifying the analogies of human order and volition, from which alone we have been able to rise to the conception of any higher Power, and by destroying that supposed connecting link between the antecedent will of the Deity and the consequent rise of the World, which, if it be not greater than the Creating Will, must at least seem to divide with it the grandeur and the glory of the Magnificent Effect.

SELECTION 5

The Real Import of the Relation of Cause and Effect[2]

The philosophy, which regards phenomena, as they are successive in a certain order, is the philosophy of every thing that exists in the universe.

The world is one mighty system of changes. The great masses – the atoms which compose them – whatever is destitute of organization, as much as the organized beings, that are vegetating, or living, or dying; all are the subjects and exhibiters of unceasing variety. What seems to our eyes to be rest is continued motion. There is not a particle of the planet on which we dwell, that continues in the same point of space, during the instant in which we strive most rapidly to think of it. Life and death, as far as the same identical mass is concerned, are dissolution alike; or rather, in the same space of time, there is a more varied decomposition, while we live, than when we die. In the internal world, though the phenomena are of a different order, there is a variation of them as perpetual. At every moment of our consciousness, some sensation, or thought, or emotion, is beginning in the mind, or ceasing, or growing more or less intense; and if the bodily functions of life continue only while the particles of the frame are quitting one place to exist in another, the functions of the spirit, which animates it, may be said as truly to subsist only by the succession of feeling after feeling.

The great character of all these changes, however, is the regularity which they exhibit; a regularity, that enables us to accommodate our plans, with perfect foresight, to circumstances which may not yet have begun to exist. We observe the varying phenomena, as they are continually taking place, around us, and within us; and the observation may seem to be, and truly is, of a single moment: but the knowl-

---

[2] [Extracted from *Inquiry into the Relation of Cause and Effect*, Edinburgh: Archibald Constable and Company, 1818, pp. 9-17]

edge which it gives us is far more extensive. It is, virtually, information of the past and of the future, as well as of the present. The change which we know, in the actual circumstances observed, we believe to have taken place, as often as the circumstances before were similar; and we believe also, that it will continue to take place, as often as future circumstances shall in this respect have an exact resemblance to the present. What we thus believe is always verified by subsequent observation. The future, when it arrives, we find to be only the past under another form; or, if it seem to present to us new phenomena, we do not consider these as resulting from any altered tendencies of succession in the substances which thus appear to be varied, but only from the new circumstances in which the substances themselves have been brought together; circumstances, in which if they had existed before, we have no doubt that they would have exhibited phenomena precisely the same.

We are truly, then, prophets of the future, while we may seem to be only observing what is before us, or remembering what has been formerly observed; and, in whatever way this prophetic gift may have been conferred on us, it must be regarded as the most valuable of all gifts, since, without it, every other gift would have been profitless. In vain might Nature, at every moment, pour around us the riches of her bounty, if we were to remain in perpetual ignorance of the uses of the wealth which was thus profusely lavished on us; and, to know its uses, we must know what it is capable of affording for our accommodation, at a time that is as yet unexisting.

The world is not a resting place of a moment; it is the home of many generations for the many long years of their mortal life; and for the purposes of that life it is fitted, in magnificent abundance, with what is necessary for sustenance, for shelter, for the prevention of many pains, and the enjoyment of innumerable pleasures: but if, when ease or pleasure at any moment followed the casual introduction of a new object, we had no other impression of relation than of a priority and subsequence that were limited to that particular moment, and had no belief, therefore, that the ease or delight would be renewed, as often as in similar circumstances, we should avail ourselves of the presence of the object which had before been attended with the gratifying result, it is evident, that, in the midst of a thousand means of luxury or alleviation, we might lose as much enjoyment, and suffer as much pain, as if the present means themselves, which required only a little voluntary adaptation on our part, had been wholly withheld. It is our faith itself, which, in a great measure, makes the surrounding objects what they truly are to us, by rendering permanent, in our voluntary use of them, what otherwise might have seemed to pass away, in the moment in which we had chanced to be under their influence.

It is not to science only, then, but to all the practical arts of life, and consequently to the preservation of life itself, that the faith is essential, which converts the passing sequences of phenomena into signs of future corresponding sequences. In whatever manner it may arise, and whatever circumstances may or may not be necessary for giving birth to it, the belief itself is a fact in the history of the mind, which it is impossible to deny, and a fact as universal as the life which depends on it.

It is this mere relation of uniform antecedence, so important and so universally believed, which appears to me to constitute *all* that can be philosophically meant, in the words *power* or *causation,* to whatever objects, material or spiritual, the words may be applied. If events had succeeded each other in perfect irregularity, such terms never would have been invented; but, when the successions are believed to be in regular order, the importance of this regularity to all our wishes, and plans, and actions, has of course led to the employment of terms significant of the most valuable distinctions which we are physically able to make. We give the name of *cause* to the object which we believe to be the invariable antecedent of a particular change; we give the name of *effect,* reciprocally to that invariable consequent; and the relation itself, when considered abstractly, we denominate *power* in the object that is the invariable antecedent; *susceptibility* in the object that exhibits, in its change, the invariable consequent.

We say of fire, that it has *the power* of melting metals, and of metals that they are *susceptible* of fusion by fire — that fire is the *cause* of the fusion, and the fusion the *effect* of the application of fire; but, in all this variety of words, we mean nothing more than our belief, that when a solid metal is subjected for a certain time to the application of a strong heat, it will begin afterwards to exist in that different state which is termed liquidity — that, in all past time, in the same circumstances, it would have exhibited the same change, and that it will continue to do so in the same circumstances in all future time. We speak of two appearances which metals present, one before the application of fire, and the other after it; and a simple but universal relation of heat and the metallic substances, with respect to these two appearances, is all that is expressed.

A cause, therefore, in the fullest definition which it philosophically admits, may be said to be, *that which immediately precedes any change, and which, existing at any time in similar circumstances, has been always, and will be always, immediately followed by a similar change.*[3] Priority in the sequence observed, and invariableness of antecedence in the past and future sequences supposed, are the elements, and the only elements, combined in the notion of a cause. By a conversion of terms, we obtain a definition of the correlative *effect*; and *power*, as I have before said, is only another word for expressing abstractly and briefly the antecedence itself, and the invariableness of the relation.

SELECTION 6

Mr Hume's Definition of a Cause[4]

"Similar objects," says Mr Hume,

> are always conjoined with similar. Of this we have experience. Suitably to this experience, therefore, we may define a cause to be, *An object followed by another, and where all the objects, similar to the first, are followed by objects similar to the second. Or, in other words, where, if the first object had not been, the second never had existed.*[5]

This last circumstance, if very rigidly examined, is not admissible into a just definition of a cause, in circumstances like those of the physical universe, in which there is at the same moment a concurrence of many trains of phenomena; however just it might have been, if there had been only a series of antecedents and consequents in one simple train. Though there may be no permanent and uniform relation of the concurring trains to each other, there is yet no improbability in the supposition, that there may often be such a relation of the antecedent in one of the trains to the phenomenon which is immediately consequent in another of the trains, that the change might have taken place, though the antecedent to which we refer it in that particular sequence, had been absent: and every definition, therefore, must be erroneous, that excludes the possible agency of co-existing

[3] [See also Selection 6]
[4] [Extracted from *Inquiry into the Relation of Cause and Effect*, Edinburgh: Archibald Constable and Company, 1818, pp. 493-497]
[5] [Hume, *Enquiry Concerning Human Understanding*, VII.ii]

objects, which, separately, might have been sufficient to produce the particular phenomenon, that is referred to any one of them. A hand, for example, may hold a piece of iron, and may approach a loadstone with it, in exactly the same direction, and with exactly the same velocity, as that with which the iron, if free, would itself have approached it. In this case, it is evident, that, whether we regard the motion of the iron as produced by the hand, or by the loadstone, *the first object might not have been, and yet the second might have existed.* The addition of this circumstance is, however, of no essential consequence to the theory of causation, which depends only on the believed invariableness of the sequence, in past, present, and future time, and does not require of us to take into account, what might, or might not, have been, in other situations, in which the antecedent was different from that of which, and of which alone, the relation to the particular consequent is felt by us.

In the same spirit of rigid scrutiny, I may remark, that the phrase, in Mr Hume's definition of a cause, *one object followed by another,* is inaccurate, if the word Object be used synonymously with Substance, and is not sufficiently precise, if it have any other meaning. There may be causation, where there is one substance, and only one substance, the changes of which are reciprocally antecedent and consequent; as, in other cases, the changes to which we give the name of Effects, are produced in one substance, on the presence of another. Such is the species of causation, in a very large proportion of the affections of the mind, that do not result from the direct influence of external things, but from previous feelings of the mind itself. The contemplation of some distant good, which is one state of the mind, is followed by the desire of that good, which is a different state of the same mind; and the one feeling is the cause of the subsequent feeling, as much as the presence of a lens on which a sun-beam falls, is the cause of the convergence or dispersion of the rays. In like manner, when a body continues in motion, the cause of the motion at any one moment, is not the primary impelling force, which has ceased, but the state of the moving body itself, at the moment preceding that in which the motion is observed by us. The cause and effect, therefore, in a sequence of changes, are not necessarily different substances; they may be only the same substance, in successive states, either different or similar.

Still, however, whether the cause and effect be different substances, or different states of the same substance, the cause must always be *a substance existing in a certain state,* and the effect too *a substance existing in a certain state.* We sometimes, indeed, in speaking of cause and effect, apply the terms to *objects,* sometimes to *events:* but there is in this case no real difference. *Events* are *objects* beginning to exist in different circumstances; and the word has no meaning, but as significant of the objects themselves in these altered circumstances. When we say, then, that one event is the cause of another, we do not mean, that an event is any thing different from the objects that are before us at the time of its occurrence. There are some objects, the presence of which, in all circumstances, is attended with a certain effect; there are other objects, of which the presence is only in certain circumstances productive of change; and it is in this latter case, that we are accustomed to speak of an *event,* as the cause of a change; because the reference signifies, that the *object,* which is the real cause, *has* begun to exist *in the particular circumstances,* in which alone it has been formed by nature to be the antecedent of the particular change. When a certain change is the consequence of the presence of an object in all circumstances, even the vulgar think only of the object itself, in their reference of causation. Thus, as the sun is never visible without an increase of heat, they have no hesitation in saying, that *the sun* is a cause of heat. But, when it is only in certain circumstances, that an object is productive of change, we almost lose sight of the simple object itself, in our reference, and transfer the causation to that change of circumstances, by which the object has begun to exist in the particular state of fitness. A single word is, in this way, sufficient to express, what might otherwise require the paraphrastic use of many words. When gunpowder, which is inert, as long as it remains a dark mass before us, becomes a destructive force when kindled, we ascribe the violent concussion, in common language, not to the gaseous products in their state of high elasticity, which are the antecedent *objects* or real causes, but to the *explosion* of the gunpowder; expressing briefly, in a few syllables, what would require many hard words, if we were to endeavour to express it with chemical precision. Yet it is evident, that to consider an *event,* rather than an *object,* as the cause of any change, is only to go back an additional step in our reference, and to ascribe the effect, not to those circumstances immediately preceding it, which in scholastic language are termed the proximate cause, but to the circumstances immediately preceding that proximate cause.

SELECTION 7

Physical and Efficient Causes and the Will of the Deity[6]

In a former Section, I endeavoured to show, that we have no other notion of power, than as that which is instantly and constantly followed by a certain change. That, which has been always followed by a certain change, is immediately followed by it, and, as we believe, is to be in all future time immediately followed by it, is the cause of that change, in the only sense in which the word *cause* seems to have any meaning. The *physical* cause, then, which has been, is, and always will be, followed by a certain change, is the *efficient* cause of that change; or, if it be not the efficient cause of it, it is necessary that a definition of *efficiency* should be given us, which involves more than the certainty of a particular change, as consequent in instant sequence. Causation is efficiency; and a cause, which is not efficient, is truly no cause whatever. It is possible, indeed, that what we may have before considered as the physical or efficient cause of a particular phenomenon—that is to say, its immediate and constant antecedent—may prove not to have been so; for it is possible, that a better analysis of a complex phenomenon may show a series of changes, where we had supposed only one. We before considered A as the immediate antecedent of D; but we find afterwards, that B and C are interposed: and we cease, therefore, to regard A as the cause of D; and give that name, first perhaps to B, and afterwards, on a still nicer analysis, to C. But we do not, on account of our minuter discoveries, call A or B the physical cause of D, and C its efficient cause. We consider physical and efficient antecedence as exactly of the same meaning, or, rather, as both superfluous, when coupled with the word Cause, that, of itself, expresses every thing which they can be employed to signify. C is the cause of D; for it has D as its invariable consequent: and, whatever verbal distinctions may be made, this is all which we can understand by the term; since no other import is assigned to it, even by those who make verbally the distinctions, to which we strive in vain to attach some accurate notion.

If, indeed, the asserters of the difference of Physical and Efficient causes had explained what they meant by the difference asserted, and proved that there is something more, involved in the notion of

---

[6] [Extracted from *Inquiry into the Relation of Cause and Effect*, Edinburgh: Archibald Constable and Company, 1818, pp. 113-132]

Power, than the invariableness of a particular consequent, which may be expected instantly, as often as the antecedent itself recurs, their doctrine might have had some claim to be admitted. But they have contented themselves with asserting the distinction, without any very great effort, or rather, I may say, without any effort whatever, to explain to us, in what the asserted difference consists.

If the distinction relate to a supposed difference of Matter and Mind; and if the meaning be, that matter is, in all circumstances, by its very nature, essentially incapable of being the direct antecedent of any changes, in other masses of matter, or in mind, and that these changes must, in every case, be produced by a spiritual being, as the sole imaginable Efficient — they, in the first place, take for granted, without the slightest proof, that matter is thus destitute of *qualities* of every species, since qualities are only another name for efficiency of change; and, in the second place, by introducing a spiritual operator in every change, they only lengthen a sequence of physical phenomena, and do not produce any thing different from a sequence of regular antecedents and consequents. We before supposed, that the approach of a loadstone to a piece of iron was the immediate antecedent of the motion of the iron. We have now, according to this view of it, a more complex phenomenon; in the first place, the approach of the loadstone, in whatever manner that may have been produced; in the second place, the volition of the Deity, or of some subordinate spirit; and, in the third place, the approach of the iron to the loadstone. But it is quite evident, that, in this lengthened series, we have only obtained a new antecedent; and instead of supposing, that the introduction of a loadstone is followed, has always been followed, and will always be followed, by the motion of all the iron that may be within a certain degree of vicinity to it, we must now suppose, that it is, has been, and always, will be, followed by some spiritual volition, and that of this volition, or spiritual energy, whatever it may be, the motion of the iron, within a certain degree of vicinity to the loadstone, is, has been, and always will be, the consequent.

The asserters of the doctrine, then, even when they suppose that they are contending for a cause of a different species, under the name of efficient, are in truth introducing into the sequence observed by us, a new physical cause; and they are introducing it, as I have before said, without any proof; for, the causes, which they term physical, they admit to be the only causes that come under our observation. They not merely introduce it without proof, however, but they introduce what, if proved to exist, would prove also the uselessness of almost every thing which exists.

That the changes which take place, whether in mind or in matter, are all ultimately resolvable into the will of the Deity, who formed alike the spiritual and material system of the universe — making the earth a habitation worthy of its noble inhabitant, and Man an inhabitant almost worthy of that scene of divine magnificence in which he is placed — I have already frequently repeated. That, in this sense, as the Creator of the world, and Willer of those great ends, which the laws of the universe accomplish, God is himself the Author of the physical changes which take place in it, is, then, most true; as it is most true, that the same Power, which gave the universe its laws, can, for particular purposes of his provident goodness and wisdom, suspend, if it be his pleasure, any effect that would flow from these laws, and produce, by his own immediate volition, a different result.[7] But, however deeply we may be impressed with these truths, we cannot find in them any reason for supposing, that the objects without us, which he has made surely for some end, have, as made by him, no efficacy, no power of being instrumental to his own great purpose, merely because whatever power they can be supposed to possess must have been derived from the fountain of all power. We have seen, indeed, that it is only as possessing this power, that they are conceived by us to exist; and their powers, therefore, or efficiencies, are, relatively to us, their whole existence. It is by affecting us, that they are known to us; and, if they were incapable of affecting us, or — which is the same thing — if we were unsusceptible of any change on their presence, it would be in vain, that the gracious benevolence which has surrounded us with them, provided and decorated for us the splendid home in which it has called us to dwell; a home, that may be splendid indeed, as planned by the Omnipotent who made it, but which must for ever be invisible, and unknown to the very beings for whom it was made. Such, reciprocally, is the nature of our mind, and of light, that light cannot be present, or at least the sensorial organ cannot exist in a certain state in consequence of its presence, without that instant sensation which constitutes vision.

If light have *not* this power of affecting us, it is with respect to us nothing; for we know it only as the cause of the visual sensation.

---

[7] [See also Selection 8]

That which excites in us all the feelings, which we ascribe to certain qualities of matter, is matter; and to suppose that there is nothing without us, which excites these feelings, is to suppose that there is no matter without, as far as we are capable of forming any conception of matter. The doctrine of universal spiritual efficiency, then, in the sequences of physical causes, seems to be only an awkward and complicated modification of the system of Berkeley; for as, in this view of physical causes that are inefficient, the Deity, by his own immediate volition, or that of some delegated spirit, is the Author of every effect which we ascribe to the presence of matter; the only conceivable use of the inanimate masses, which cannot affect us more than if they were not in existence, must be as remembrancers, to Him who is Omniscience itself, at what particular moment he is to excite a feeling in the mind of some one of his sensitive creatures, and of what particular species that feeling is to be: as if the Omniscient could stand in need of any memorial, to excite in our mind any feeling which it is his wish to excite, and which is to be traced to his own spiritual agency. Matter, if we must still continue to use that name, has no relations to *us*: all its relations are to the presiding and operating Spirit alone. The asserters of the doctrine, indeed, seem to consider it as representing in a more sublime light the Divine Omnipotence, by exhibiting it to our conception, as the only *power* in nature: but they might in like manner affirm, that the creation of the infinity of worlds, with all the life and happiness, that are diffused over them, rendered less, instead of more sublime, the *existence* of Him who till then was the sole Existence: for power that is derived derogates as little from the primary power, as derived existence derogates from the being from whom it flows. Yet the believers of inefficient physical causes, who conceive that light is powerless in vision, are perfectly willing to admit that light exists, or, rather, they are strenuous affirmers of its existence, as essential to the very distinction on which their doctrine is founded; and are anxious only to prove, in their zeal for the glory of Him who made it, and who makes nothing in vain, that this, and all, or the greater number of his works, exist for no purpose. Light, they contend, has no influence whatever: it is as little capable of exciting sensations of colour, as of exciting a sensation of melody or fragrance; but still it exists. The production of so simple a state as that of vision, or any other of the modes of perception, with an apparatus which is not merely complicated, but, in all its complication, absolutely without efficacy of any sort, is so far from adding any sublimity to the Divine nature in our conception, that it can scarcely be conceived by the mind, without lessening in some degree the sublimity of the Author of the universe, by lessening, or rather destroying, all the sublimity of the universe which he has made. What is that idle mass of Matter, which cannot affect us, or be known to us, or to any other created being, more than if it were not? If the Deity produces, in every case, by his own immediate operation, all those feelings which we term Sensations or Perceptions, he does not first create a multitude of inert and cumbrous worlds, invisible, and incapable of affecting any thing whatever, that He may know when to operate, in the same manner as he would have operated, though they did not exist. This strange process may indeed have some resemblance to the ignorance and feebleness of human power; but it is not the awful simplicity of that Omnipotence,

> Whose word leaps forth at once to its effect;
> Who calls for things that are not—and they come.[8]

In those cases, however, in which the direct agency of the Supreme Being is indubitably to be believed—as in that greatest of all events, when the Universe arose at his will—what notion are we capable of forming of such a change, and are we to consider that Highest Energy as different in nature, as well as in degree, from the humble delegated energies, which are operating around us?

The Omnipotence of God, it must indeed be allowed, bears to every created power the same relation of awful superiority, which his infinite wisdom and goodness bear to the humble knowledge and virtue of his creatures. But, as we know his wisdom and goodness, only by knowing what that human wisdom and goodness are, which, with all their imperfection, he has yet permitted to know and adore him; so, it is only by knowing created power, weak and limited as it is, that we can rise to our feeble conception of His Omnipotence. In contemplating it, we consider only His will, as the direct antecedent of those glorious effects, which the Universe displays. The power of God is not any thing different from God, but is the Almighty himself, willing whatever seems to him good, and creating, or altering, by his very will to create or alter. It is enough for our devotion, to trace every where the characters of the Divinity—of provident arrangement, *prior* to this system of things—and to know,

---

[8] [William Cowper, *The Task,* Book V, "The Winter Morning's Walk", §685]

therefore, that, without that Divine will as antecedent, nothing could have been. Wherever we turn our eyes — to the Earth, to the Heavens, to the myriads of beings, that live and move around us, or to those more than myriads of worlds, which seem themselves almost like animated inhabitants of the infinity through which they range — above us, beneath us, on every side, we discover, with a certainty that admits not of doubt, Intelligence and Design, that must have preceded the existence of every thing which exists. Yet, when we analyze those great but obscure conceptions, which rise in our mind while we attempt to think of the creation of things, we feel that it is still only a sequence of events which we are considering, though of events the magnitude of which allows us no comparison, because it has nothing in common with those earthly changes, which fall beneath our view. We do not imagine any thing existing intermediately, and binding as it were the will of the Omnipotent Creator to the things which are bursting upon our gaze: we conceive only the Divine Will itself, as if made visible to our imagination, and all nature at the very moment rising around.

It is evident, that, in the case of the divine agency, as in every other species of causation, the introduction of any circumstance of supposed efficiency, as furnishing a closer bond of connection, would, in truth, furnish only a new antecedent, to be itself connected. But, even though it were possible to conceive the closer connection of such an additional circumstance, as might be supposed to intervene, between the will of the Creator, as antecedent, and the rise of the Universe, as consequent — it would diminish indeed, but it certainly could not be supposed to elevate the majesty of the person and of the scene. Our feeling of his Omnipotence is not rendered stronger by the slowness of the complicated process. It is, on the contrary, the immediate succession of the object to the desire — of an object so vast and so magnificent, to a simple volition — which impresses the force of the Omnipotence on our mind; and it is to the divine agency, therefore, that the representation of instant sequence seems peculiarly suited, as if it were more emphatically powerful.

In the works of man, if we consider only the progressive changes, as they rise after each other, each effect is equally the immediate consequent of its particular antecedent. But the change, first produced, may not be that which was primary in the mind of the operator — the finished result which he contemplated at a distance, in his plan.

Before this can arise, a multitude of gradual changes may be necessary; and quick, therefore, as each sequence may be, there is an appearance of slowness when we consider the whole successive parts of the train; because we have constantly in our mind one great sequence, of the desire itself, and the object of the desire, which a process, that is complicated with so many instrumental changes, seems tardy to present. Man is not omnipotent. What *he* wills does not arise, merely because he has willed it; and often, therefore, to gratify a single wish, he must toil to produce sequence after sequence, and, in many cases, toil to produce them in vain. But there is a Being, who *is* Omnipotent; and His boundlessness of power, as distinctively opposed to human feebleness, seems best marked by a rapidity in which there is nothing that intervenes between the will itself, and its perfect fulfilment.

In the liveliness of the impression produced by a change so rapid, is to be found the chief sublimity of the celebrated passage in Genesis, descriptive of the creation of light; whatever charm additional it may receive, from the ethereal purity of the very object that is imaged to us — which seems itself of a nature so heavenly, as to have been worthy of being the first material emanation of the divine glory, to connect it afterwards with the grosser forms of earth. It is by stating nothing more than the antecedent and consequent, that the description is majestically simple. God speaks, and it is done. We imagine nothing intermediate. In our highest contemplation of his power, we believe only, that, when he willed creation, a world arose, and that, in all future time, a similar volition will be followed by the rise of whatever he may will to exist — that his will to destroy any of his works, will be in like manner followed by its nonexistence — and his will to vary the course of things, by miraculous appearances. The will is the only necessary previous change; and that Being has *almighty power,* whose *every will* is immediately and invariably *followed* by the existence of its object.

SELECTION 8

Mr Hume's Essay on Miracles[9]

The *possibility* of the occasional direct operation of the Power which formed the World, in varying the usual course of its events, it would be in the highest degree unphilosophical to deny: nor can we presume to estimate the degree of its probability; since, in many cases, of the wide bearings of which on human happiness we must be ignorant, it might be the result of the same benevolent motives which we must suppose to have influenced the Divine Mind, in the original act of creation itself. But the theory of the Divine government, which admits the possibility of such occasional agency, is very different from that which asserts the necessity of the perpetual and uniform operation of the Supreme Being, as the immediate or efficient cause of every phenomenon. The will of the Deity, whether displayed in those obvious variations of events, which are termed Miracles, or inferred from those supposed secret and invisible changes, which are ascribed to his Providence, is itself, in all such cases, to be regarded by the affirmer of it, as a new physical antecedent, from which, if it really form a part of the series of events, a difference of result may naturally be expected, on the same principle, as that on which we expect a change of product, from any other new combination of physical circumstances.

It is on this view of the Divine Will — as itself, in every case in which it may be supposed to operate directly in the phenomena of the universe, a new circumstance of physical causation — that every valid answer to the abstract argument of Mr Hume's Essay on Miracles must, as I conceive, be founded. The great mistake of that argument does not consist, as has been imagined, in a miscalculation of the force of testimony in general: for the principle of the calculation must be conceded to him, that, whatever be the source of our early faith in testimony, the rational credit, which we afterwards give to it, in any case, depends on our belief of the less improbability of the facts reported, than of the ignorance or fraud of the reporter. If the probabilities were reversed — and if it appeared to us less probable, that any fact should have happened as stated, than that the reporter of it should have been unacquainted with the real circumstances, or

---

[9] [Extracted from *Inquiry into the Relation of Cause and Effect*, Edinburgh: Archibald Constable and Company, 1818, pp. 500-511]

desirous of deceiving us—it matters little, from what principle our faith in testimony may primarily have flowed: for there is surely no one, who will contend, that, in such a case, we should be led by any principle of our nature to credit that which appeared to us, at the very time at which we gave it our assent, unworthy of being credited, or, in other words, less likely to be true than to be false.

Whether it be to experience that we owe our belief of testimony in general, or whether we owe to it only our knowledge of the possibilities of error or imposition, which makes us hesitate in admitting any particular testimony, is of no consequence then to our belief, in the years in which we are called to be the judges of the likelihood of any extraordinary event that is related to us. It is enough, that we know, as after a very few years of life we cannot fail to know, that it is possible for the reporter to be imperfectly acquainted with the truth of what he states, or capable of wishing to deceive us. Before giving our complete assent to any marvellous tale, we always weigh probability against probability; and if, after weighing these, it appear to us more likely, on the whole, that the information is false, than that the event has really happened, in the manner reported, we should not think ourselves, in the slightest degree, more bound to admit the accuracy of the narrative, though a thousand arguments were urged, far more convincing than any which have yet been offered, to persuade us, that there is an original tendency in the mind, before experience, to believe whatever is related, without even the slightest feeling of doubt, and consequently, without any attempt to form an estimate of its degree of probability.

It is not in any miscalculation, then, of the force of general testimony, whether original or derived, that the error of Mr Hume's abstract argument consists. It lies far deeper, in the false definition of a miracle, which he has given, as "a violation of the laws of Nature;" a definition, which is accordant, indeed, with the definitions that have been usually given of it by theologians, but is not on that account more accurate and precise, as a philosophic expression of the phenomena intended to be expressed by it. To the theologian himself it is, I conceive, peculiarly dangerous; because, while it makes it essential to the reality of a miracle, that the very principle of continued uniformity of sequence should be false, on which our whole belief of causation, and consequently of the Divine Being as an operator, is founded, it gives an air of inconsistency, and almost of absurdity, to the very assertion of a miracle, and at the same time deprives the doctrine of miracles of its principal support against an argument, which, if his definition of them were philosophically a just one, Mr Hume must be allowed to have urged very powerfully against them.

In mere philosophy, however, the definition, though we were to consider it, without any theological view, simply as the expression of certain phenomena of a very peculiar kind, is far from being just. The laws of Nature, surely, are not *violated,* when a new antecedent is followed by a new consequent; they are violated, only when, the antecedent being exactly the same, a different consequent is the result: and if such a violation—which, as long as it is a part of our very constitution, to be impressed with an irresistible belief of the uniformity of the order of Nature, may be said to involve, relatively to this belief, a physical contradiction—were necessarily implied in a miracle, I do not see, how the testimony of any number of witnesses, the wisest, and most honourable, and least interested from any personal motive in the truth of what they report, could afford evidence of a miracle that might amount to proof. The concurring statements might, perhaps, be sufficient to justify a suspension of judgment between belief and disbelief; but this suspension is the utmost, which the evidence of a fact so monstrous, as the sequence of a different consequent when the antecedent had been exactly the same, could reasonably claim. When we have once brought our mind to believe in the violation of the laws of Nature, we cannot know what we should either believe or disbelieve, as to the successions of events; since we must, in that case, have abandoned for the time the only principle on which the relation of cause and effect is founded: and, however constant the connection of truth with testimony, in the most favourable circumstances, may be, it cannot be more, though it may be less, constant, than the connection of any other physical phenomena, which have been, by supposition, unvaried in their order of sequence, till the very moment of that supposed violation of their order, in which the miracle is said to consist.

Let us suppose a witness, of the most honourable character, to state to us a fact, with which he had every opportunity of being perfectly acquainted, and in stating which *he* could not have any interest to deceive us, but might, on the contrary, subject himself to much injury, by the public declaration; it must be allowed, that it is in the highest degree improbable, that his statement should be false. To express this improbability, in the strongest possible manner, let us admit, that the falsehood of his statement, in such circumstances, would be an absolute miracle, and therefore, according to the definition that is given of a miracle, would be a violation of a law of Nature. It would be a miracle, then, if, in opposition to his former veracity and to his own interest in the case supposed, he should wish to deceive us; but, if it be a miracle, also, which he asserts to have taken place, we must equally, whether we credit or do not credit his report, believe that a law of Nature has been violated, by the sequence of an unaccustomed effect after an accustomed cause; and if we must believe such a change as constitutes an absolute violation of some law of Nature, in either case, it is impossible to discover, in the previous equal uniformity of Nature, in both cases — without the belief of which regular order of sequence we cannot form the notion of physical probabilities at all — any ground of preference of one of these violations to the other.

Though we were to admit, then, to testimony in general all the force, for which Dr Campbell and other writers have so laboriously, and, as I conceive, in relation to the present argument, so vainly contended — and though we were to imagine every possible circumstance favourable to the veracity of the reporter to be combined — the utmost that can be implied in the admission is, that it would be a violation of a law of nature, if the testimony were false; but, if it would not be more so, than the alleged violation of a law of Nature, concerning which the testimony is offered, and if, beyond the uniformity of antecedence and consequence in the events of the universe, we cannot form a notion of any power whatever, a suspension of judgment, and not positive belief, in a case, in which, before we can believe either of the violations, we must have abandoned the very principle on which our whole system of physical belief is founded, is all which the propounder of a miracle, in this view of it, can be supposed reasonably to demand.

It would be vain, in such a case of supposed opposite miracles, to endeavour to multiply the improbabilities on one side, and thus to obtain a preference, by counting the number of separate witnesses, all wise, all possessing the means of accurate information, all honourable men, and all perfectly disinterested, or having personal motives, that, if they were less honourable, would lead them rather to refrain from giving evidence; since the only effect of this combination of evidence would be to add to the probability of the statement, which, if once we have admitted the falsehood of it to be miraculous, is already as great as it is possible to be. It is a miracle, that one witness, who has had perfect opportunities of accurate observation, and every motive of personal interest to give a true representation of an event, should yet, in opposition to his own interest, prefer to give a false account of it. That a hundred, or a thousand, or a hundred thousand witnesses, should, in the same circumstances, concur in the same false account, would be a miracle indeed, but it would only be a miracle still. Of probability there are many degrees, from that which is merely possible to that which is almost certain; but the miraculous does not admit of gradation. Nobody thinks, that the conversion of water into wine at the marriage-feast in Galilee, would have been a greater miracle, if the quantity of transmuted water had been doubled; and a commentator would surely render himself a little ridiculous, who, in descanting on the passage of the Israelites through the Red Sea, should speak of the myriads of liquid particles of the mass that were prevented from following their usual course, as rendering more miraculous the passage itself, than if the number of drops had been less by a few scores or hundreds. But, if this numerical calculation would be absurd in the one case, when applied to a number of particles of matter, each of which, individually, may be considered as exhibiting the influence of a miraculous interposition of a Power surpassing the ordinary powers of nature, it is surely not less absurd, when applied to a number of minds, in each of which, in like manner, a violation of an accustomed law of nature is supposed. It is a miracle, that one drop of water should become wine: it is a miracle, that a thousand drops of water should he so changed. It is a miracle, that a single witness, with many motives to declare the truth, and not one motive to utter a falsehood, should yet, with great peril to himself, prefer to be an impostor: it is a miracle, that a thousand witnesses, with the same motives, should concur, at the same risk, in the same strange preference. In miracles, there are truly, as I have said, no degrees. The Deity either must act or not act; or, according to the false definition which I am opposing, a law of Nature must either be violated or not violated. There may be less than a miracle; but there cannot be more than a miracle.

As long as a miracle is defined to be a violation of the law of Nature, it is not wonderful, that it should shock our strongest principles of belief; since it must require from us the abandonment, for the time, of the only principle by which we have been led to the belief of any power whatever, either in God himself, or in the things which he has created: while, at the same time, it is defined to be that which must, by the very terms of the definition, be as improbable as false testimony can be in any circumstances. It may be less, but it cannot be more, worthy of the name of a miracle, that we should be deceived by the testimony of the best and wisest of mankind, as to a fact of which they had means of the most accurate knowledge, than that any other event should have happened, which is admitted by the reporters of it to be a violation of the order of Nature, as complete, as the falsehood of the testimony which reports it to us, in these or in any circumstances, itself could be.

With Mr Hume's view of the nature of a miracle, then—if we rashly give our assent to his definition—it seems to me not very easy to get the better of his sceptical argument. The very assertion of a violation of a law of Nature is, as we have seen, the assertion of something that is inconsistent with every principle of our physical faith: and, after giving all the weight which it is possible to give to the evidence of concurring witnesses, with the best means of knowledge, and no motives of interest that could lead them to wish to deceive, we may perhaps succeed in bringing one miracle against another—the miracle of their falsehood against the physical miracle reported by them—but we cannot do more than this: we cannot render it less a violation of a law of Nature—and less inconsistent, therefore, with the principle, which, both speculatively and practically, has guided us in all our views of the sequences of events—that the reported miracle should have happened, than that the sage, and amiable, and disinterested reporters, should, knowingly and intentionally, have laboured to deceive us.

The definition, however, which asserts this apparent inconsistency with our experience, is not a just one. A miracle is *not* a violation of any law of Nature. It involves, therefore, primarily, no contradiction, nor physical absurdity. It has nothing in it which is inconsistent with our belief of the most undeviating uniformity of Nature: for it is not the sequence of a different event when the preceding circumstances have been the same; it is an effect that is new to our observation, because it is the result of new and peculiar circumstances. The antecedent has been, by supposition, different; and it is not wonderful, therefore, that the consequent also should be different.

While every miracle is to be considered as the result of an extraordinary antecedent—since it flows directly from a higher Power, than is accustomed to operate, in the common trains of events which come beneath our view—the sequence, which it displays, may be regarded, indeed, as out of the common course of Nature, but not as contrary to that course; any more, than any other new result of new combinations of physical circumstances can be said to be contrary to the course of events, to which, from the absolute novelty of the circumstances, it has truly no relation whatever, either of agreement or disagreement. If we suppose any one, who is absolutely unacquainted with electrical apparatus and the strange phenomena which that apparatus can be made to evolve, to put his hand accidentally near a charged conductor, so as to receive from it a slight shock, though his sensation may be different from any to which he had been accustomed, we do not believe that he will on that account consider it as a proof of a violation of a law of Nature, but only as the effect of something which was unknown to him before, and which he will conceive therefore to be of rare occurrence. In a miracle, in like manner, nothing more is to be supposed. It is the Divine Will, that, preceding it immediately, is the cause of the extraordinary effect which we term miraculous; and, whatever may be the new consequent of the new antecedent, the course of nature is as little violated by it, as it was violated by the electrician, who for the first time drew lightening from the clouds, or by the aeronaut who first ascended to a region of the air of more ethereal purity than that which allows the gross substance of a cloud to float in it.

SELECTION 9

Mr Hume on Customary Conjunction[10]

In a former Part of this Work, when I inquired into the circumstances in which the belief of the relation of Cause and Effect arises in the mind, I thought it sufficient, to appeal to our consciousness, as the great source of evidence on the subject; and I remarked, that, as far back as our memory reaches to the earliest events, that occupied us either actively or passively in childhood, we do not remember a time, in which the belief of some permanent relation of this kind was not immediate on the observation of change. Even before the period

---

[10] [Extracted from *Inquiry into the Relation of Cause and Effect*, Edinburgh: Archibald Constable and Company, 1818, pp. 351-388]

which memory is afterwards to comprehend—as soon as the little sensitive being seems capable of distinct perception—his actions are indicative of this accompanying belief. There is not the slightest evidence, then, of a single moment in which events are regarded as wholly loose and casual, but, on the contrary, the fullest evidence of every moment which affords any indication whatever, that events are always regarded as signs of future uniformity of sequences, that are to be the same as often as the circumstances which recur are the same. It is, therefore, by a very strange licence of gratuitous assertion, it is maintained, in opposition to the whole continued evidence of observation and consciousness, that the belief of the relation of Cause and Effect is so far from being coextensive with the changes observed, that there is not a single change, which does not require the influence of custom or frequent repetition, to invest it with that character of invariable relation, which it seems to us to bear in the moment, or almost in the very moment in which the phenomenon is perceived by us.

If Mr Hume had been able to adduce a single instance of that belief of casual subsequence, without any accompanying notion of power, which he has asserted to be the belief of all mankind as to every change of every species, before the new feeling of the relation of the change as an effect has arisen from customary observation of the same phenomenon in the same circumstances; his doctrine then, indeed, would not have been founded on a supposition *wholly* unwarranted, and inconsistent with *every* fact which it professes to explain. But, till an instance, though it were only a solitary instance, of such belief could be fairly adduced—however suitable it might be, and even indispensable, for his theory, to suppose a state of the mind on the observation of every change absolutely different from any of which we have had experience—there could be no reason on that account to consider the supposition as more accordant with the experience which has so uniformly contradicted it.

Even if, by the supposition of a state of mind in every case different from any of which memory or observation affords the slightest evidence, we could be supposed to free ourselves from any peculiar mystery which might appear to hang over the intuitive belief of causation, the theory might have some claim to easier admission. But even this scanty recommendation is more than it possesses. What is mysterious, if there be any peculiar mystery, before the admission, is equally mysterious after it; and the supposed difficulty, therefore, is exactly what it was, when the influence of custom was not called in to remove it. A single moment of the past, and a thousand moments of the past, or, in other words, a single observation of a phenomenon, and a thousand observations of the same phenomenon — if we attempt to speculate abstractly from the light of intuition itself — are, relatively to the unexisting future, equally incapable of affording us any discovery of that unknown course of Nature which is still beyond us, and independent of our thought. Experience is always of the past; and the longest custom can tell us only what changes have been, in the phenomena with which we have been familiar; while the belief of Power is the belief of changes that are to be, when we may no longer exist to observe them, and of changes that have been, when there was, perhaps, no human observer to witness them. In this indefiniteness of extension the whole difficulty consists; and Custom, which is of the past alone, does not render the extension through futurity less indefinite, nor the future itself a more distinct object of our knowledge. It leaves us the past, which we know, and the future, which we do not know; but it remains with us still, on the side on which we stand, of the great gulf that is between; while it is Intuition only, that passes over the darkness which is impenetrable to our vision, and speaks to us, as from another world, of the things which are beyond.

If, as Mr Hume himself maintains, no experience of the past, however long and uniform, entitle us to infer the similarity of the course of nature in future, with any greater evidence to our reason, than may be drawn from the first single instance of sequence, there is no presumption, at least, afforded by this equality, that circumstances which are to our reason the same, are not equally fit also to be the medium of intuition: and, at whatever stage of observation our belief begin, whether at the first or the thousandth succession of the same events, the belief itself must still, as I have said, be intuitive; for the propositions *B has once succeeded A,* and *B will for ever succeed A,* are not more different, nor less comprehensive the one of the other, than the propositions *B has a thousand times succeeded A* and *B will for ever succeed A.* Why should the future resemble the past? At every stage of observation, this question may be equally put; and, at every stage, it is equally unanswerable. If we can give any reason for our belief of the similarity, we do not need custom to convince us of it; and, if we cannot give any reason for it, it is surely vain to appeal to custom, which is only a portion of that very past, concerning which there is no difficulty whatever, and not a portion of that unexisting future, in the believed similarity of which is to be found the only difficulty that perplexes us.

As far as we have yet seen, then, the assertion of Mr Hume, with respect to the necessary influence of custom or frequent observation of the same change, before any belief of the relation of Power can arise, is not warranted, in the slightest degree, by the evidence of what we remember to have felt in ourselves or observed in others; and, even though it were accordant with this evidence, instead of being completely opposed to it, it would not lessen in any degree the mystery of that conversion of the past into the future, which is involved in our belief of the continued uniformity of the order of Nature, and in the various terms of Power or Causation, which are used by us to express that belief....

It is not necessary, to be a practiced experimentalist, to have felt this confutation of Mr Hume's theory. The belief of regularity of sequence is so much the result of an original principle of the mind, that it arises constantly, on the observation of change, whatever the observed antecedents and consequents may have been, and requires the whole counteracting influence of our past knowledge, to save us from the mistakes into which we should thus, at every moment, be in danger of falling. In the common circumstances of life, how often have we felt this struggle, between our tendency to conjoin events, as invariably consecutive, and the past experience, which shows us that they have no permanent and uniform connection! It is a struggle, like that which we feel with another very strong principle of belief, when we look through an optical instrument, on a landscape that is familiar to us. The church, and the lake, and the wood that overhangs it, appear to us indeed to be near; but we have a stronger conviction, from past experience, that they are far off: and we, therefore, do not consider the meadows between as less extensive than they are, nor hasten, as if he were before us, to meet the friend, whom we see approaching at the very end of our telescope.

If one train of phenomena alone were taking place in nature, it is probable that our feeling of the relation of cause and effect would in every case be unmingled with doubt of any kind; but we learn, from varied disappointment, that innumerable trains are taking place together; and, with this confusion before us, we feel a want of certainty – but it is in this only, that we are ignorant, to which of the trains the particular phenomenon of which we may be thinking belongs.

The very knowledge that there are separate trains in the mixed phenomena, is itself almost a sort of proof, that the belief of causation is immediate, or at least that, before custom can have influence, the similarity of future sequences is in some degree anticipated. There is no sensation, perhaps, which is entirely simple. Various objects at the same moment affect us, and form an aggregate, which is, probably, at no other period exactly the same, but intermingled with other antecedents and consequents, in ceaseless diversity. If, therefore, there were no presumption that Z, which once before succeeded C, would succeed it again, more than X or Y, which we had never before observed to succeed C, it would be impossible, when A, B, C, were, at one moment, producing X, Y, Z, to determine, of which part of the aggregate, Z, thus renewed, was the regular consecutive effect. The analysis and distribution depend on the belief, or presumption, which followed the observation of the first sequence; and, without this, the mixed sequence would still be loose as before.

Even with all the doubts, which the experience of many years has given us, we never hesitate, in simple cases, in which we have little reason to suspect the interference of concurring trains, to rank the consequent which we know, with the antecedent which we know. Such is the case in far the greater number of the direct affections of our organs of sense, where the circumstances are usually of easy limitation, with little chance of the admixture of foreign bodies with those which we are particularly considering. When a new fruit is presented to us, and we apply it to our organ of taste, though altogether deprived of the aid of customary connection, and therefore, if custom be necessary for our belief of power, incapable of any relative notion but that of casual sequence, we have no scruple in ascribing the new sensation to the new object, and we say instantly, that it is sweet, or acid, or bitter. The epicure, who relishes a new ragout, knows well, that the source of his pleasure is in the particular dish before him; and, if he wish to enjoy it again, it is to that dish alone he returns, though twenty new objects be around it. When, on plucking a flower, which we have never before seen, we are sensible of a disagreeable odour, we throw away the flower, without the slightest doubt that it was from it the odour arose. The boy, who for the first time catches a bee, and is astonished to feel its sting, does not wait for a second, and third application of the poison, before he learn to fear it in future. Whether his belief be consistent with reason, is not the inquiry. It has been already admitted, that the uniformity of the course of Nature, in the similar returns of future events, is not a conclusion of reason, derived from the perceived agreement of propositions, but is a single intuitive judgment, that, in certain circumstances, rises in the mind, inevitably, and with irresistible conviction. Whether true or false, the belief is in these cases felt, and it is felt without even the possibility of a perceived customary conjunction of the particular antecedent and the particular consequent.

Would Mr Hume himself have considered the sequences as purely accidental? He owns, that, "when a child has felt the sensation of pain from touching the flame of a candle, he will be careful not to put his hand near any candle;" yet the child, even though old enough, to have acquired an accurate knowledge of the places of objects, and to be certain that it is the candle which is burning him at that particular moment, should, in such circumstances, if custom were necessary for enabling him to extend the past to the future, think no more of removing his finger from the flame, than of shaking off the bandage of his foot.

There is another form of the instant original belief, which might of itself almost be considered as decisive of the question. We often see a phenomenon, for the first time, without having attended to the particular circumstances which preceded it. If it be the experience of custom alone, then, which can give us that belief of connection, by which we denominate a change an *effect,* we are, in this case, as observers, not merely without a customary sequence: we have not even a single case of it; since we know the consequent only, not the antecedent, which was unmarked. Yet there is no one, who does not believe the change to be *an* effect, as completely as if he had witnessed every preceding circumstance. On this one point he is in no suspense, and waits, only to discover *what* object, in the uniform and regular order of succession, was its correlative cause. ...

If the preceding reasoning be just, the error of Mr Hume evidently consists, not in affirming too much, but in affirming too little: for, if any succession of events can suggest the expectation of future similarity, there is surely nothing in the frequent recurrence of the succession, which can reasonably be supposed to diminish the expectation. It may not be greater, after it has been often confirmed, but it certainly cannot be less; and the theory is therefore objectionable, only as confining to sequences that have been often observed, a belief, which is common to them with all other sequences. Yet, by a singular mistake, Mr Hume has been censured by his opponents, as if his affirmation had been too large. Thus, it has been maintained by Dr Reid, that there are cases of uniform succession, in which the belief of causation is never felt; since, from the very commencement of our existence, day has succeeded night in endless return, without any supposition arising, that night is the cause of day.[11] But it should be remembered, that *day* and *night* are not words which denote two particular phenomena, but are words invented by us to express long series of phenomena. What various appearances of Nature, from the freshness of the first morning beam, to the last soft tint that fades into the twilight of the evening sky, changing with the progress of the Seasons, and dependent on the accidents of temperature, and vapour, and wind, are included in every day! These are not one, because the word which expresses them is one; and it is the believed relation of physical events, not the arbitrary combinations of language, which Mr Hume professes to explain.

If, therefore, there be any force in the strange objection of Dr Reid, it must be shown, that, notwithstanding the customary conjunction, we do not believe the relation of Cause and Effect to exist, between the successive *pairs* of that multitude of events, which we denominate night and day. What then are the great events included in those terms? If we consider them philosophically, they are the series of positions in relation to the sun, at which the earth arrives, in the course of its diurnal revolution; and, in this view, there is surely no one who doubts, that the motion of the earth, immediately before sun-rise, is the cause of the subsequent position, which renders that glorious luminary visible to us. If we consider the phenomena of night and day in a more vulgar sense, they include various degrees of darkness and light, with some of the chief changes of appearance in the heavenly bodies. Even in this sense, there is no one who doubts, that the rising of the sun is the cause of the light which follows it, and that its setting is the cause of the subsequent darkness.

---

[11] "The third argument is, that what we call a cause, is only something antecedent to, and always conjoined with the effect. It is sufficient here to observe, that we may learn from it that night is the cause of day; and day the cause of night : for no two things have more constantly followed each other since the beginning of the world." *Essays on the Intellectual Powers*, Essay vi. chap. 6.

That darkness and light mutually produce each other, they do not believe: and if they did believe it, their belief, instead of confirming the truth of Mr Hume's theory, would prove it to be false; since it would prove the relation of Cause and Effect to be supposed, where there has been no customary connection. How often, during a long and sleepless night, does the sensation of darkness—if that phrase may be accurately used, to express a state of mind that is merely exclusive of visual affections of every sort—exist, without being followed by the sensation of light! We perceive the gloom, in this negative sense of the term *perception*—we feel our own position in bed, or some bodily or mental uneasiness, which prevents repose—innumerable thoughts arise, at intervals, in our mind, and with these the perception of gloom is occasionally mingled, without being followed by the perception of light. At last light is perceived, and, as mingled with all our occupations and pleasures, is perceived innumerable times during the day, without having, for its immediate consequence, the sensation of darkness. Can we then be said, to have an uniform experience of the conjunction of the two sensations; or do they not rather appear to follow each other loosely and variously, like those irregular successions of events, which we denominate Accidental? In the vulgar, therefore, as well as in the philosophic sense of the terms, the regular alternate recurrence of day and night furnishes no valid objection to that theory, with the truth of which it is said to be inconsistent.

But other objections, as we have seen, may be urged against it; objections founded on the evidence of our consciousness itself, and of a kind which it seems scarcely possible to resist.

The general conclusion, accordingly, to which we are led, on this part of Mr Hume's doctrine, is that the experience of customary succession is not, as he contends, necessary to the belief of future similarity of sequence; but that where, from a supposed concurrence of many trains of phenomena, any doubt is felt as to the parts of each separate train, the influence of the experience of customary succession is always to diminish the doubt, till, by frequent exclusions of foreign circumstances in many varied repetitions of the observation, we are at length enabled to determine the particular antecedents and their particular consequents.

SELECTION 10

Mr Hume and Dr Reid on the Idea of Power[12]

In the preceding statement of Mr Hume's theory of Power, and the endeavour to discriminate those parts of it which alone deserve our approbation, the office of philosophic criticism might seem to be fulfilled. But it is not enough, to have shown what his theory *is*: the universal misconception of it renders it necessary, to show also what it *is not*. The author of the Essay, "on the idea of necessary connection," has been uniformly represented, as denying the existence of the very idea of necessary connection; and though so many years have elapsed, since the publication of the work which contained his inquiry into the *origin* of the idea of power, it is still necessary to show, that the Word *power* is not considered by him as altogether without meaning. That he does maintain it to be a word altogether without meaning, is the positive assertion of Dr Reid, and of the other philosophers by whom the doctrine was originally opposed; and this opinion, under the authority of respectable names, has become in our Schools of Metaphysics a sort of traditionary article of faith, and of wonder at the possible extent of human scepticism, so as to preclude even that very slight examination, which alone seems necessary to confute it.

That we have no idea of power whatever, which can enable us to form any distinction of the sequences of events, as casual or invariable, is, indeed, so completely opposite to the feelings of which every mind is at almost every moment conscious, that the presumption is very strong, against the possibility of such an opinion. In the case of Mr Hume, this presumption is verified. He does not deny, that we have an idea of *power* or of *invariable priority* in sequences: he denies only that we can *perceive* or *infer* it, as inherent in the subjects of a sequence.

All our *ideas*, I have already frequently said, are considered by him, as copies of *impressions*. A very simple syllogism has therefore been formed for him, to express briefly the result of his inquiry: *We have no idea which is not a copy of some impression; we have no impression of power; we therefore have no idea of power.* The major proposition of this syllogism is unquestionably maintained by him: and by those,

---

[12] [Extracted from *Inquiry into the Relation of Cause and Effect*, Edinburgh: Archibald Constable and Company, 1818, pp. 440-467]

who know nothing more of Mr Hume's doctrine, than that he held that proposition, and had also some peculiar sceptical opinions on the subject of power, the remaining propositions of the syllogism may be readily supposed to have formed a part of his theory. But, when the mind has not been prepossessed by such an inference, it seems scarcely possible to read with ordinary attention the Essays on the subject, without perceiving, that the minor and the conclusion should be reversed. The syllogism, which is truly involved in the reasoning of those Essays, is the following: *We have no idea which is not a copy of some impression; but we have an idea of power; there must therefore be some impression, from which that idea is derived.* The major proposition, as we have seen, is drawn from too narrow an induction, or is founded on a vague and very fallacious definition of the word Idea: but the mode, in which it has rendered his subsequent reasoning inaccurate, is very different from what has been supposed. It has not led him to deny the idea of power, or the belief itself, as a feeling of the mind; but it has led him, from the necessity of finding its corresponding "impression," to satisfy himself with a very erroneous theory of the "idea," and to imagine, that he had discovered its real prototype, where, but for the supposed necessity of finding a prototype of some sort, he could not have imagined that he had discovered the similarity that is stated by him.

In his Essays on the subject, Mr Hume advances first his "Sceptical Doubts," in which he establishes the impossibility *of perceiving* or *inferring any* necessary connection in the parts of a sequence; an impossibility, which *seems* to render power a word without meaning. He then offers his "Sceptical Solution of these Doubts," in which he argues that power *is not* a word without meaning, since we have an impression, from which it may be supposed to be copied, in the feeling of a customary connection of ideas, by which, after the experience of the sequence of two events, the mind passes readily from the idea of one to the idea of the other. That the *Sceptical Solution,* which asserts the *actual existence* of the idea of power is, by being the subject of a new Section, separated from the *Sceptical Doubts,* which assert the *seeming non-existence* of the idea of power, cannot surely disqualify it from being considered as a part of the theory, which is composed of both; and indeed, in the single Section "Of the idea of necessary connection," they are recapitulated, in one continuous argument. Yet, by an oversight that is altogether unaccountable, Dr Reid, and the other writers who have considered Mr Hume's theory, neglect the solution of the doubts, as if it formed no part of the theory, and thus gain an easy triumph over a scepticism, which its author himself had been the first to overthrow.

It is surely no very uncommon mode of analytic disquisition, to proceed, step by step, in search of a particular element, supposed to be present; to remark at intervals, that there as yet *seems* to be no such element, but that in our remaining progress we shall perhaps discover it; and afterwards, when some new circumstances evolve it to us, to conclude with remarking, that we have now discovered the element which we sought: yet, in all such cases, if a part of the analysis were considered alone, when the important discovery had not yet been made, the indisputable inference would be, that the existence of the supposed element was denied by the sceptical inquirer. The mode of investigation described is exactly that which Mr Hume has pursued. His inquiry is into the source of the *universal belief of causation*.[13] He first seeks the source of the idea of necessary connection, in single instances of sequence: but in these he observes only one event preceding another, without being able to perceive any circumstance, from which he can *infer* similarity of their future successions: and the *doubts,* therefore, which arise at this stage of the inquiry, may truly, *at this stage of inquiry,* be considered as well-founded; since perception and reasoning are evidently as incapable as he states them to be, of showing us what the unexisting future is to present, and therefore of affording us the notion of Power, which comprehends the future as well as the past.

> All events seem entirely loose and separate. One event follows another; but we never can observe any tie between them. They seem *conjoined,* but never *connected.* And as we can have no idea of any thing, which never appeared to our outward sense or inward sentiment, the necessary conclusion *seems* to be, that we have no idea of connection or power at all, and that these words are absolutely without any meaning, when employed either in philosophical reasonings, or common life. But there still remains one method of avoiding this conclusion, and one source which we have not yet examined. When any natural object or event is presented, it is impossible for us, by any sagacity or penetration, to discover, or even con-

---

[13] "All reasonings concerning matter of fact, seem to be founded on the relation of Cause and Effect."
"Here it is constantly supposed, that there is a connection between the present fact, and that which is inferred from it."

jecture, without experience, what event will result from it, or to carry our foresight beyond that object which is immediately present to the memory and senses. Even after one instance or experiment, where we have observed a particular event to follow upon another, we are not entitled to form a general rule, or foretell what will happen in like cases; it being justly esteemed an unpardonable temerity to judge of the whole course of nature from one single experiment, however accurate or certain. *But when one particular species of event has always, in all instances, been conjoined with another, we make no longer any scruple of foretelling one upon the appearance of the other, and of employing that reasoning, which can alone assure us of any matter of fact or existence. We then call the one object,* Cause; *the other,* Effect. We suppose, that there is some connection between them; some power in the one, by which it infallibly produces the other, and operates with the greatest certainty and strongest necessity. It appears, then, that this idea of a necessary connection among events arises from a number of similar instances, which occur, of the constant conjunction of these events.[14]

It is indeed most strange, that he who thus endeavours to show, how the idea of necessary connection arises, should be the very person who is asserted and believed to deny, that we have any idea of necessary connection, which can thus arise. He proceeds to point out more particularly the original *impression,* in that connection of the ideas of objects which he supposes to be felt by the mind, after experience of their sequence, and remarks, in a passage already quoted: "This connection therefore which we feel in the mind, this customary transition of the imagination from one object to its usual attendant, is the sentiment or impression from which we form the idea of power or necessary connection." If it be still requisite, to produce further evidence of his acknowledgment of the idea of power, it may be found, in the short summary of the whole doctrine, with which he concludes the Essay.

> To recapitulate, therefore, the reasonings of this section; every idea is copied from some preceding impression or sentiment; and where we cannot find any impression, we may be certain that there is no idea. In all single instances of the operation of bodies or minds, there is nothing that produces any impression, nor consequently can suggest any idea, of power or necessary connection. But when many uniform instances appear, and the same object is always followed by the same event; we then begin to entertain the notion of cause and connection.

---

[14] [Hume, *Enquiry Concerning Human Understanding*, VII.ii.]

We then *feel* a new sentiment or impression, to-wit, a customary connection in the thought or imagination between one object and its usual attendant; And this sentiment is the original of that idea which we seek for.[15]

The whole argument is nothing more, than an expansion of that syllogism, which I proposed, as the key to Mr Hume's speculations in his Essays on the subject: *We have no idea which is not a copy of some impression; we have an idea of power; there is therefore an impression of it to be somewhere found.*

Since the doctrine was not originally delivered by Mr Hume, in the form, in which it now appears in his Essays, it may perhaps be thought, that some considerable change was made in it, and that, originally, it may have been such, as with reason to give rise to the opinion of it, which still prevails. But, if we examine the Treatise of Human Nature, we shall find the doctrine to be the same in this respect — implying the belief of the idea of power, as a feeling to which the mind is in certain circumstances necessarily determined, and *appearing* sceptically, at certain stages, to doubt its existence, only because at certain stages the supposed requisite prototype has not been found. The Section "*Of the idea of necessary connection*" commences with the following summary:

> Having thus explained the manner, *in which we reason beyond our immediate impressions, and conclude that such particular causes must have such particular effects*; we must now return upon our footsteps to examine that question which first occurred to us, and which we dropped in our way, viz. *what is our idea of necessity, when we say that two objects are necessarily connected together.* Upon this head I repeat, what I have often had occasion to observe, that as we have no idea, that is not derived from an impression, we must find some impression, that gives rise to this idea of necessity, if we assert we have really such an idea. In order to this, I consider, in what objects necessity is commonly supposed to be; and finding that it is always ascribed to causes and effects, I turn my eye to two objects supposed to be placed in that relation; and examine them in all the situations of which they are susceptible. I immediately perceive that they are *contiguous* in time and place, and that the object we call cause, *precedes* the other we call effect. In no one instance can I go any farther, nor is it possible for me to discover any third relation betwixt these objects. I therefore enlarge my view to comprehend several instances; where I

---

[15] [Hume, *Enquiry Concerning Human Understanding*, VII.ii.]

find like objects always existing in like relations of contiguity and succession. *At First sight* this seems to serve but little to my purpose. The reflection on several instances only repeats the same objects; and therefore can never give rise to a new idea. But *upon farther inquiry* I find, that the repetition is not in every particular the same, but produces a new impression; and by that means the idea, which I at present examine. For after a frequent repetition, I find, that upon the appearance of one of the objects, the mind is *determined* by custom to consider its usual attendant, and to consider it in a stronger light upon account of its relation to the first object. It is this impression, then, or *determination*, which affords me the idea of necessity.[16]

In various other passages of the Treatise, *the existence of the idea of power or necessary connection* is equally admitted; and, even when doubts of its existence are expressed, they are qualified by phrases, that limit the application of the doubt to those mere words of mystery, which our scholastic nomenclature has combined with the expression of the simple fact of the belief of invariableness of antecedence, in the order of the phenomena of Nature.

The history of the origin of the idea of power, which is thus delivered by Mr Hume, is, as I have endeavoured to show in a former part of this work, altogether inaccurate and inadmissible. The belief of power is an original feeling, intuitive and immediate on the perception of change; not borrowed from any *resemblance* in the transitions of thought. But, *whether the theory of power advanced by him be a just theory,* is one question: *whether he deny that we have any idea of power,* is another question. He may be right in the latter question, and be as wrong as I conceive him to be in the former. An error in the former question does not necessarily involve any dangerous consequences; for, if we be irresistibly determined, as he allows, to ascribe to the antecedent in a sequence that invariableness of priority which constitutes power, we have all which is necessary for any physical or moral, or theological arguments, that are founded on the belief of power. The denial of the very idea of any permanent relation, in the latter question, however, would necessarily involve the most dangerous consequences; for, if we could conceive it possible, that a doctrine so false to the first principles of our nature should be adopted by any one, it would immediately deprive him of that foresight of the future which is necessary for the physical purposes of life, and of all the consolation and peace, and happiness, and virtue, of a filial secu-

[16] [Hume, *Treatise of Human Nature*, XIV.]

rity in the existence of the Father and Sovereign of the Universe. It is, therefore, no common misrepresentation of a theory, to ascribe to it falsely a denial of the idea of power; and to ascribe it to the theory of Mr Hume is assuredly a misrepresentation.

The circumstances, which Dr Reid has urged, in opposition to this almost inconceivable scepticism, which he ascribes to Mr Hume, are, we shall accordingly find, equally consistent with the theory which he wished to overthrow, as with that which he has himself asserted. Nor is this harmony of the theories at all wonderful: for, that we are determined irresistibly to the belief of *invariableness of antecedence,* is allowed by Mr Hume—that our belief of *power* is intuitive, is the opinion of Dr Reid—and, however opposite his language may be, *invariableness of antecedence* is the very *power* for which Dr Reid contends. His arguments for the existence of the idea of power, therefore, instead of being, as he supposed, demonstrative of fallacy in the negative part of Mr Hume's reasoning, must be allowed to form a strong additional support of its truth; since it will appear, on examination, that the belief of *invariableness of antecedence* is all which is essentially comprised in those very arguments, that are adduced as involving necessarily the existence of the idea of *power.* To prove the one, is, indeed, to prove the other; but it is not to afford the slightest proof of any thing additional.

For the purpose of examination, I copy from Dr Reid the paragraph, in which he recapitulates his arguments.

> The arguments I have adduced, are taken from these five topics: 1. That there are many things that we can affirm or deny concerning power, with understanding. 2. That there are, in all languages, words signifying, not only power, but signifying many other things that imply power, such as action and passion, cause and effect, energy, operation, and others. 3. That in the structure of all languages, there is an active and passive form in verbs and participles, and a different construction adapted to these forms, of which diversity no account can be given, but that it has been intended to distinguish action from passion. 4. That there are many operations of the human mind familiar to every man come to the use of reason, and necessary in the ordinary conduct of life, which imply a conviction of some degree of power in ourselves and in others. 5. That the desire of power is one of the strongest passions of human nature.[17]

---

[17] Essays on the Active Powers, Ess. i. chap. 2.

It is scarcely possible to read these arguments, without perceiving immediately, that they confound *loose and variable* with, *invariable* sequences. If there be any bold sceptic, who denies that we expect, in future, a similarity of result, from circumstances similar to the past, the force of the proof must be allowed to be irresistible: but it is of no force, when directed against that very different theory, which allows that we are determined, by the very nature of our mind, to expect, in all future time, from similar circumstances, a similarity of result.

That there are "many things which we can affirm or deny concerning power, with understanding," is an evident consequence of this principle. We may say, of a loadstone, that it *has the power* of attracting iron, which gold *has not*; because we have observed the past difference of the sequence, when, after making the experiment with gold, a loadstone was substituted, and because we believe, that the approach of a loadstone will *continue* to be followed by the motion of iron, which gold, *as before*, will suffer to remain at rest. In like manner we rely on the muscular strength of one man, as greater than the strength of another, because we have seen the one to sink beneath a burden, which the other sustained with ease. We expect again what we have before observed in the same circumstances; but we do not expect, in these circumstances, what we did not observe before.

The minor observations on Power, included by Dr Reid in the reasonings of this primary argument, may perhaps be thought to deserve our attention.[18] 1. "Power is not an object of any of our external senses, nor even an object of consciousness." This agrees completely with what has been stated in Mr Hume's Sceptical Doubts. 2. "A second observation is, That as there are some things of which we have a direct, and others of which we have only a relative conception, power belongs to the latter class. Our conception of power is relative to its exertions, or effects. Power is one thing; its exertion is another thing." This is only to say, that *invariableness of antecedence* is one thing, and *one single fact of antecedence* is another thing. 3. "It is evident that power is a quality, and cannot exist without a subject to which it belongs." Assuredly there can be no invariableness of sequence, without antecedents and consequents. 4. "We cannot conclude the want of power from its not being exerted ; nor from the exertion of a less degree of power, can we conclude that there is no greater degree in the subject." Invariableness of sequence

---

[18] [For the following see Reid, *Active Powers*, I.i]

is supposed, *when the previous circumstances are similar;* but we cannot predict events, when the circumstances are different. From the mere silence of any one, we cannot infer that he is dumb, in consequence of organic imperfection. He may be silent, only because he has no desire of speaking, not because speech would not have followed his desire; and it is not with the mere existence of any one, but with his desire of speaking, that we suppose utterance to be connected. A man, who has no desire of speaking, has truly, if we are to express ourselves with strict philosophic precision, no power of speaking, as long as the mind continues in that state; since he has not the circumstance, which, as always immediately prior, is essential to speech, as much as any other antecedent is essential to any other consequent; but, since he has that power, as soon as the new circumstance of desire arises, and since the presence or absence of the desire cannot be perceived but in its effects, there is no inconvenience in the common language, which ascribes the power of utterance as a faculty possessed at all times, and in all circumstances of the mind; though, unquestionably, nothing more is meant, in this more extensive reference, than that the desire, when it exists, will be followed by the words which correspond with it.

5. "There are some qualities that have a contrary, others that have not; Power is a quality of the latter kind." This is a proposition of no value, and has no relation to the general argument.

In all languages, there *must* be such words, as *action, passion, cause, effect,* &c. if in all nations the sequences of events be supposed to be invariable. That, which existing is always followed by a change, is very different from that of which the change always follows something prior; and it, therefore, is not wonderful that different names should have been invented, to express the difference. But the deflagration of gunpowder will be expected from the contact of a spark, with equal certainty, whether we say, that a spark, in such circumstances, *is always followed* by deflagration, or, merely using different words, say, that the spark has *an active power* of deflagrating gunpowder.

To the same principle are to be traced the different forms of verbs. A spark *kindles* gunpowder: gunpowder *is kindled by* a spark. It is as little wonderful, that there should be active and passive verbs, as that there should be such words, as *before* and *after, first* and *second.*

We proceed on the belief of power, both in ourselves and others, because we proceed on the belief, that similar circumstances will have similar results. I resolve to walk with my friend; for I believe, that my desire of moving my limbs will be followed by their motion: I trust, that my friend will accompany me; for I believe, that in him there will be a similar sequence of motions to volitions, and that the separate volitions or desires, which precede the separate motions, will follow his general expressed intention, in the same manner as they have usually followed it.

Ambition is the desire of power; and ambition is a passion that is felt by us. But the desire of power is nothing more than the desire of being obeyed: and we trust, that, in certain circumstances, we shall be obeyed by the multitude; because we have observed the circumstances which have led to obedience, and believe that similar motives of fear and hope will continue to be followed, on their part, by similar actions. Since we are capable of anticipating those sequences of human conduct, it is not more wonderful, that power should be desired, and that there should thus be a passion of ambition, than that food should be desired by the hungry or by the luxurious, who expect from it the same relief from uneasiness, and the same pleasure, which they remember to have received from it before.

Such are the arguments of Dr Reid, which, though they may be allowed to prove, if proof were necessary, that we do not regard the successions of events as altogether irregular, cannot surely be considered, as establishing any relation, which is not implied in the theory of Mr Hume, and in every theory, which proceeds on an irresistible determination of the mind to the belief of uniformity of order in the physical changes of the universe. *Power* is only a shorter synonymous expression of *invariableness of antecedence*: and the invariableness is not any thing separable or distinguishable from the antecedents and consequents themselves. In all the changes which the substances in nature undergo, the substances themselves alone have any real existence; and what we term Power, in the anticipation of any future change, is itself the antecedent substance, or it is nothing.

SELECTION 11

Scepticism, Atheism, and the Existence of God[19]

To ascribe the origin of the belief to a principle of intuition, it appears then, is, if the intuition be real, to fix it on the firmest possible foundation. Whatever may be thought of the truth of such a reference, it is surely not to be confounded with that vain and frivolous scepticism, which would affect to deny the reality of the belief itself: and yet, it has been so confounded by the opponents of Mr Hume, who uniformly argue, as if, not content with denying the possibility of perceiving, *a priori*, or of inferring by reason, the invariable future sequence of any two objects, he had denied also, that such a sequence is an object of our belief. The misconception of this part of his doctrine has been already, however, pointed out. The universality of the intuition, and the irresistible influence on our reasoning and conduct, with which it is accompanied, are stated by him in the fullest and liveliest manner, and are, in truth, as has been shown, the very difficulty, which, inconsistently, but industriously, he labours to solve.

It would not be easy, indeed, to imagine language on the subject, stronger and more explicit, than that of Mr Hume himself. "This belief," he observes,

> is the necessary result of placing the mind in such circumstances. It is an operation of the soul, when we are so situated, as unavoidable as to feel the passion of love, when we receive benefits; or hatred, when we meet with injuries. All these operations are a species of natural instincts, which no reasoning or process of the thought and understanding is able, either to produce or to prevent.[20]

On whatever principle the force of experience depend, "none but a fool or a madman," he says, "will ever pretend to dispute the authority of experience, or to reject that great guide of human life." His scepticism, therefore, as to the relation of cause and effect—if the suspicious name of *scepticism* must be given to a question of the justest philosophic analysis—consists, not in denying any one of our first principles, but in tracing to one of them, as its ultimate source,

---

[19] [Extracted from *Inquiry into the Relation of Cause and Effect*, Edinburgh: Archibald Constable and Company, 1818, pp. 476-489]
[20] Essays. Sect v. Part 1.

the force of our various reasonings on the uniformity of the order of Nature.

When Berkeley, not content with hesitating as to the grounds of our belief in an external world, boldly denied its existence, what dangerous consequences might have been supposed to flow from the denial! How absurd, it might be said, did all social virtue become, to man, who was to be for ever in a state of solitude; and what magnificent arguments for the existence of a Deity were annihilated in the general desolation produced by a *few* propositions! These desolating propositions it is not easy for mere logic to confute: yet no evil consequence can flow from them; because they are opposed by feelings, akin to those which are the ultimate source of all conviction, and paramount to demonstration itself. The principle, by which, in the state of mind that is termed perception, we consider our sensations as *marks* of the existence of an external world, has a force too powerful to be weakened by any theory; and even the celebrated sceptic who opposed it, inconsistently but amiably pious and benevolent, was, at the time of his opposition, so completely under its influence, as to deliver his theory, professedly for the confutation of those very freethinkers and atheists, whose actual existence his theory, if rigidly examined, might be considered almost as denying, or at least as rendering in the highest degree doubtful.

When we address a philosopher, who speculatively has no doubt that it is to a principle of this kind alone our sensations are evidence of things external, we believe, as much as when we address the vulgar, that he will be moved by the reasonings which are founded on the belief of external things; because it is his belief alone, not the source of it, which we address. If that belief be the same, whether it be intuitive or demonstrative, his judgments, and emotions and actions will be the same. He will approve and disapprove, and hate, and fear, and despise, and love, alike in either case. In the same manner, if a philosopher believe the relation of cause and effect, every reasoning founded on that belief will be the same, whether the evidence of the relation, as felt in its irresistible force, be intuitive or demonstrative; and we have exactly the same reason to fear, that the common duties of social life will be altogether omitted by him, because he regards as intuitive his belief of the external existence of the persons and places, and things to which his duties relate, as that he will deny any power whatever, because he regards as intuitive his belief of the relation of Cause and Effect.

How many perplexities are involved, in the whole doctrine of infinities! Yet we do not less believe the doctrine of the infinite divisibility of matter, because the most ludicrous absurdities may be inferred from it. It may be proved unanswerably, as far as mere logic is concerned, that no portion of the earth's surface, however small in appearance, can ever be traversed by a moving body, however rapid its motion may be: for, to pass from one point to another, some time, however small, is requisite; and therefore, since the space supposed is infinitely divisible, to pass over an infinite number of parts must require an infinite number of times. Yet, though the conclusion be logically irresistible, it is a conclusion, at which we smile only, without admitting it; and we certainly should be astonished at the zeal of any devout theologian, who should be shocked with the dangerous consequences of the doctrine of the infinite divisibility of matter, because it might be shown from it, that the Children of Israel must have spent a whole eternity, before they could have passed through the wilderness, or even through the Red Sea. There are principles independent of reasoning, in the mind, which save it from the occasional follies of its own ratiocinations. By these, we can believe, where there is no argument, and can disbelieve, where there is argument, without a single demonstrative imperfection. It is from them, indeed, as we have seen, that every argument derives its force; and therefore, if there were no belief without reasoning, there could be no reasoning whatever, and Demonstration itself would be a word altogether meaningless.

In ascribing the belief of efficiency to such a principle, we place it, then, on a foundation, as strong as that on which we suppose our belief of an external world, and even of our own identity, to rest. What daring atheist is he, who has ever truly disbelieved the existence of himself and others? For it is he alone, who can say, with corresponding argument, that he is an atheist, because there is no relation of cause and effect. The doctrine of the intuitive belief of that relation may, indeed, have been dangerous, to him who does not go to bed that he may sleep, nor rise that he may enjoy another day, nor stretch out his hand to grasp an object, nor eat that he may satisfy his hunger: but it is only to an individual so unlike all the human beings around us, that the doctrine can have had any evil consequence; for he who performs a single action of daily life, in reliance on the similarity of the future to the past, has already confessed the existence of God – as far as the belief of the existence of God depends on the belief of mere causation. If, as Mr Hume confesses, "none but a fool or a madman" will deny the authority of that principle, he confesses that none but a fool or a madman will deny the just reasonings, which are founded on that principle.

The theism, which flows from it, will, therefore, be as much believed by him, as the simple proposition, which also flows from it, that fire will warm him tomorrow; or, if he affect to disbelieve the theism, he will state, as the reason of his disbelief, some supposed inconsistency in parts of the ratiocination, not his doubt of that fundamental principle, by which alone, he can expect warmth from the fire of tomorrow. "Nature," as Mr Hume has well observed,

> will always maintain her rights, and prevail, in the end, over any abstract reasoning whatsoever. Though we should conclude, for instance, that, in all reasonings from experience, there is a step taken by the mind, which is not supported by any argument or process of the understanding; there is no danger, that these reasonings, on which almost all knowledge depends, will ever be affected by such a discovery. If the mind be not engaged by argument to make this step, it must be induced by some other principle, of equal weight and authority; and that principle will preserve its influence as long as human nature remains the same.[21]

When we examine the systems of atheism, which have been given to the world, and which have produced any impression on the weak and unfortunate minds that have been subject to their influence, we find some, which are founded on false and extravagant analogies of productive powers in matter, or on narrow views of the Universe, and on an unwillingness to discover in it marks of creative design and goodness; but we do not find any which are founded on a general disbelief, that prevents the expectation of warmth from fire, and of relief of hunger from food. Even he, who professes to discover no traces of the designs of a Creator, is himself a designer every moment; and little reason is there, therefore, to fear the atheistic effects of any doctrine, which does not prevent us, if the theological argument be well stated, from having as much belief in the existence of God, as we have in our own continued existence, or in the existence of the friend who may be sitting beside us, or in the warmth of fire, and the coldness of snow.

---

[21] [Hume, *Enquiry Concerning Human Understanding*, V.i.]

While Mr Hume, then, admits, and expresses as strongly as any other philosopher, the force of that determination of the mind, by which we are led irresistibly to the belief of power; the suspicion, attached to his doctrine with respect to it, must have arisen from the general character of his writings, not from attention to this particular part of them; for, since all are able to understand the words of praise or censure, in which a general character may be conveyed, and few are able to weigh and appreciate the works from which that character has arisen, there are many, who hate and dread a name, without knowing why it is that the name should be dreaded, and tremble at the consequences of opinions, which, if they knew what those opinions were, might seem to them as void of danger as their own, from which they have, perhaps, no other difference than of the mere phrases employed to express them.

That, in Mr Hume's view of the origin "of the idea of necessary connection," many errors are intermixed with his assertion of the irresistible determination of the mind to the belief of power, I need not repeat, after the exposition of those errors in so many of the preceding pages. But, when he states, as the result of his Sceptical Doubts, the general proposition, "that in all reasonings from experience, there is a step taken by the mind, which is not supported by any argument or process of the understanding," he asserts nothing more in this doctrine than his opponents themselves assert. The followers of Dr Reid, and the followers of Mr Hume, are in this respect in perfect harmony. The only remarkable circumstance is, that while Dr Reid admits our belief of uniformity of order in the sequences of events in Nature to be the belief of "a contingent truth," that is not susceptible of proof by reasoning, as having itself the evidence of "a first principle," he still thinks that he is the asserter of a doctrine very different from that with which he completely agrees—attacking in Mr Hume a scepticism, which does not differ in any respect from his own, and asserting most strenuously the force of that instinctive belief of power, of the irresistible force of which Mr Hume is himself an equally strenuous asserter.[22]

---

[22] "As this belief is universal among mankind, and is not grounded upon any antecedent reasoning, but upon the constitution of the mind itself, it must be acknowledged to be a first principle, in the sense in which I understand that word." *Essays On The Intellectual Powers*, Essay vi. chap. 5. On the First Principles of Contingent Truths.

The just analysis, then, which reduces our expectation of similarity in the future trains of events to intuition, we may safely adopt, without any fear of losing a single argument for the existence of God, or for the existence of any of the humbler causes, that are continually operating around us; till it be shown, that physical demonstration itself is not dependent, for all its force, on some primary truth of the same order, and that, hence, if the belief of power had depended, not on an immediate and irresistible determination of the mind, but on reason, it would have rested on a principle of surer evidence.

IV
Sketch

SELECTION 12

Mental Phenomena[1]

The great defect of the System of Philosophy of the Mind, which has been generally prevalent in the northern part of the Island, so as to distinguish it as the seat of a particular School of Metaphysics, seems to me to be a redundancy of division, arising partly indeed from imperfect analyses of the complex phenomena of thought which a nicer observation might have shown to be in their elements the same, but still more from indistinct notions attached to the words *Faculty* or *Power* of the Mind, and to the processes that are termed *Operations* or *Acts* of those Powers; by which a sort of mystery has been thrown over the simple sequences of the Phenomena of the Mind, the relations of which to each other or to certain bodily changes, are all which those words can be justly employed to denote.

The view of the mental phenomena which I have taken in the following pages — a view which it appears to me of the utmost importance for simplicity and accuracy of investigation to have constantly before us while we are endeavouring to philosophize on them — is that which considers all our feelings of whatever order, Sensations, Thoughts, Emotions, simply as *states of the mind,* that bear to each other, or to corresponding affections of our bodily frame, certain relations, either of *reciprocal antecedence and consequence,* by which we distinguish them as Causes and Effects, or of *virtual comprehensiveness,* by which it is impossible for us not to regard some of them as complex and involving, virtually at least, certain simpler feelings as their elements. From the beginning of life to its close the mind has

---

[1] [Extracted from *Sketch of a System of the Philosophy of the Human Mind*, Edinburgh: Bell & Bradfute, Manners & Miller, and Waugh & Innes, 1820, pp. x-xiii]

existed, and is known to us only as thus existing, in various states of changeful feeling; the feeling at each moment being its state at each moment, that continued till the new state of some other feeling was more or less rapidly induced. The whole series of these feelings, therefore, has been the whole series of its states: and it is in our power to philosophize on these changes of mental state, as we philosophize on any of the changeful phenomena of the material world which they indirectly indicate to us; to fix by internal observation the order of their succession, or to mark any other relation which they may seem mutually to bear.

When this view of all the processes of sensation, thought and emotion, as mere states in which the mind is capable of existing in certain circumstances—and of the laws of mind as the laws which regulate the mere succession of these states, or, in other words, as the general circumstances in which alone the changes of state take place—has once been made familiar, there will, I conceive, be far less difficulty in comprehending the principle of my arrangement, and the various analyses on which the minuter parts of that arrangement are founded. I know, indeed, that it is very possible, to become still more obscure, in striving to get rid of the darkness of mystery which may thicken on us in our very struggle to escape from it; and I cannot flatter myself with the certainty of exemption from this danger. But it is a danger which all must encounter who endeavour to give greater simplicity to science: and it fortunately happens in such cases, that, while the evil of the failure may be personal only, the advantage of success may have a wideness of distribution, to which, in the light that is gradually spread from inquirer to inquirer, there may be no limits but the limits of philosophy itself.

SELECTION 13

Philosophy of the Human Mind Comprehensive of Many Sciences[2]

The Philosophy of the Human Mind, in its fullest extent, may be regarded as comprehensive of many sciences.

---

[2] [Extracted from *Sketch of a System of the Philosophy of the Human Mind*, Edinburgh: Bell & Bradfute, Manners & Miller, and Waugh & Innes, 1820, pp. 1-7]

I. *That which perceives* is a part of nature as truly as *the objects of perception* which act on it, and, as a part of nature, is itself an object of investigation purely *physical*. It is known to us only in the successive changes which constitute the variety of our feelings: but the regular sequence of these changes admits of being traced, like the regularity which we are capable of discovering in the successive organic changes of our bodily frame. There is a Physiology Of The Mind, then, as there is *a, physiology of the body* — a science, which examines the phenomena of our spiritual part simply as phenomena, and, from the order of their succession, or other circumstances of analogy, arranges them in classes under certain general names; as, in the physiology of our corporeal part, we consider the phenomena of a different kind which the body exhibits, and reduce all the diversities of these under the names of a few general Functions.

II. If these arrangements could be conceived to be so fully and accurately made, that not a single phenomenon of the mind or of the living body had been unobserved, nor an injudicious systematic place been in any one instance assigned, from a preference of a less important to a more important relation of the kindred phenomena, the Physiology of the Mind and of the Body would be alike complete. But some of the mental phenomena are of such a nature, as of themselves to give rise to a distinct science. After inquiring what has generally been the conduct of mankind, and therefore what may generally be again expected in certain circumstances, we have still to inquire, in relation to that conduct, what *should have been*, and what *should be*, in those circumstances, as morally fit to be done: and though this Ethical Science, if very minutely traced to its source, may be found to be only a mode of stating the physical order of succession of certain feelings that arise on the contemplation of certain actions, it still relates to feelings of so peculiar a kind, and of such comprehensive influence on the whole of human life, as justly to deserve a separate consideration.

The science of Ethics is itself twofold; as it is purely *speculative*, and as it is *practical*: in the one case, inquiring into the feelings to which we owe our general notions of moral propriety or impropriety of conduct; in the other case, applying this knowledge to the various circumstances in which man can be placed, and stating, with relation to these circumstances, what it would be right or wrong for him, in the particular situation supposed, to do or to omit.

III. It is not to the individual agent alone, that such views of conduct, in the greater number of instances, relate. The happiness of others, as far as it is in any degree within our power to promote it, is a primary object of moral regard, which it is guilt to violate or neglect. But the duty of consulting for the good of others, obvious as its directions may be in the ordinary cases of domestic life, is in many cases, particularly in those which relate to remote and extensive interests, of very difficult application. The happiness of our country, or of the still greater community of mankind, is not reducible with the same ease to its simple elements, as the happiness of the individuals that are dwelling around us, whose very wants almost point out, of themselves, the means by which they may be remedied. It is not enough, therefore, to be a patriot or a general philanthropist in design: before we can expect truly to benefit the world, we must know in what way it is possible to benefit it; for, without this knowledge, which comprehends the distant as well as the near, we may, in lessening the misery of days or months, produce or prolong the misery of ages. A sedulous study of the means by which public happiness may be most effectually increased and preserved, is hence a part, and a most important part, of public virtue; and the science of Politics, in all its extensive bearings on the wealth, the virtue, the liberty, and the security of nations, may be said accordingly, to be comprehended in that general science of moral duty, which it is the object of *Practical Ethics* to develop and apply.

IV. It is not with mankind only, however, and with the other creatures that may be benefited by our kindness, or may suffer from our cruelty, that we are morally connected. The most important of all our relations is that which connects us with the Great Being who formed us, and under whose continued government we live. If it be our duty to look with gratitude to our earthly benefactors, and to love to contemplate their goodness, the same sentiment must lead us, with still more powerful obligation, to contemplate with grateful love that Highest Beneficence to which we owe whatever we possess. In this sense, the investigations of Natural Theology may be said almost to be included in *Practical Ethics*. Our moral sentiment alone, though there were no other reason to influence us, should prompt us to a devout study of the nature of the Supreme Being, in all his manifestations of it to the creatures whom he has deigned to render capable of adoring him; and while, with the deep conviction of our dependence on his power, we endeavour humbly to trace his character as the Creator and Governor of the Universe, we are led, by that very character which we trace, to a more confident expectation — the grounds of which, even exclusively of the light of Revelation, it must be one of the most interesting of inquiries to examine — that our spiritual existence is not to cease in the mere decay of the bodily elements which surround us, but that He who has been our God in our brief earthly life, will be our God also in the endless ages of a life that is immortal.

Such are the various lights in which the human mind may be regarded — *physiologically, ethically, politically, theologically*. It is thus the object of many sciences — but of sciences that, even when they seem most remote, have still one tie of intimate connection, in the common relation which they all directly bear to the series of feelings of the inquirer himself.

SELECTION 14

Analysis of Mind and Matter[3]

I. All physical inquiry, with respect to the material universe, has one or both of two great objects in view – the *composition of bodies,* and the *sequence of changes* by which they are made known to us as reciprocally *causes* and *effects*. We consider the substances, into the nature of which we inquire, in these two lights alone, *as they exist in space,* or *as they exist in time;* in the one case, endeavouring to discover what the separate elementary bodies are, that are comprehended in any aggregate before us, and that, under the common name of this aggregate, derive from their mere juxtaposition a unity that is not in them, but only in our imperfect mode of perceiving them — in the other case, endeavouring to discover what new appearances they exhibit, and may be expected to exhibit again, in all the variety of circumstances in which they have been, and may be, placed.

1. We term a body *one,* when, from the imperfection of our senses, we are incapable of perceiving the spaces that divide its elementary atoms from each other. But these atoms, which, with finer organs, we might distinguish as separate, are not to be considered as less truly independent substances, because our sight and touch are too gross

---

[3]   [Extracted from *Sketch of a System of the Philosophy of the Human Mind*, Edinburgh: Bell & Bradfute, Manners & Miller, and Waugh & Innes, 1820, pp. 12-23.]

to discern the exact place and boundary of each. It is not absolute unity, then, which we have in view, but relative unity—a unity that is wholly relative to us the percipients. The body which we before termed *one,* therefore, we term *two, three, four,* without the addition to it of a single atom, as soon as we have divided, by any mechanical process, the larger mass into the number of separate masses expressed by those terms—that is to say, as soon as we have made distinctly perceptible the spaces which divide the smaller masses, that can now without any difficulty be placed at a distance from each other. Such is the species of division that is termed *mechanical,* when masses of atoms, without any internal change, are merely separated, or placed at a greater distance from other masses of similar atoms, that formed with them, before the separation, one larger aggregate; and it is sufficiently evident, that, in this case, the change is merely in the separating spaces, and that the atoms themselves in each separated mass are, after the operation, exactly what they were before it.

There is another species of division, however, more intimate than this—the division which is termed *chemical* – that does not merely separate a mass into smaller masses, which may easily be placed near to each other again in close apposition, and of which the atoms continue in the same relative position to each other, but extends to the corpuscles themselves, or at least to congeries of them too minute, even in their combination, to be distinguishable by the senses, and to be separable by a process purely mechanical. But still, though the chemical process be a finer and more extensive one than the mechanical, it is, like it, only a process of separation. It affects the relative position of a larger number of atoms, but it affects their position only, and leaves them, in every respect, the same substances as before. There is nothing creative in mere analysis: what was before, is. We now see in one place the sulphuric acid, in another place the soda, which, in a solution of the neutral salt, were so intimately mixed as to appear to us homogeneous; but when we looked on the solution, we saw, if that word may be applied to a perception so indistinct, every thing which we now see. The mixed atoms which are now separate from each other were separate then, though at distances too minute to come within the sphere of our imperfect vision; and we require, therefore, the subsidiary art of the chemist, to show us what has been at every moment before our eyes. Such is the result, or at least the object, of *every* inquiry into the mere composition of bodies. We wish to know matter as it exists before us in space: and we avail ourselves of many complicated processes of chemical analysis, to know what it is which we have been holding perhaps on the palm of our hand, and considering with the most attentive gaze — the various corpuscles that existed together undistinguishably at invisible distances, in the space which then seemed to us to be occupied by one continuous body.

2. To know matter *as it exists in time,* is to know more than this juxtaposition of elements with elements. It is to know it as susceptible of various changes — of all those changes which, in the variety of their ceaseless succession, are commonly termed the *phenomena* of the material world. The great law, which regulates alike our practical expectations and our systems of philosophy, in this respect, is a principle of our nature, intuitive, or independent of all reasoning — since reasoning, when it is extended from the moment of actual observation to the unobserved past or the unobserved future, must itself be founded on it — a principle by which it is impossible for us not to believe that the course of nature has been uniform, and will be uniform, in all the simple sequences that have composed, or may hereafter compose it, and that the same antecedents, therefore, have always been followed, and will continue to be followed, by the same consequents. Whatever we observe becomes at once, by the influence of this principle, representative to us of the past and of the future, as well as of the present. We arrange phenomena, accordingly, not merely as parts of one casual sequence, but as *causes* and *effects,* or, in other words, as the invariable antecedents and consequents of the same phenomena in the same circumstances; and, expecting this uniformity of result, we invent the term *power,* not to express any thing distinct and separable from the antecedent itself, but to express the simple relation which we feel of its uniform immediate antecedence to a certain change — our undoubting belief, that whenever it has occurred, or may again occur, the event which we have once observed to be consequent, has always followed, and may always, in similar circumstances, be expected to follow again.

To know Matter fully, in accordance with these two views, both as it exists in space, and as it exists in time — that is to say, to know all the elements of every compound, and all the changes of which they may be reciprocally antecedent and consequent — would be to know every thing which can be physically known of the whole surrounding system of material things. We may think that it is possible for us to speculate still further; but our speculation, in that case, will be without a distinct object, and its result, if it have any, will be some distinction that is purely verbal, and nothing more.

II. In the philosophy of the other great department of nature, the physical inquirer has the same objects in view, or objects that are at least very closely analogous—the *analysis* of what is *complex,* and the arrangement of the various feelings or *successive* states of mind, in the regular order of their sequence, as *causes* and *effects*.

That *successive* phenomena, whether of matter or of mind, may alike admit of being arranged as antecedents and consequents in the order in which they occur, no one can doubt; and in this respect, therefore, the similarity of the objects of inquiry in the two departments of nature will be readily allowed. But that there should be inquiries in the physics of mind, corresponding with those of the chemist into the *composition* of bodies, may seem inconsistent with the simplicity and indivisibility which are universally regarded as essential to our very notion of the mind itself: and it may be the more necessary to dwell a little on this difficulty, as philosophers have been accustomed rather to pass over it without notice, than to treat it with the attention which it deserves.

There would, indeed, be the inconsistency supposed, if the analysis, in Mind, were professed to be strictly the same as in Matter. The mind *is* simple and indivisible. Every feeling of the mind, therefore, being only the mind itself existing in a certain state, must be equally simple and indivisible; and hence, as there is no real plurality in a sensation or thought or emotion, to admit of integral separation, the analysis, which is real, where self-subsisting elements of matter are detached from other self-subsisting elements, must in mind be virtual only, like the virtual complexity of the feelings on which it is exercised. It must always be remembered, that the feelings which we term *complex,* are, as truly as the feelings which we term *simple,* states of a substance that cannot be divided into elementary parts. But, while we admit this distinction, we must be conscious at the same time, that it is the very nature of certain feelings to *seem* to involve certain other feelings as elements of themselves; and this *seeming complexity,* which it is impossible not to feel, is sufficient for the analysis of the inquirer into mind, who does not attempt to divide a feeling into distinct parts, which it has not, but only traces the feelings to which, on reflection, certain other feelings are thus regarded as virtually equivalent. He knows, that the conception of a Centaur, or the notion of the abstract number four, is one state of one simple substance, as much as the conception of the trunk and limbs of a horse, or of the upper parts of a man, or the notion either of unity or of the abstract number three; but he knows also, that it is the very nature of that conception, and of that notion, to seem to be comprehensive of the other two; and the virtual analysis, by which he reduces this or other seeming compounds to their seeming elements, is, relatively to those of whose very nature such feelings of equivalence or comprehensiveness are a part, the same thing, as if there were a separate and distinct existence of the objects of thought thus regarded as equivalent, and elementary feelings as distinct, which were truly, and not virtually only, included in the more general feeling that seems to comprehend them.

In the Philosophy of Mind, then, as often as we speak of the analysis of complex feelings, it must never be forgotten, that the analysis of which we speak is virtual, not real – that it has not for its object what is truly compounded of parts, but a mere relation of seeming comprehensiveness, which, in certain circumstances, it is impossible for us not to feel, of one state of mind to other states in which the mind has before existed. It is not the less important, however, on that account, as a branch of physical inquiry, nor the less inexhaustible in the results which it affords. Almost every feeling is susceptible of this reflective analysis, in some greater or less degree; and inquirer after inquirer, in the field of mind, may evolve to us unsuspected elements of thought and passion, as chemist after chemist, in the world of matter, presents to us elements that never had been perceived by us, in substances which may have been before us from the moment of our birth.

III. The foregoing remarks have, I trust, prepared us in some measure for the discussions which are to follow. We have seen the nature of the two objects of inquiry in the Philosophy of Mind, analogous to the objects of the physical inquirer in the other department of nature, whose search is directed to the composition of bodies, and to the successive changes which they exhibit; and we have now to proceed to the consideration of the mental phenomena in this twofold view – analyzing what is felt by us as complex – and arranging them in the order of their succession, as reciprocally antecedent and consequent.

SELECTION 15

Of the Sensations Commonly Ascribed to Touch[4]

In the senses as yet considered by us, we have seen only the sources of certain feelings, pleasing, painful or indifferent, which might begin and pass away like any other affections of the mind, without affording the slightest information, as to the existence of a system of external things.

I. What is true of fragrance, and sweetness, and melody, is not less true of warmth and coldness, considered as mere sensations that arise from affections of our organ of touch.

But there are other feelings, commonly ascribed to touch, which are peculiarly distinguished by a reference to external corporeal causes, and which are supposed to have afforded, primarily and immediately, to the infant mind the knowledge which is implied in that reference.

With the exception of warmth and coldness — which, as they have nothing peculiar to distinguish them from the varieties of sensation before considered by us, may in the present inquiry be laid out of account — the perceptions ascribed to touch are only of modes of *extension* and *resistance,* the very compound which we have in view in all our definitions of matter. There may be in matter various other tendencies to excite various other feelings. But whether those other qualities be absent or present, we term Matter what is composed of parts and resists our effort to compress it.

To what organ, then, are we to ascribe the external influences, which give occasion to these feelings of resistance and extension?

II. It is not to touch, as I conceive, that either of these is to be traced.

Our feeling of *resistance,* in all its varieties of hardness, softness, roughness, smoothness, solidity, liquidity, &c. I consider as the result of organic affections, not tactual, but muscular; our muscular frame being truly, as I have before stated, an organ of sense, that is affected in various ways, by various modifications of external resistance to the effort of contraction.

If we had never used a single muscle, and knew nothing of the existence of things without, the pressure of a hard substance by any

---

[4] [Extracted from *Sketch of a System of the Philosophy of the Human Mind,* Edinburgh: Bell & Bradfute, Manners & Miller, and Waugh & Innes, 1820, pp. 77-144.]

foreign force that directed it on the palm of our hand, might have occasioned an unpleasant feeling; as the cut of a knife, or the application of fire to the same part, would in like manner have produced an unpleasant feeling. But this pain of the bruise would have been all. We should as little have known, in the one case, that the compressing mass was hard, as we should have supposed, in the other case, that the flame which burned us was hard. What we now mean, as often as we use that word, is a tendency to resist compression—a tendency to resist our muscular effort. It has its source in the peculiar muscular feeling which arises in that case; or at least the resulting sensation is a compound of a tactual and muscular feeling, the latter part of which is that which we have particularly in view as often as we employ the word.

The feeling of resistance, then, as a primary sensation, is a feeling of our muscular frame. It is the feeling which arises, when we endeavour to perform an accustomed contraction, and the contraction is impeded—a feeling which does not require any very nice discernment to distinguish it from that which arises on the mere touch of bodies, when no muscular effort has been made; though, from the uniform concurrence of the tactual feeling with the muscular, the one may afterwards become representative of the other, and suggest it, in the same way as the primary sensations of vision, by the influence of similar co-existence and suggestion, become representative of distance.

III. But, though *resistance* may not be a direct tangible quality, is not *extension* a quality of this kind? Does not touch, immediately and originally, inform us of superficial shape?

Though it appears to me very evident, that it is not from touch we obtain, primarily, our knowledge of form, I am aware that the denial of that which has had the sanction of universal belief, may have some chance, like every opinion, however well founded, that is regarded as paradoxical, of being counted little worthy of examination for that reason alone. It is certainly very possible, as the history of philosophy abundantly shows, to dispute long on distinctions purely verbal, and go through the forms of analysis, where there is nothing to be analyzed: but the tendency to reject every subtle inquiry, on that account, is one of the many prejudices with which we are accustomed to flatter our intellectual indolence. It is a tendency, however, so strong in most minds, that there are few errors, for which, if they be akin to the mixed mass of truth and error that forms the system of general belief, it would not be easier to obtain admission, than for truths that result from the justest analysis, if they be in opposition to errors which have been generally received.

That we at present seem to perceive figure immediately by touch, I do not deny; though I conceive our tactual perception of it to be far less accurate, than our visual perceptions of the magnitude and position of external things, which it is now no longer a paradox to consider as secondary or acquired perceptions of vision.

As little do I deny, that, when any hard surface is pressed on the surface of our body, a part of the tactual organ is affected, equal in extent to the impressing surface; and that, if we had any previous means of knowing the figure of our impressed organ as the result of the impression, there could not be any doubt as to the external form. But, if we assume this previous knowledge, we assume the very point in question, and take for granted, as previous to touch, what we yet ascribe to touch as its source. It must not be forgotten, that, before the knowledge of extension has been acquired in some way or other, the infant knows as little of the existence and form of his own organ of touch, as he knows of the existence and form of other external things, and that he cannot, therefore, have any knowledge of a similarity, which can be known only through a knowledge of the similar forms themselves, that are, by supposition, as yet unknown.

Above all, it must be remembered, that the feeling of extension, like every other feeling, is a state of mind, not of matter – a state of a substance, which, by its very nature, cannot be of any shape whatever, but is as little square when the bodily surface touches a square, as when it simply grieves or rejoices. The squareness of a portion of the palm of the hand is not a squareness of the sentient spirit. Till the mind, therefore, have acquired, in some other way, a knowledge of the bodily frame with which it is connected, no similarity of configuration of that which is not mind can be known to it; and when it knows this configuration, it has already received its knowledge of extension, and does not need any impression from without, to give it this elementary knowledge.

The confusion in our notions of the mind itself, which is capable of sensation, but unsusceptible of figure, and of the body, which is susceptible of change of figure, but incapable of sensation, is then, as we have seen, one great source of error with respect to the primary mode of acquiring the knowledge of extension.

Another source of error, of the same species, is to be found in the very general neglect by philosophers of circumstances in the other senses, which are truly common to them with touch, but which, from the permanence of the objects of touch, are very falsely supposed to be peculiar to it, or at least to belong to it in a greater degree than to the others.

It is not in the organ of touch only, that the sensorial matter is of a certain shape when affected. In all the other organs of sense, there is an expansion of similar matter; and when sensation of any kind takes place, there is always a portion of the expanse affected, which, being limited, must always be of a certain figure, whatever its boundary may be. If mere extension of nervous matter affected, therefore, were the only thing necessary to give the knowledge of extension, we should, by smell or hearing alone, have a perception of olfactory or auditory figure, in the same way as we are supposed to acquire the knowledge of tangible figure, from an affection of a similar expanse of nervous matter on the surface of the body.

These arguments, though only of a negative kind, appear to me, I confess, of very considerable strength. But, as they are negative only, let us next examine, more particularly, the phenomena themselves, and consider whether the perceptions, by which touch is supposed to convey to us the knowledge of magnitude and form, be of a kind which marks them more peculiarly as primary or secondary.

If touch be truly the direct and primary sense of magnitude and form, as hearing is the sense of sound, and smell the sense of fragrance, it should be equally the sense of every variety of these, as hearing is the sense of every variety of sound, and smell of every variety of fragrance. It would surely appear either a very singular doctrine of philosophy, or a very absurd abuse of language, to say of the sense of sound, that it is the sense of hearing a violin, but not equally the sense of hearing a harp, which are yet equally direct and primary objects of hearing, as far as the mere sounds of both are concerned; or to say of the sense of smell, that we distinguish by it the fragrance of a rose, but not equally any other fragrance as powerful. We may not be capable, indeed, of saying of some odours, that they are the fragrance of particular flowers, or of determining of some sounds, by what instruments they have been produced. But the reason of this difficulty is, that the external forms of flowers and instruments are not the direct objects of the senses of hearing and smell, which are affected only by the vibratory particles, in the one case, and the odorous particles, in the other case; and which never, but for other senses, could have told us of any flowers or instruments whatever. By the aid of other senses, indeed, we are able often to determine, that many flowers have mingled their odours, and many instruments their concurring vibrations. But in the varieties of sound, whether simple or complex, and the varieties of fragrance, whether simple or complex, all which was original in the particular sensations must have been felt with equal acuteness, if of equal intensity; or rather is itself the only measure which we possess of such intensity of the corresponding qualities of things without. There is no indistinctness in the immediate sensation: it is only in what is secondary or acquired in the perception, that any indistinctness is felt.

Now, if, on the supposition that magnitude and figure are direct objects of touch, this sense should give us perceptions as instant of every magnitude and figure, as hearing of every sound, and smell of every odour, let us consider, whether the phenomena agree, or do not agree, with this general description.

With this view, let an irregular figure, of any shape, and of the same temperature with the hand, to render the experiment as simple as possible, be pressed on the palm of any one whose eyes have previously been closed; and let him be required, in these circumstances, to state its magnitude and figure. It will be found, that he will form a very obscure and inaccurate guess as to its magnitude; and that he will very seldom, or, I may say never, be exactly right as to its outline. In no instance will he be able, even after the longest tactual study, if I may so term it, to state the magnitude and figure with the accuracy with which he is able to state them on a single glance; though the perception by vision is itself acknowledged not to be primary, but to be derived from the original perceptions of this very sense. In proportion as the figure is more regular, his perception will be quicker, and his approach to accuracy will be greater; though still far inferior to the rapid accuracy of that visual glance which is said to derive from it its whole power.

If we were to judge from the phenomena themselves, then, and determine the question by the evidence which they afford, it would surely seem to be stronger in support of the opinion, that the tactual perception of figure is secondary, not primary—that we learn by touch to distinguish actual magnitude, as we learn visually to distinguish actual magnitude—and that the simplest forms, therefore, being most familiar, are, as might have been anticipated, in such circumstances, most readily and surely learned. ...

3. Let us once more consider the circumstances in which the infant first exists, when he is the subject indeed of various feelings, but is ignorant of the existence of his own organic frame, and of every thing external. If we observe him as he lies on his little couch, there is nothing which strikes us more than his tendency to continual muscular motion, particularly of the parts which are afterwards his great organs of touch. There is scarcely a moment while he is awake, at which he is not opening or closing his little fingers, or moving his little arms in some direction. Now, though he does not know that he has a muscular frame, he is yet susceptible of all the feelings that attend muscular contraction in all its stages. From the moment at which his fingers begin to move towards the palm, to the moment at which they close on it, there is a regular series of feelings, which is renewed as unceasingly as the motion itself is renewed. The beginning of this series, as in every other regular sequence of events in after life, leads to the expectation of the parts which are to follow; and, like any other number of continuous parts, the whole series, whether merely remembered as past, or anticipated as future, is felt as of a certain length. The notion of a certain regular and limited length is thus acquired, and very soon becomes habitual to the mind of the infant — so habitual to it, that the first feeling which attends the beginning contraction of the fingers, suggests, of itself, a length that may be expected to follow.

It must be remembered, that it is the mere length of a sequence of feelings, attendant on muscular contraction, of which I speak, and not of any knowledge of muscular parts contracted. The infant does not know that he has fingers which move, even when, from an instinctive tendency, or other primary cause to which we are ignorant how to give a name, he sets them in motion: but, when they are thus in motion, and a consequent series of feelings already familiar to him has commenced, he knows the regular series of feelings that are instantly to follow.

In these circumstances, let us imagine some hard body to be placed on his little palm. The muscular contraction takes place, as before, to a certain extent, and with it a part of the accustomed series; but, from the resistance to the usual full contraction, there is a break in the anticipated series of feelings, the place of the remaining portion of which is supplied by a tactual feeling combined with a muscular feeling of another kind—that feeling of resistance which has been already considered by us. As often as the same body is placed again in the hand, the same portion of the series of feelings is interrupted by the same new complex feeling. It is as little wonderful, therefore, that this new feeling should suggest or become representative of the particular length of which it supplies the place, as that the reciprocal suggestion of one object by another should be the result of any other association as uniform. A smaller body interrupts proportionally a smaller part of the accustomed series—a larger body a larger portion—and, while the notion of a certain length of sequence interrupted varies thus exactly with the dimensions of the external object felt, it is not very wonderful, that the one should become representative of the other; and that the particular muscular feeling of resistance, in combination with the tactual feeling, should be attended with notions of different lengths, exactly according to the difference of the length of which it uniformly supplies the place.

The only objection which I can conceive to be made to this theory —if the circumstances be accurately stated, and if the inadequacy of touch as itself the direct sense of figure, have been sufficiently shown—is, that the length of a sequence of feelings is so completely distinct in character, as to be incapable of being blended with tactual notions of space. But this objection, as I flatter myself I have proved, arises from inattention, not to a few only of the phenomena of tactual measurement, but to all the phenomena: for in the measurement even of the most familiar object, as we have seen, a difference of the mere rapidity or slowness with which we pass our hand along its surface, and therefore of the mere length or shortness of the accompanying series of feelings, is sufficient to give in our estimate a corresponding difference of length or shortness to the surface which we touch. Length, indeed, considered abstractly, whether it be of time or of space, is nothing more in our conception than a number of continuous parts; and this definition is equally applicable to it, in the one case as in the other.

We see, then, how, in the mind of the infant, notions of length may be acquired, by the retrospect and anticipation of a continued series of feelings—a portion of that long line of time, which seems to us, as often as we look to the past and the future, to connect one remote event with another, like the lines of which geometricians speak, that, without any substantial reality, connect point with point in imaginary space.

4. In the early half-instinctive contractions of the fingers, sometimes more, sometimes fewer, of these are brought down upon the palm; and though the complex feeling, which arises from the simultaneous contraction of the whole fingers, would be, relatively to the sentient mind, like one simple feeling, if the contraction of the whole were uniform, it ceases to be regarded as simple, when frequent repetitions of the partial contractions have shown the elements of which that complex whole was composed. This internal analysis may be supposed to be rude and indistinct at first; but it will gradually become less and less obscure, like every other analysis which we are able to make of the first complex sensations of our infancy.

When the analysis has been made to a certain degree — and when the inward movement of each finger has been felt, in the series of the muscular sensations that attend its contraction, like a particular length — the similar movements of the others, when the whole fingers are bent, will be felt as a number of concurring lengths. The analysis on which this distributive belief depends, will be aided by the very circumstances to which we have traced the feeling of resistance, that is afterwards combined with that of length in the complex notion of matter: for, when any small mass is placed in the infant's hand, and when the ordinary contraction of all the fingers has begun, more or fewer of these will be impeded in their course, according to the breadth of the mass; and the series of muscular feelings of the unimpeded fingers will thus be more strongly distinguished from the other concurring series, of which the very different feeling of resistance has supplied the place.

Even in that rude state of intellectual being, which we are considering at present, we must not suppose, that the mind is incapable of reasoning, or is exempt from the influence of those principles of intuition which it obeys in after life. Let us endeavour, then, to trace that mixed result of sensation and intuition and reasoning, which may be supposed to arise in the circumstances that have now been under our review.

5. In whatever manner the first motions of the fingers may be produced, the infant will soon discover, that they are renewable by his will; and he will often exercise this power. From the accustomed antecedents he will expect the accustomed consequents, exactly as in after life; since this anticipation, which is independent of all reasoning, seems to flow from a law of our physical being. Certain series of feelings, then, begin and end in uniform order; the anticipation of

which is fulfilled as often as he does not will to suspend them. At last, however, they are suspended, without any will on his part, when some external substance has been placed in his hand. He expected the whole of the accustomed series: but the place of a portion of it is now supplied by another feeling; and since all of which he was conscious in himself at the moment preceding the interruption, was exactly the same as in the many former instances when the regular sequence took place, he ascribes the feeling of resistance to something that is foreign to him. There is something, then, which is not himself — something that represents a number of concurring lengths — something that gives rise to the feeling of resistance; and we have thus, however obscure they may be as first conceived by him, the rude elements, which afterwards become more distinct in his notion of a system of external things. Matter is that which is without us — which has parts — which resists our effort to compress it.

6. The notion of concurring lengths external to us, which I have traced only to contractions of the fingers, might be traced in like manner to other muscular contractions, especially to those of the arms, as sometimes terminating in certain tactual feelings, and sometimes interrupted by external objects: and the concurrence of these varieties of muscular contraction of the fingers and arms, and also of the impediments to accustomed series of feelings, when the contraction is interrupted, may be naturally supposed to aid the process, by which each singly might have evolved the same notions with less distinctness.

7. Another element of the complex feeling arises from the continuity of the surface of the tactual organ. I do not suppose this surface to be primarily known to the infant; for he would then have the knowledge which we are endeavouring to trace to its source: but, though he has no knowledge of his own organs, either as continuous in surface or separate, he has certain tactual feelings, which are not the same from similar pressure on different parts of the organ, but vary to a certain extent with the part of the organ affected; and of these some are always proximate to each other in time, when the hand is made to pass along any external surface. This proximity in succession of certain tactual feelings, when the same motion of the hand along similar surfaces has been very frequently repeated, gives another series for affording the notion of length, and a series that is equally capable of being anticipated and expected, as the muscular feelings in contraction. When one finger bends upon the palm, the

series of muscular feelings terminates in a certain tactual feeling; when two or more fingers bend on it, they impress other portions of the tactual surface; the feelings consequent on which impressions have before been found to be continuous or proximate, in the manner already stated, when part after part of the surface of the hand had frequently been moved along the same surface: and the union of all these concurring lengths, if I may so term them, in the feeling of external resistance, in which they all terminate, when any mass within the hand supplies the place of the accustomed contraction, seems to afford the elements, from which that compound notion of outness, and extension and resistance, which are truly all that is meant by us when we speak of matter, may gradually be evolved. That the first notions of this kind will be very rude, may naturally be supposed; as we cannot but suppose, in like manner, that the first visual perceptions of distance and magnitude are very rude. But the child will learn to distinguish forms by touch, as he learns to distinguish them by vision; and the elements of the perceptions, that are afterwards to become more and more distinct in progressive evolution, are all which the physiologist has to find, in the one case, as much as in the other.

It is not, then, to any peculiar intuition, that I am inclined to ascribe our knowledge of external things, as if the knowledge were primary and immediate. I suppose it, on the contrary, to be progressive in touch, as it is allowed to be in vision; and I conceive, that the gradual acquirement of this knowledge implies only such associations, inferences, and intuitions, as are common to all our physical reasonings. There is an intuitive belief of uniformity of the order which has once been observed. There is a consequent expectation, when all the antecedent circumstances have been the same, in a part of an accustomed series of muscular feelings, that the remaining part of the series will follow. There is an inference, therefore, when, without any difference of previous consciousness, the accustomed series is broken, by a new complex feeling which arises on the interposition of some hard substance, that the cause of this change is something different from the little sentient being himself — and there are the ordinary influences of association or suggestion, by which the complex feeling of touch and of resistance that is thus supposed to arise from a cause external or foreign, and that uniformly supplies the place of a certain length, or number of concurring lengths, becomes itself blended with the notion of those lengths of which it is the uniform representative. Outness, Extension, Resistance, are thus mingled in one complex feeling; and these, in our conception, are Matter.

VI. In whatever manner the belief of external corporeal causes of our sensations may arise, the universality of the belief, as far back as we are able to trace our perceptions, is a physical fact, as true of the sceptic himself as of all the rest of mankind. In our reasoning hours, we may speculate on it variously: but in the moment of perception, it is equally impossible for us not to believe that there are external things around us, as to believe that we are ourselves, unexisting.

1. That this impossibility does not arise from any primary intuition which accompanies our first sensations, but is the gradual result of other general influences, I have endeavoured to show. The argument, however, in this respect, is of no consequence as to the justness of the belief; for the evidence, if that word may be used in such a case, is precisely of the same kind, whether the intuition be primary and peculiar to our sensations, or common to them with other feelings, and will be, neither of greater nor of less force, whether other principles of the mind do or do not concur with the simple intuition. Though our first sensations, of whatever kind, may have been regarded by us, as I conceive they truly were regarded, only as feelings that began and died away; and though, for many weeks, the notions of external causes of our sensations may have been as vague and indistinct as I conceive them to have been, a short time is sufficient to evolve them gradually into greater clearness: and we are believers in external nature, long before we are capable of thinking whether the existence of that world which appears to be around us wherever we are, be a question for philosophic inquiry. Our belief becomes at last, on the one supposition, what it is asserted to have been on the other supposition, in the first sensations of our infancy. The intuition, which in the one case is primary, is secondary in the other case, and combined with the influence of other principles of our nature: but, in both cases, the belief depends on intuition in one stage or other; and in both alike, if it were possible for us to abandon our faith in every seeming truth that is not demonstrable by reasoning, the belief of a system of external causes of our sensations would cease with that abandonment.

This faith, however, it is by the very nature of intuition, or, as I should rather say, by the very nature of the human mind, impossible for us to abandon. The most sceptical inquirer is a sceptic only in years in which it is absolutely impossible for him to reject mentally what he professes to regard as illusive; or at least, in asserting that his feelings are under the influence of illusion, he must also admit, that it is an illusion to which he is at the very moment forced by his nature to yield, while he strives, in all the forms of reasoning, to appear to have escaped from it. In arguing against the reality of external things, he takes for granted that he has a disputant in the world without, on whose senses of sight or hearing he is to operate; and he avails himself instrumentally of substances which he regards as corporeal, at the very moment of his using them to prove that there is nothing which is worthy of that name.

2. It is not in the writings of Berkeley, as I conceive, that any just view of the sceptical argument on this subject is to be found. On many other subjects, the acuteness of this amiable and excellent philosopher cannot be too highly praised: but the praise which he has received even from his antagonists, for the ingenuity of his reasonings against the existence of matter, seems to me to have been far greater than was merited. These reasonings are truly little more than the development of one or two errors as to the nature of the mind and its affections; errors, that were nearly allied, indeed, to opinions which had prevailed for many ages, but that were little in the spirit of the sound general views which had been introduced in intellectual science by the eminent philosophers who more recently preceded him. His errors, I have said, were primarily and fundamentally errors as to the mind itself: for it is in his false views of it, that all which is fallacious in his view of matter is to be found. Even in rejecting a fixed material universe, and asserting the reality only of minds and their ideas, he carried into mind and confounded with it the properties of the universe which he had rejected; and, in this mixture of their common qualities, was almost as much a materialist as a spiritualist. He denies the existence of matter, in the common sense of that term: but he denies it, only by ascribing to the mind qualities, that are inconsistent with our very notions of spiritual being, and that, if really possessed by it, would bring it within a very near approach of that grosser substance to which it is commonly opposed.

Ideas, according to him, are not states of the mind: they are separate things, capable indeed of existing in a mind only, but contained within the mind, and capable of passing in some undescribed way from one mind into another. It is by ascribing recipiency, in this real unmetaphorical sense, to the mind, and a separate existence to the ideas of which it is the recipient, that he appears to me to have subjected himself to the charge of the semi-materialism which I have ventured to impute to him. He does not truly spiritualize the objects of perception, by making them thus fugitive; since, whether brief or lasting, whether termed Matter or termed Ideas, they are still said to be things capable of being contained within something else — he only converts the mind itself into a spacious vessel for containing them. Recipiency, in this gross sense of holding things that enter it and remain in it for a while, is as incompatible with our notion of mind, as concavity; with which, indeed, it may be said, in this sense, to be synonymous. The spiritual nature, of which Berkeley speaks, containing within itself an unbounded number of the things which he terms Ideas, that quit one mind to find their way into another mind, has scarcely any greater claim to be regarded as the pure Intelligence of which we are accustomed to think in using that phrase, than the mass of the brain to which materialists ascribe a similar office.

3. The only philosophic scepticism with respect to an external world, is that which, rejecting the separate existence of ideas, regards them in their true light, as states of the mind itself, and nothing more. Our perceptions, it may be said, are mere states of the mind, as much as any of our other vivid feelings — a part of the series of states in which the mind has existed, from its first sensation in infancy to the present moment. What we call our knowledge of matter, is either this mental state, which we term Perception, or an inference from this mental state, that must be itself equally a modification of the mind. If consciousness had not been, knowledge could not have been; and, beyond the mind itself, there is no consciousness; for consciousness, whatever variety of names we may give it, in sensation, in thought, in emotion, is itself in all these, only a state in which the mind is existing at the moment. All of which we are conscious, therefore, when we have a notion of external things, and give to that notion the name of Perception, is a feeling of the mind itself; and though it proves certainly, that the mind is capable of existing in this as in other states, it is that mental capacity alone which it proves.

4. To this scepticism, as to a world of masses that have qualities corresponding with our perceptions, there is no evidence of mere reasoning which can be opposed, except that which is founded on our actual impossibility of disbelieving the existence of such masses. The feeling, to which we give the name of the Perception of a Rose, is indeed a state of the mind, and of the mind only: but this very state of

the mind, which arises in certain circumstances, independently of any volition on our part, is a state of belief of the existence of something distinct from ourselves, and corporeal, to which we give the name of a Rose. To perceive is to make this very reference, and to make it undoubtingly. The state of the mind does not lead to the belief, but is the belief; and therefore, while the mind continues to be impressed with this and similar feelings, that are as much beyond the control of our reason as of our will, it must, by the very nature of the feelings, be a believer in the outward things which its perceptions seem to point out to it.

This is what we feel in perception, and must always feel, till, by some change of our physical nature, perception cease to be a state of the mind. Beyond the irresistible faith that is involved in the feeling, there is indeed nothing, it may be allowed, on which a reasoner can found his demonstration: but faith so universal, and so irresistible, has in it all the force of demonstration itself; because it has all the qualities of those primary truths which demonstration itself only evolves more fully in unsuspected applications of them, but does not render of stronger evidence, than they were felt to possess before the demonstration began.

VII. It is only in this way, as it appears to me, that the sceptical argument as to the existence of Matter admits of being answered: and the answer and the scepticism, it is evident, are alike independent of any false notions which may be entertained, with respect to the nature of Ideas; since both proceed equally on the belief that ideas are mere affections or states of the mind. There is one philosopher, however, of very high celebrity, especially in the northern part of the Island, who has been generally considered as the establisher of the positive doctrine of the existence of a system of material things, by his overthrow of what has been termed the Ideal Theory of Perception. The philosopher of whom I speak is Dr Reid, who regarded this supposed discovery of the errors of a former system as the source of almost every thing which can be considered as original in his own views of the mental phenomena, and who, whatever we may think of the general rank which he should hold as an intellectual inquirer, or of the justness of this particular pretension, must be allowed at least to have had a mind far too candid and honourable to lay claim to any praise to which he did not believe himself to be justly entitled.

The ready admission which his claim has received; the ample praise which has been in consequence bestowed on him; and the eminence of that School of Philosophy which was in a great degree founded on the opinions entertained by him on this leading subject; render necessary some examination of the grounds, on which so much merit has in this respect been ascribed to him.

We may consider, then, in the *first* place, the opinions entertained by Dr Reid himself with respect to perception; in the *second* place, the justness of the title which these opinions have been supposed to give him, to be regarded as the overthrower of that very absurd theory of perception which has been distinguished by the name of the Ideal System; and, in the *third* place, the effect which this supposed overthrow, if real, would have had, or might justly be expected to have, in obviating or lessening the force of the scepticism as to an external world.

1. According to Dr Reid, there are, in the process by which we become acquainted with external things, two distinguishable "acts of the mind" — in the *first* place, Sensation, by which various feelings are excited in the mind, simply as feelings — fragrance, sweetness, sound, for example; and, in the *second* place, Perception, which accompanies these sensations, and refers them to objects existing without — a particular fragrance, for example, to a quality of the rose which we smell, a particular sweetness to a quality of the honey which we taste, a particular sound to a quality of the trumpet which we hear. The trumpet, the honey, the rose, in all their variety of qualities, might be for ever unknown to us, if we were capable of sensation only: for sensation does not go beyond the feeling itself, which those objects excite. It is Perception, which, passing from the internal momentary feeling to the world without, discovers there some object to which it refers the feeling as its effect. There is, in short, according to him, a peculiar Power of the Mind, by the operation of which we have an immediate conviction of qualities of external things, that excite our sensations: and this Power, which is in every instance distinct from Sensation itself, is Perception.

If nothing more were meant by this distinction of Sensation and Perception, than that certain feelings, induced by external things, may, or may not, be considered by us with reference to their external causes, and that the word Perception is used to express the complex state of mind, when such a reference is made; the word might be allowed to be a very convenient one: but, when it is intended to convey the belief of a peculiar Faculty of the mind, under the name of Perception, that is distinct from Sensation, though commensurable with it in all the variety of the feelings which are recognized as the results of external influences, and that is at the same time essentially different from every other Power or tendency of the mind, the assertion of such a Faculty cannot be admitted; because it is founded on a very imperfect analysis of the phenomena, which a more minute examination would show to be referable to other sources.

What we term Perception is, in the greater number of cases, if not in all, a suggestion of memory, and nothing more. I have already shown, that, if we had had no other sense than smell, no other sense than taste, no other sense than hearing, and I might add, no other sense than that of colour, we should as little have suspected the existence of an external cause of our sensations, as of a direct external cause of any of our internal emotions. When we have previously acquired, whether by touch, as is commonly supposed, or less directly, in the manner which I have endeavoured to point out, the notion of external form and resistance, we have then, indeed, the complex notion, which we term the Notion of Matter; and this notion is capable of being suggested in certain trains of thought, as much as any other feeling of the mind. When we have previously seen and handled a rose, then, at the same time that we were sensible of its fragrance, or listened to a flute, with the existence of which, as a hard figured body, we had previously become acquainted, it is not very wonderful, that, on hearing the flute again, or again smelling the rose, we should be reminded of those external forms, with the presence of which the sound and the fragrance had before seemed to be connected in intimate union. The supposed perception, in these cases, is obviously nothing more than a simple suggestion of Memory or Association, or such an inference as is made in any of the simplest ordinary cases of reasoning. It is only in the phenomena ascribed to Touch, that any thing like the peculiar perception, of which Dr Reid speaks, is to be found: and even in the supposed perceptions of Touch, as I have endeavoured to show, a finer analysis may detect elements still more minute, that do not render it necessary to refer them to a peculiar Faculty. But, though we should admit the phenomena of perception in touch to be what he states them to be, it is in this one order of our sensations alone, as I have said, that the distinct perception takes place; and in all the other orders of our sensations, what is termed Perception is the mere suggestion of the form and hardness, which the single sense of Touch is supposed to have made known to us intuitively. Why this particular intuition, if it is to be considered as one, should be ranked differently from other intuitions, under the name of a Power or Faculty, it is not easy to discover. When we believe in our own identity, or believe that the future course of nature will resemble the past, the belief is not ascribed to the operation of a peculiar Intellectual Power; and yet these intuitions would as justly deserve the name of a Faculty, as the intuition which alone we suppose to impress us with the belief, that our sensations of touch have an external cause which is hard and figured.

All the phenomena of the mind, by whatever names expressed, are, as I have already often repeated, nothing more than the mind existing in certain states, and exhibiting, therefore, certain susceptibilities of it, or tendencies to exist in these successive states, after certain other antecedent circumstances, external or internal. What Dr Reid terms *Acts* or *Operations* of the mind, are nothing more than the development of these tendencies, when the antecedent circumstances necessary for their development have taken place. The "act" of Sensation, and the "act" of Perception, express, indeed, different states of the mind; for the one expresses a simple feeling, the other a reference of this feeling to some external cause, suggested by former association, or perhaps in one order of our sensations discovered intuitively: but, however different they may be, they are still, like all our different feelings, a portion of the series of states in which the mind has existed at different times, that have been various, as the antecedent circumstances which induced them, have themselves been various.

Dr Reid, however, considering all the processes of thought in a more mysterious view, and attaching to the words *act* and *operation* no very precise meaning, was influenced by an error of the same kind, in supposing the word *object* to express a relation different from that relation of simple and invariable antecedence, which is all that is meant when we speak of causation, in other sequences of events, material or mental. Yet perception is surely a mere feeling or state of the mind, like any other part of our varied consciousness – a state of mind, which is induced, directly or indirectly, by its external cause, as any other feeling is induced by its particular antecedent. If the external cause or object be absent, the consequent feeling, direct or indirect, which we term Perception, will not be induced; precisely as any other feeling will not arise without its peculiar antecedent. The relation of Cause and Effect, in short, is exactly the same in perception as in all the other mental phenomena — a relation of invariable sequence of one change after another change. I have already shown, that in all our affections of sense, with the exception, perhaps, of the single order of them commonly ascribed to Touch, perception is nothing more than a suggestion of the past; and that what we term the Object, therefore, in these cases, is merely what we remember to have been present on some former occasion: while in Touch itself, the belief or perception of something hard and figured, if it be not, as I suppose, the result of similar associations and inferences, is merely an intuition like any other intuition, in which we do not suppose the relation of the intuitive feeling to the feeling that preceded it, to be at all different from the relation of any other feeling to any other antecedent feeling. When certain circumstances have taken place, certain sensations arise; when certain other circumstances have taken place, there is a sequence as immediate of certain intuitions. The consequent feelings in the two cases are different as the antecedent circumstances are different; but there is no difference in the nature of the relation itself which the particular consequent in the train bears to the particular antecedent.

2. The mysterious obscurity of the meaning attached by Dr Reid to the relation of the object of perception to the percipient mind, as different from that of the ordinary sequences of events in causation, tended greatly, as I conceive, to aid the illusion with which he flattered himself that he was the overthrower of a great system of error, in his exposure of the absurdity of the Ideal System of Perception. That such a claim should have been made by him is indeed wonderful: but far more wonderful is it, that the claim should have been admitted, and should still continue to be admitted, by the general assent of philosophers.

The narrow limits of a sketch like the present, which must necessarily be restricted to a brief view of the phenomena themselves in their various relations, or to a notice only of such theories as derive peculiar importance from the high estimation in which they continue still to be held, do not allow room for a full discussion of the circumstances which seem most probably to have led to that ancient theory of perception by intervening species or images of things, the spirit of which, in its most important applications, Dr Reid conceived himself to be the first who had effectively combated. I may state, however, in general, that this, like various other theories, ancient and modern, of the same mental process, seems to me to have arisen chiefly from a false supposition of two great difficulties — the difficulty of accounting for the perception of objects at a distance, and the difficulty also of accounting, with respect to substances so little kindred in their nature as matter and mind, for such a link of mutual connection, as was supposed to be necessary for their reciprocal agencies in causation. Of these two imaginary difficulties, which have been so perplexing to philosophers, and so productive of wild and extravagant fancies, one vanishes instantly, when it is shown, by an analysis of what is falsely called the medium when it is truly the direct object of the particular sense, that there never is, in the strict philosophic meaning of the phrase, perception of distant things; and the other difficulty vanishes in like manner, when it is shown that causation does not imply any intermediate link of connection, but is the simple relation of one change, as invariably antecedent, to another change that is invariably consequent.

The views, therefore, on which the Ideal theory was founded, were false: but, while such false views of perception at a distance, and of the necessity of connecting links in causation prevailed, the doctrine of Species was a very natural consequence of them; since, however faulty in other respects, it had at least the advantage of appearing to obviate the two great difficulties which perception was thus erroneously believed to involve. By flowing from the object to the organ, and affecting the organ only when in contact with it, the Species virtually destroyed the interval between external things and our sensitive frame, and at the same time, from its exquisite tenuousness, as of a nature almost intermediate between that of matter and of mind, seemed admirably adapted for such a common link as was supposed to be necessary to intervene and connect them.

While the difficulties which I have now stated were felt, then, it does not appear to me wonderful, that a doctrine like that of perception by Species should have prevailed; since the facility which it afforded of obviating these difficulties would naturally, as we may well suppose, procure an indulgent allowance for the imperfections which it involved in other respects. If the belief of such little images, as the real objects of perception, had prevailed down to the time of Dr Reid, he would have been most unquestionably a benefactor to science, in exposing the futility of the hypothesis. But though, during the reign of the Commentators on Aristotle, this error may be said to have been universal in the Schools, it had gradually sunk away, chiefly by the influence of the Cartesian philosophy,[5] in which the absurdity of the supposition of such intermediate images was very strongly shown. From the period of this memorable reform in science—if we except Malebranche, who, though a Cartesian in many important respects, had not adopted his great master's simple theory of perception, and Berkeley, who, as we have seen, had notions on this subject, which in many respects were not very unlike to those of Malebranche—I do not know any great writer, who professed a belief of the necessity of images as things intervening in perception, or who considered the idea as something altogether distinct both from the mind and from the external object. They were accustomed indeed to speak of ideas in their minds, as we are accustomed still to use the same phrase; but they meant nothing more by it then, than we mean by it now, and could as little have suspected, that the use of such a metaphor would, at the interval of a century, subject them to the ridicule of philosophers, for believing in the existence of real images of things which were neither the external objects perceived nor states of the percipient mind, as we should now dread a similar confutation and ridicule from the philosophers who are to follow us, for a similar use of the same very obvious figure of speech.

The presence of an external object—an organic change, or series of changes of some sort, consequent on the presence of that object; the subsequent affection of the sentient mind itself—all these Dr Reid supposes to be necessary to constitute the process of perception, and

---

[5] I refer particularly to the paragraphs 197 and 198 of the 4th Part of the Principia Philosophic, and to the 1st and 4th Chapters of the Dioptrics. I have far too high a respect for Dr Reid, to suppose for a moment that he could be guilty of willful misrepresentation. But my astonishment is the greater on that account, when, after reading these and similar passages, in disproof of perception by representative images, I find that he who contends that there is no proof of such representation, "Diversos motus tenuium uniuscujusque nervi capillamentorum sufficere ad diversos sensus producendum," —" neque opus esse ut in objectis aliquid sit nostris sensibus simile," ["The diverse movements of each of the nerve fibres suffice to produce our diverse sense perceptions" —"nor is there anything in the objects themselves which is similar to the sensations we have of them"] is yet stated to have believed "that it is only a representative image, in the mind, of the external object that we perceive, and not the object itself; and this image, which the Peripatetics called a Species, he calls an Idea, changing the name only, while he admit the thing." The change of mere name would, indeed, have been of little consequence; but it seems scarcely possible to read the works of Descartes, without perceiving, that his controversy with the Peripatetics, in this respect, regarded the thing, and not the name.

contends only against the existence of "a fourth thing," which, under the name of an Idea, he affirms to have been introduced by philosophers: but the existence of this fourth thing, distinct from the object, from the organic change or series of changes, and from the mind itself, was as little maintained by Descartes, by Hobbes, by Locke, or, with the exceptions already made, by any other intervening philosopher of the slightest eminence, from the time of Descartes, as it was maintained by Dr Reid himself. The materialists indeed might reject the mental affection, which is the last part of the process, as the rejecters of matter would of course deny the presence of the external object and the consequent organic changes which form the first and second parts of the threefold process; but the *fourth thing,* distinct from the object the organ and the mind, was not supposed by any one.

How erroneous a representation Dr Reid has delivered of the opinions on perception entertained by the great philosophers preceding him, can be shown, however, only by a full review of the works themselves, in which their opinions are stated. After such an examination, the general sanction which his claim has received, will appear indeed most extraordinary: but it is a review which cannot be comprised in a few pages, and which is too extensive, therefore, to be attempted in this brief sketch.

I have already said, that the vague and mysterious meaning of the word "object," which, in the speculations of Dr Reid, is a word of peculiar importance, tended partly to aid his illusion in this respect. In the process of perception, there is always a series of changes, corporeal and mental. If we were to analyze the process with strict philosophic exactness, and to ascribe each effect in the train only to its immediate cause—as we should in that case consider the mental affection with constant reference to the sensorial change, and only to the sensorial change, by which it was immediately induced—its real object or external cause would appear to be that particular state of the nerves and brain. But we are not always so exact in our analysis and reference. It is much more convenient, for the sake of brevity, in popular and even in philosophic language, to omit many parts of the train of corporeal changes, and to speak only of the perception itself, and of the object that is external not merely to the mind but to our bodily frame; since, on the presence of this external object, the whole bodily train of changes, however numerous and various they may be, are a sequence which may always be anticipated. This separation of the object from the train of bodily changes that follow it, as if it had itself a relation to our feelings that is primary and direct, and the peculiar importance attached to its presence as that on which the other changes of the train depend, lead very naturally all who are little accustomed to nicety of analysis, to suppose the relation of the Object in perception, to be one of a peculiar kind, different from the relation which the other parts of the train bear to each other. With this view, therefore, of something peculiarly mysterious in the relation, it is not wonderful that they should imagine, when philosophers do not speak of it as of a peculiar kind, but content themselves with merely tracing the parts of the sequence of changes in the process of perception, of which the presence of the external object is a part like any of the other parts, that they who do not apply to the external object any of the accustomed phrases of mystery, must have in view something else, an image or other intermediate thing, which they regard as the real object of perception – its object not in the sense of mere antecedence or causation, but in that mysterious sense in which the more distant object has been falsely understood by themselves.

The fallacy in this respect would naturally be much strengthened by the use, in a metaphorical sense, of phrases that, while the Scholastic Philosophy prevailed, were employed with a very different meaning. To perceive ideas was, in the scholastic ages, to have "images of things," distinct from the object and the mind, truly present to the mind in perception; and though this and other similar phrases of the obsolete philosophy, like the language which we use when we speak of the rising and setting of the sun, to express only corresponding motions of our earth with respect to that great luminary, were employed to express opinions on perception corresponding exactly or almost exactly with those of Dr Reid himself, it still was *possible* to conceive them as meant to be expressive of the ancient opinions which they had long been employed to denote. In this way only can we account for the singular illusion, which, in spite of the contrary assertions in the works of the eminent philosophers who preceded him, and even of the ordinary language[6] of the elementary

---

[6] I may quote, as an example of this kind, the words of one of the most laborious and useful of elementary writers on Logic, J. P. de Crousaz, Professor of Philosophy and Mathematics at Lausanne, who is, perhaps, now better known to general readers by the line in which Pope has coupled him with 'Dutch Burgersdyck,' than by his many Works on Dialectics,

works of the schools, could lead the author of the "Inquiry into the Human Mind" to suppose, that in the systems of all the great metaphysicians who spread a light of so much glory on the century preceding him, it was assumed, that we saw and heard and smelled and touched and tasted only little images of things, distinct both from the mind itself and from the external things which surround us.

It was, perhaps, unfortunate for the accuracy of Dr Reid's Philosophy, that his view, as a controversialist, was so frequently turned to the speculations of Mr Hume; who, though worthy of high praise for his acuteness, is far from being entitled to the same praise for the precision of his metaphysical language; and who, perhaps, occasionally, for the sake of giving greater force to his sceptical reasonings, which a little verbal confusion might render more difficult to be combated, was less nice in his analyses, and in the applications of his terms, than he would otherwise have been. A particular study of his language, therefore, which was often accordant with that of the scepticism of earlier ages, was very apt to mislead an inquirer, who did not make the necessary limitations and deductions on that account. In his Essay on the Academical Philosophy, in which he states the sceptical argument against the evidence of the senses, he uses phrases, indeed, which, if we were to consider them technically, without attention to the spirit of the argument, might be adduced as proofs of his belief of images present to the mind. But it is very clear, that the image of which he speaks in such a case, is the perception itself, not any thing distinct from perception; and that the presence to the mind is only a metaphorical expression of the actuality of the momentary feeling. He calls it, therefore, an "Image or Perception;" and he says, that "the existences which we consider, when we say *this house,* and *that tree,* are nothing but perceptions in the mind;" thus evidently showing that he does not mean the image and the per-

---

which might justly have entitled him to more honourable notice. "Cogitandi modi qui in nobis sunt," he says, " quibus cogitatio nostra modificatur, quos induit alios post alios, sufficiunt ut per eos ad rerum cognitionem veniat, nec sunt fingendae ideae ab illis modificationibus diversae,." ["The ways of thinking, by which our mind is successively modified, are themselves sufficient to acquaint us with external objects, and separate ideas are not fashioned from these various mental modifications." Jean-Pierre de Crousaz, *System of Logic*, I.II.i.] It would not be easy to express more strongly the nullity of those intermediate Ideas of which Dr Reid supposed himself the overthrower: and indeed, if I were desirous of giving a view of all which Dr Reid supposed to be peculiar to himself in his system of Perception, I could scarcely do it better than in the words of De Crousaz.

ception to be distinguished. Dr Reid, however, who had been originally, by his own account, a believer in real images of things, was the more naturally led to conceive his own error to be the common belief of other philosophers, and, in conformity with this opinion, therefore, to interpret strictly in every case the phrases that were used by them with a metaphorical or limited application. His self-illusion as to his supposed overthrow of the Ideal System was thus, perhaps, the consequence of his own former belief of that very Ideal System.

3. But, even though it were granted, in accordance with the too ready general admission of this claim, that Dr Reid was truly the overthrower of that strange system, which he affirmed to be the universal belief of philosophers, would this overthrow deserve to be considered as having any effect in lessening the scepticism with respect to an external world? In this respect, too, a species of merit has been ascribed to Dr Reid's System, which it certainly is very far from deserving.

Our perceptions — or whatever other name we may give to our belief of external things as causes of our sensations — are, it must surely be allowed, states of the mind, not states of matter; and would be equally so, whether induced by things which are to be termed Ideas, or by things which are to be termed more properly Objects of Perception. If all that is mental had continued precisely what it has been in any of the individuals who live around us, and if every thing material could be supposed at the same time to have had no existence, there would still have been, as now, what we term Perceptions of external things; because perceptions are a part of the series of states of the mind. It would be of no moment in this respect, whether in the annihilation of every external object were included certain things called Ideas, or whether there never existed such things; for, as the mental state of perception, in whatever way induced, must still be only a state of the mind, the relation of this, state to its immediate external cause is all that could be affected by the annihilation, and this relation to an external cause, would be the same, whether the direct antecedent were the presence of an object external or an image external. The image would be only one external link more — an unnecessary one, it may be admitted, in the train of antecedents of perception; and the argument of the sceptic regards not the number of antecedents of perception external to the mind, but the existence of any external antecedent whatever. It is in the mental nature of the feeling which we term Perception, that the whole force of the argument consists; and that nature is not rendered less completely mental by the denial of intervening Species. On the contrary, it seems to me that the admission of such species, as it would itself be the admission of *something* external to the mind, would lessen, rather than increase, the force of the sceptical argument, which proceeds on the impossibility of any knowledge but of the various feelings of the mind itself. The only scepticism on the subject that is worthy of being confuted, is that which believes as little in things called Ideas, beyond the mind, as it believes in any thing else beyond the mind, and has, therefore, nothing to do with the controversy, whether the feeling which we term a Perception of the sun have for its cause the light which is radiated from that great orb, or the presence of some intervening thing, which is a little image of the sun. To show that there is no such little image, would be of no effect whatever in combating such scepticism: for there would still be the same necessity as before, to show that the cause of the feeling, though not an image, was a mass such as we term the Sun, or an ethereal substance like that to which we give the name of Light. This Dr Reid can do in no other way, than by stating the absolute impossibility of disbelieving the existence of external causes of our sensations — an impossibility that would be exactly the same, whether little images of things existed or not; and this impossibility of disbelieving, in perception, that there are things truly without us, the sceptics whose reasonings he supposed himself to have overthrown, would have admitted as readily as himself; though they might still have endeavoured to show that this very impossibility was the result of an illusion. Nothing can be stronger, as to the total inadequacy of the sceptical argument to produce any practical and lasting conviction, than the language of Mr Hume himself. " Nature," he says,

> is always too strong for principle: and though a Pyrrhonian may throw himself or others into a momentary amazement and confusion by his profound reasonings, the first and most trivial event in life will put to flight all his doubts and scruples, and leave him the same, in every point of action and speculation, with the philosophers of every other Sect, or with those who never concerned themselves in any philosophical researches. When he awakes from his dream, he will be the first to join in the laugh against himself.[7]

---

[7]   [Hume, *Enquiry Concerning Human Understanding* XII.ii]

It would not be easy to discover in the writings of Dr Reid himself, a stronger expression of the irresistible evidence, as he would term it, of the Senses. Indeed, the philosophy of Mr Hume and the philosophy of Dr Reid, on this subject, on which, to ordinary observers, they may seem to be wholly at variance, will appear, if we examine them more closely, to have no real discrepancy. The doctrine of both is composed only of two propositions; one of which is, That no argument can be offered to show by mere reasoning the existence of external causes of our feelings—The other, that it is absolutely impossible for us, in the various states of mind which we term Perception, not to believe in external causes of our feelings. The whole seeming difference is merely this—that each philosopher, though affirming both propositions, dwells a long time on one of them, and a short time on the other; and that the particular proposition on which they dwell the longer, is not, in both cases, the same.

SELECTION 16

Classification of Mental Phenomena: Condillac and Reid[8]

All the feelings of which the mind is susceptible, have been already divided by me into two classes, according as their causes are External or Internal; and having considered the former class of External Affections of the mind, we have now to proceed to the consideration of its Internal Affections.

These it will be necessary to subdivide into distinct orders.

I. In the classification of our feelings, as in that of any other phenomena, it is evident that we may err in two ways—by excessive simplicity or by redundancy. We may force under one name various feelings that have little general resemblance, or we may invent many verbal distinctions for seeming varieties, which a more minute analysis would have shown to be of the same general character, and to be reducible with advantage to a single division, in an arrangement of simpler phraseology.

The most striking example of the former species of error, with respect to the mind, is to be found in the system of Condillac and other French metaphysicians his followers, who consider all our

---

[8] [Extracted from *Sketch of a System of the Philosophy of the Human Mind*, Edinburgh: Bell & Bradfute, Manners & Miller, and Waugh & Innes, 1820, pp. 177-184.]

feelings, in our internal processes of thought and emotion, as mere *Sensations* variously *transformed*. What the nature of the *transformation* is, by which the affections of sense become reasonings and desires, they have not thought it necessary to explain very clearly; contenting themselves with the mere fact of the priority of our sensations to all our other feelings, as if priority and succession were enough to constitute identity — or repeating the unsupported assertion in many new forms and applications, as if mere frequency of asserting a proposition were itself a proof of its justness — or occasionally calling in the aid of authority, and professing to consider themselves as followers of Locke, in a doctrine which is wholly unsanctioned by the very different views of that great philosopher.

Such is one species of error of arrangement with respect to the phenomena of the mind. It is not an error which has been very prevalent in the intellectual philosophy of Britain. In the northern part of the Island, especially, an opposite error has prevailed: and the philosophy of Dr Reid, with its long catalogue of Intellectual and Active powers of the mind, may be considered as exemplifying one extreme, as the philosophy of Condillac exemplifies the other.

It is easier, however, to discover deficiencies or redundancies of this kind, or to suppose that we have discovered them where there truly may be none, than to catch and preserve for our continued guidance that almost invisible line, on either side of which is deviation into error. However just any arrangement of our own may appear to ourselves, we must be aware, that it cannot appear juster to us, than the arrangements to which we have preferred it, most probably appeared to their authors. Yet we are not the more on that account to adhere to a classification that appears to us faulty: it is a reason only for caution and humility in the statement of any new arrangement which we may venture to propose.

II. The class of Internal Affections I have divided into two Orders – Intellectual States of the Mind, and Emotions; — the former of which orders alone we have at present to consider.

Our Intellectual States of Mind, however much they may specifically differ, will be found, even in their minutest variations, to exhibit only two generic diversities — diversities which, in the ordinary metaphysical sense of those terms, may be expressed very nearly by the phrases, *Conceptions*, and *Feelings of Relation*. Our whole trains of thought, if we abstract from them the Sensations which external objects may occasionally induce, and the Emotions that may frequently mingle with them, will be found to be composed of these, and of these alone. It is the very nature of the mind to be susceptible of these in certain trains; one perception or conception suggesting, or, in other words, having for its immediate consequent, some other conception; as when the sight of a picture suggests the Artist who painted it, and the conception of the painter suggests, in like manner, the name of some other artist of the same School, and this afterwards the City in which that School of painting chiefly flourished. The successive conceptions, in such cases, arise in the mind, in the absence of the external objects that produced originally the corresponding perceptions; and, though capable of being modified to a certain extent by states of the bodily frame, are, as far as any discoveries of the physiologist have yet been able to throw light on their origin, Internal Affections of the Mind — results of a tendency of the mind itself, in certain circumstances, to exist in one state after existing in some other state. The tendency to this renovation of former feelings has commonly received the name of Association of Ideas — a name that is faulty in various respects, as limiting to our mere Ideas an influence which is not confined to them, and as seeming to imply some mysterious process of union as necessary before the suggestion itself; which, whether it be found to be true or not, on a more subtle analysis of the phenomena; is at least not very easy to be reconciled with the opinions of those who invented, or have continued to employ the phrase. I have preferred, therefore, for the sake of greater precision, and for avoiding the intermixture of any thing that can be considered as conjectural, the name of Simple Suggestion; meaning by that phrase to express nothing more than is actually observed by us, in the readiness of certain feelings to arise after certain other feelings, as resemblances of former perceptions or conceptions or other preceding states of the mind; and restricting the phrase uniformly to such simple sequences of the similar feelings, exclusively of all notions of relation of object to object, that may occasionally arise from them, and be intermingled with them.

Our trains of thought are not composed, then, merely of such conceptions, or other resemblances of former feelings, that begin, and continue, and pass away, as it were separately, without impressing us with any common relation which they bear. In the same manner as one conception suggests another conception, the perception or conception of two or more objects suggests or gives rise to certain feelings of relation, which, as states of the mind, differ from the mere perceptions or conceptions themselves, that have given rise to them, not merely as these perceptions or conceptions appear to differ from each other, but generically as a distinct order of feelings.

There is an original tendency of the mind to the one species of suggestion, in certain circumstances, as much as to the other; and as to the one of these, which affords us mere copies of former feelings, I have given the name of Simple Suggestion; to the other, which develops a new order of states of mind, in our feelings of relation, I give the name of Relative Suggestion; using the term Suggestion in both cases, as that which expresses most simply the mere general fact of the rise of the feelings in succession, without involving any hypothesis as to processes of former association, or any other circumstances, that may be justly or erroneously supposed to connect them.

That our trains of thought, as purely intellectual states of the mind, are indicative of these two tendencies alone, and that it is only from imperfect analysis, which seems to present differences when there truly is no generic difference whatever, that they have been referred to a greater number of supposed Faculties, will appear, I flatter myself, on a review of the phenomena, to which we are next to proceed, under the two heads to which I have referred them.

V
Lectures

SELECTION 17

Consciousness[1]

In the systems of philosophy, which have been most generally prevalent, especially in this part of the island, consciousness has always been classed as one of the intellectual powers of the mind, differing from its other powers, as these mutually differ from each other. It is accordingly ranked by Dr Reid, as separate and distinct, in his Catalogue of the intellectual powers; and he says of it, that

> it *is* an operation of the understanding of its own kind, and cannot be logically defined. The objects of it are our present pains, our pleasures, our hopes, our fears, our desires, our doubts, our thoughts of every kind; in a word, all the passions, and all the actions and operations of our own minds, while they are present.[2]

And in various parts of his works, which it would be needless to quote, he alludes to its radical difference from the other powers of the mind, as if it were a point on which there could be no question. To me, however, I must confess, it appears, that this attempt to double, as it were, our various feelings, by making them not to constitute our consciousness, but to be the objects of it, as of a distinct intellectual power, is not a faithful statement of the phenomena of the mind, but is founded, partly on a confusion of thought, and still more on a confusion of language. Sensation is not the object of consciousness different from itself, but a particular sensation is the consciousness of the moment; as a particular hope, or fear, or grief, or resentment, or simple remembrance, may be the actual consciousness of the next moment.

---

[1] [Extracted from *Lectures on the Philosophy of the Human Mind*, London: William Tegg, 1860, Lecture XI, pp. 67-70]
[2] [Reid, *Essays on the Intellectual Powers*, VI.iii]

In short, if the mind of man, and all the changes which take place in it, from the first feeling with which life commenced, to the last with which it closes, could be made visible to any other thinking being, a certain series of feelings alone, that is to say, a certain number of successive states of the mind, would be distinguishable in it, forming, indeed, a variety of sensations, and thoughts, and passions, as momentary states of the mind, but all of them existing individually, and successively to each other. To suppose the mind to exist in two different states, in the same moment, is a manifest absurdity. To the whole series of states of the mind, then, whatever the individual momentary successive states may be, I give the name of our consciousness – using that term, not to express any new state additional to the whole series, (for to that, which is already the whole, nothing can be added, and the mind, as I have already said, cannot be conceived to exist at once in two different states) but merely as a short mode of expressing the wide variety of our feelings; in the same manner as I use any other generic word for expressing briefly the individual varieties comprehended under it. There are not sensations, thoughts, passions, and also consciousness, any more than there is quadruped or animal, as a separate being, to be added to the wolves, tigers, elephants, and other living creatures, which I include under those terms.

The fallacy of conceiving consciousness to be something different from the feeling, which is said to be its object, has arisen, in a great measure, from the use of the personal pronoun *I*, which the conviction of our identity, during the various feelings, or temporary consciousnesses of different moments, has led us to employ, as significant of our permanent self – of that being, which is conscious, and variously conscious, and which continues, after these feelings have ceased, to be the subject of other consciousnesses, as transient as the former. *I am conscious* of a certain feeling, really means, however, no more than this – I feel in a certain manner, or, in other words, my mind exists in that state which constitutes a certain feeling; the mere existence of that feeling, and not any additional and distinguishable feeling that is to be termed consciousness, being all which is essential to the state of my mind, at the particular moment of sensation; for a pleasure, or pain, of which we are not conscious, is a pleasure or pain, that, in reference to us at least, has no existence. But when we say, I am conscious of a particular feeling, in the usual paraphrastic phraseology of our language, which has no mode of expressing, in a single word, the mere existence of a feeling, we are apt, from a prejudice of grammar, to separate the sentient *I* and the feeling, as different—not different, as they really are, merely in this respect, that the feeling is one momentary and changeable state of the permanent substance I, that is capable of existing also, at other moments, in other states; but so radically different, as to justify our classing the feeling in the relation of an object, to that sentient principle which we call I—and an object to it, not in retrospect only, as when the feeling is remembered, or when it is viewed in relation to other remembered feelings; but in the very moment of the primary sensation itself; as if there could truly be two distinct states of the same mind, at that same moment, one of which states is to be termed sensation, and the other different state of the same mind to be termed consciousness.

To estimate more accurately the effect which this reference to self produces, let us imagine a human being to be born with his faculties perfect as in mature life, and let us suppose a sensation to arise for the first time in his mind. For the sake of greater simplicity, let us suppose the sensation to be of a kind as little complex as possible; such: for example, as that which the fragrance of a rose excites. If, immediately after this first sensation, we imagine the sentient principle to be extinguished, what are we to call that feeling which filled and constituted the brief moment of life? It was a simple sensation, and nothing more; and if only we say, that the sensation has existed – whether we say, or do not say, that the mind was conscious of the sensation—we shall convey precisely the same meaning; the consciousness of the sensation being, in that case, only a tautological expression of the sensation itself. There will be, in this first momentary state, no separation of self and the sensation—no little proposition formed in the mind, *I feel* or *I am conscious of a feeling*—but the feeling, and the sentient I, will, for the moment, be the same. It is this simple feeling, and this alone, which is the whole consciousness of the first moment; and no reference can be made of this to a self, which is independent of the temporary consciousness; because the knowledge of self, as distinct from the particular feeling, implies the remembrance of former feelings—of feelings, which, together with the present, we ascribe to one thinking principle; recognizing the principle, the self, the *me*, as the same, amid all its transient diversities of consciousness.

Let us now, then, instead of supposing life, as in the former case, to be extinguished immediately after the first sensation, suppose another sensation to be excited, as for instance that which is produced by the sound of a flute. The mind either will be completely absorbed in this new sensation, without any subsequent remembrance—in which case the consciousness of the sensation; as in the case of the fragrance that preceded it, will be only another more paraphrastic expression of the simple sensation—or the remembrance of the former feeling will arise. If the remembrance of the former feeling arise, and the two different feelings be considered by the mind at once, it will now, by that irresistible law of our nature, which impresses us with the conviction of our identity, conceive the two sensations, which it recognizes as different in themselves, to have yet belonged to the same being: that being, to which, when it has the use of language, it gives the name of self and in relation to which it speaks, as often as it uses the pronoun *I*.

The notion of self, as the lasting subject of successive transient feelings, being now, and not till now, acquired, through the remembrance of former sensations or temporary diversities of consciousness, the mind will often again, when other new sensations may have arisen, go through a similar process, being not merely affected with the particular momentary sensation, but remembering other prior feelings, and identifying it with them, in the general designation of self. In these circumstances the memory of the past will often mingle with and modify the present; and, now, indeed, to form the verbal proposition, *I am conscious of a particular sensation*—since the very word *I* implies that this remembrance and identification has taken place—may be allowed to express something more than the mere existence of the momentary sensation, for it expresses also that the mind, which now exists in the state of this particular sensation, has formerly existed in a different state. There is a remembrance of former feelings, and a belief that the present and the past have been states of one substance. But this belief, or in other words, this remembrance of former feelings, is so far from being essential to every thought or sensation, that innumerable feelings every moment arise, without any such identification with the past. They are felt, however, for this is necessarily implied in their existence; but they exist, as transient thoughts or sensations only, and the consciousness, which we have of them, in these circumstances, is nothing more than the thoughts or sensations themselves, which could not be thoughts or sensations if they were not felt.

In the greater number of our successions of momentary feelings, then, when no reference is made to former states of the mind, the consciousness is obviously nothing more than the simple momentary feeling itself as it begins and ceases; and when there is a reference to former states of the mind, we discover on analysis only a remembrance, like all our other remembrances, and a feeling of common relation of the past and the present affection of the mind to one permanent subject. It is the belief of our continued identity which involves this particular feeling of relation of past and present feelings; and consciousness, in this sense of the term, is only a word expressive of that belief.

That the fragrance of a rose, the sound of a flute, and in general all the other objects of sense, might have excited precisely the same immediate sensations as at present, Doctor Reid admits, though the belief of our personal identity had not been impressed upon us; for he ascribes this belief to an instinctive principle only, and acknowledges, that there is nothing in our sensations themselves, from which any such inference could be drawn by reason. If, then, this instinctive belief of identity had not been, as at present, a natural law of human thought—operating irresistibly on the remembrance of our different feelings—we should have had no notion of *self*, of *me*, the sentient and thinking being, who exists at the present moment, and who existed before the present moment: and what, then, would have been the consciousness, accompanying, and different from, our sensations, when they merely flashed along the mind and vanished? The most zealous defender of consciousness, as a separate intellectual power, must surely admit, that, in such circumstances, it would have been nothing more than sensation itself. It is the belief of our identity only, which gives us the notion of self, as the subject of various feelings, and it is the notion of self, as the subject of various former feelings, which leads us to regard the consciousness of the moment, as different from the sensation of the moment; because it suggests to us those former feelings, which truly were different from it, or at least that subject *mind*, which unquestionably existed before the present sensation.

If it be said, that the faculty of consciousness is nothing more that this reference to the past, and consequent belief of identity, we may in that case very safely admit its existence; though the classification of it, as a peculiar intellectual power, would in that case be a most singular anomaly in arrangement, and would involve a very absurd, or at least a very awkward use of a term. To assert this signification of it, however, would be to admit every thing for which I have contended. But it certainly is not the sense which has been attached to it by philosophers; and indeed, in this sense, consciousness, instead of having for its objects, as Doctor Reid says, all "our present pains, our pleasures, our hopes, our fears, our desires, our doubts, our thoughts of every kind; in a word, all the passions, and all the actions and operations of our own minds, while they are present," would be limited to the comparatively few, of which the consideration of our personal identity forms a part.[3] In far the greater number of our feelings, as I have already said, the sensation dies away, almost in the moment—not, indeed, without being enjoyed or suffered, but without any reference to self, as the subject of various feelings, or remembrance of any prior state of mind, as distinct from the present. The belief of our identity is surely not the only belief that arises from an instinctive principle; and if its existence entitle us, in our systematic arrangements, to the possession of a new intellectual power, every other belief that arises instinctively from a principle of our constitution, must give us a similar title to enlarge the catalogue of our faculties. The never-failing and instant faith, by which we expect, without the slightest doubt of the similarity of the future, that events will continue to follow each other, in the same order as at present—that bodies will fall to the ground, fire burn, food satisfy the craving of our appetite; that immediate intuitive principle of belief, on which all our foresight depends, and according to which we regulate our whole conduct in providing for the future—should certainly, in that case, be ascribed by us to some peculiar intellectual power, for which it would be easy to invent a name. It is not by any inference of our reason we believe that the sound of a flute which preceded the fragrance of a rose, and the fragrance of a rose which followed the sound of a flute, excited sensations that were states of the same identical mind; for there is nothing, in either of the separate sensations, or in both together, from which such an inference can be drawn; and yet, notwithstanding the impossibility of inferring it, we believe this at least as strongly as we believe any of the conclusions of our reasoning. In like manner it is not by any inference of reason we believe,

---

[3] [Reid, *Essays on the Intellectual Powers*, VI.iii]

that fire will warm us tomorrow, as it has warmed us today; for there is nothing, in the fire of today, or in the sensation of warmth, considered as a mere sequence of it, from which the succession of a similar sensation to the fire of tomorrow can be inferred; yet we also rely on this future sequence, at least as strongly, as we believe any of the conclusions of our reasoning. In both cases the parallel is complete; and, in both, the evidence of a particular intellectual faculty must consequently be alike—or in neither is there sufficient evidence of such a power.

There is, indeed, one other sense, in which we often talk of our consciousness of a feeling and a sense, in which it must be allowed that the consciousness is not precisely the same as the feeling itself. This is, when we speak of a feeling, not actually existing at present, but past: as when we say, that we are conscious of having seen, or heard, or done something. Such a use of the term, however, is pardonable only in the privileged looseness and inaccuracy of familiar conversation; the consciousness, in this case, being precisely synonymous with remembrance or memory, and not a power different from the remembrance. The remembrance of the feeling, and the vivid feeling itself, indeed, are different. But the remembrance, and the consciousness of the remembrance, are the same: as the consciousness of a sensation, and the sensation, are the same; and to be conscious that we have seen or spoken to any one, is only to remember that we have seen or spoken to him.

Much of this very confusion with respect to memory, however, I have no doubt, has been always involved in the assertion of consciousness as a peculiar and distinct power of the mind. When we think of feelings long past, it is impossible for us not to be aware that our mind is then truly retrospective; and memory seems to us sufficient to account for the whole. But when the retrospect is of very recent feelings—of feelings, perhaps, that existed as distinct states of the mind, the very moment before our retrospect began—the short interval is forgotten, and we think that the primary feeling, and our consideration of the feeling, are strictly simultaneous. We have a sensation—we look instantly back on that sensation—such is consciousness as distinguished from the feeling that is said to be its object. When it is anything more than the sensation, thought or emotion, of which we are said to be conscious, it is a brief and rapid retrospect. Its object is not a present feeling, but a past feeling, as truly as when we look back, not on the moment immediately preceding, but on some distant event or emotion of our boyhood.

SELECTION 18

Classification of the Phenomena of Mind[4]

The science of mind, as it is a science of analysis, I have more than once compared to chemistry, and pointed out to you, and illustrated its various circumstances of resemblance. In this, too, we may hope the analogy will hold – that, as the innumerable aggregates, in the one science, have been reduced and simplified, the innumerable complex feelings in we other will admit of a corresponding reduction and simplification. The classes which we form, in the mental as well as in the material universe, depend, as you cannot but know, on certain relations which we discover in the phenomena; and the relations according to which objects may be arranged, are of course various, as they are considered by different individuals in different points of view. Some of these relations present themselves immediately, as if to our very glance; others are discoverable only after attentive reflection; and though the former, merely as presenting themselves more readily, may seem, on that account, better suited for the general purpose of arrangement, it is not the less true that the classification, which approaches nearest to perfection, is far from being always that which is founded on relations, that seem, at first sight, the most obvious. The rudest wanderer in the fields may imagine, that the profusion of blossoms around him — in the greater number of which he is able, himself, to discover many striking resemblances — may be reduced into some order of arrangement. But he would be little aware, that the principle, according to which they are now universally classed, has relation, not to the parts which appear to him to constitute the whole flower, but to some small part of the blossom, which he does not perceive at the distance at which he passes it, and which scarcely attracts his eye when he plucks it from the stem.

To our mental classifications the remark is equally applicable. In these, too, the most obvious distinctions are not always those which

---

[4] [Extracted from *Lectures on the Philosophy of the Human Mind*, London: William Tegg, 1860, Lecture XVI, pp. 97-103]

answer best the purposes of systematic arrangement. The phenomena of the mind are only the mind itself existing in certain states; and, as many of these states are in their nature agreeable, and others disagreeable, this difference, which is to the sentient being himself the most important of all differences, may be supposed to afford the most obvious principle of classification. What is pleasant, what is painful, are perhaps the first classes, which the infant has formed long before he is capable of distinguishing them by a name; and the very imbecility of idiotism itself, to which nothing is true or false, or right or wrong — and to which there is no future beyond the succeeding moment — is yet capable of making this primary distinction, and of regulating, according to it, its momentary desires.

> The love of pleasure is man's eldest born,
> Born in his cradle, living to his tomb.
> Wisdom — her younger sister, though more grave,
> Was meant to minister, not to dethrone[5]
> Imperial Pleasure, queen of human hearts.[6]

The distribution, which we should be inclined to make, of our mental phenomena, according to this obvious principle, would be into those which are pleasing, those which are painful, and those which are neither painful nor pleasing. But, however obvious this first distinction may seem, as a principle of arrangement, the circumstances, on which the differences depend, are so very indefinite, that the distinction — though it may be useful to have it in view, in its most striking and permanent cases — cannot be adopted as the basis of any regular system. To take the mere pleasures and pains of sense, for example — to what intelligible division could we reduce these, which are not merely fugitive in themselves, but vary, from pain to pleasure, and from pleasure to pain, with a change of their external objects so slight often as to be scarcely appreciable, and in many cases, even when the external objects have continued exactly the same? How small, and how variable a boundary separates the warmth which is pleasing from the heat which pains! A certain quantity of light is grateful to the eye. Increase it — it becomes, not indifferent (though that would be a less change) — but absolutely painful; and, if the eye be inflamed, even the small quantity of light — which was agreeable before and which seemed, therefore, to

---

[5] Instead of "not to dethrone" the original has "and not to mar."
[6] [Edward Young,] *Night Thoughts*, viii. 595-599.

admit of being very safely classed among the sources of pleasure — is now converted into a source of agony. Since it is impossible, therefore, to fix the limits of pain and pleasure, and every affection or state of mind, agreeable, disagreeable, or indifferent, may, by a very trifling change of circumstance, be converted into an opposite state, it is evident that any division, founded on this vague and transient distinction, must perplex and mislead us, in our attempts to systematize the almost infinite diversities of thought and feeling, rather than give us any aid in the arrangement.

The great leading division of the mental phenomena which has met with most general adoption by philosophers, is into those which belong to the understanding and those which belong to the will; a division which is very ancient, but, though sanctioned by the approbation of many ages, very illogical; since the will, which, in this division, is nominally opposed to the intellect, is so far from being opposed to it in reality, that, even by the asserters of its diversity, it is considered as exercising, in the intellectual department, an empire almost as wide as in the department allotted to itself. We reason, and plan, and invent, at least as voluntarily, as we esteem, or hate or hope, or fear. How many emotions are there too, which cannot, without absolute torture, be forced into either division! To take only a few instances, out of many: to what class are we to reduce grief, joy, admiration, astonishment, which certainly are not phenomena of the mere understanding, and which — though they may lead indirectly to desires or volitions — have nothing, in themselves, that is voluntary, or that can be considered as in any peculiar degree connected with the will. The division of the mental phenomena into those which belong to the understanding, and those which belong to the will, seems, therefore, to be as faulty as would be the division of animals into those which have legs and those which have wings; since the same animals might have both legs and wings, and since whole tribes of animals have neither one nor the other.

Another division of the phenomena of mind, similar to the former, and of equal antiquity, since it corresponds with the very ancient division of philosophy into the contemplative and the active, is into those which belong to the intellectual powers and those which belong to the active powers. "Philosophia et contemplativa est et activa; spectat simulque agit."[7] I must confess, however, that this division of the mental phenomena, as referable to the intellectual and the active powers of the mind, though it has the sanction of very eminent names, appears to me to be faulty, exactly in the same manner as the former, which, indeed, it may be considered almost as representing, under a change of name. Its parts are not opposed to each other, and it does not include all the phenomena which it should include. Is mere grief, for example, or mere astonishment, to be referred to our intellectual or to our active powers? I do not speak of the faculties which they may or may not call into action; but of the feelings themselves as present phenomena or states of the mind. And, in whatsoever manner we may define the term *active,* is the mind more active, when it merely desires good, and fears evil, when it looks with esteem on virtue, and with indignation, or disgust and contempt, on vice, than when it pursues a continued train of reasoning, or fancy, or historical investigation; when, with Newton, it lays down the laws of planetary motion, and calculates in what exact point of the heavens any one of the orbs, which move within the immense range of our solar system, will be found to have its place at any particular moment, one thousand years hereafter; when, with Shakespeare, it wanders beyond the universe itself, calling races of beings into existence, which nature never knew, but which nature might almost own; or when, with Tacitus, it enrols slowly, year after year, that dreadful reality of crimes and sufferings, which even dramatic horror, in all its license of wild imagination, can scarcely reach: the long unvarying catalogue of tyrants, and executioners, and victims that return thanks to the gods and die, and accusers rich with their blood, and more mighty, as more widely hated, amid the multitudes of prostrate slaves still looking whether there may not yet have escaped some lingering virtue, which it may be a merit to destroy, and having scarcely leisure to feel even the agonies of remorse in the continued sense of the precariousness of their own gloomy existence?

When it thus records the warning lessons of the past, or expatiates in fields, which itself creates, of fairy beauty or sublimity, or comprehends whole moving worlds within its glance, and calculates and measures infinitude—the mind is surely active, or there are no

---

[7] ["Philosophy is both theoretical and practical; it contemplates and also it acts." Seneca, *Epistulae Morales ad Lucilium*, XCV.10.]

moments in which it is so. So little, indeed, are the intellectual powers opposed to the active, that it is only when some intellectual energy coexists with desire, that the mind is said to be active, even by those who are unaccustomed to analytical inquiries, or to refinements of metaphysical nomenclature. The love of power, or the love of glory, when there is no opportunity of intellectual exertion, may, in the common acceptation of the word, be as passive as tranquillity itself. The passion is active only when, with intellectual action, it compares means with ends, and different means with each other, and deliberates, and resolves, and executes. Chain some revolutionary usurper to the floor of a dungeon, his ambition may be active still, because he may still be intellectually busy in planning means of deliverance and vengeance; and, on his bed of straw, may conquer half the world. But, if we could fetter his reason and fancy, as we can fetter his limbs, what activity would remain, though he were still to feel that mere desire of power or glory, which, though usually followed by intellectual exertions, is itself, as prior to these exertions, all that constitutes ambition as a passion? There would indeed still be, in his mind, the awful elements of that force which bursts upon the world with conflagration and destruction; but though there would be the thunder, it would be the thunder sleeping in its cloud. To will, is to act with desire; and, unless in the production of mere muscular motion, it is only intellectually that we can act. To class the active powers, therefore, as distinct from the intellectual, is to class them, as opposed to that, without which, as active powers, they cannot even exist.

It may certainly be contended, that, though the mental phenomena, usually ranked under this head, are not immediately connected with action, they may yet deserve this generic distinction, as leading to action, indirectly — and, if they led, in any peculiar sense, to action, however indirectly, the claim might be allowed. But, even with this limited meaning, it is impossible to admit the distinction asserted for them. In what sense, for example, can it be said, that grief and joy, which surely are not to be classed under the intellectual powers of the mind, lead to action even indirectly, more than any other feelings, or states, in which the mind is capable of existing? We may, indeed, act when we are joyful or sorrowful, as we may act when we perceive a present object, or remember the past; but we may also remain at rest, and remain equally at rest in the one case as in the other. Our intellectual energies, indeed, even in this sense, as indirectly leading to action, are, in most cases, far more active than sorrow, even in its very excess of agony and despair; and in those cases in which sorrow does truly lead to action, as when we strive to remedy the past, the mere regret which constitutes the sorrow is not so closely connected with the conduct which we pursue, as the intellectual states of mind that intervened—the successive judgments, by which we have compared projects with projects, and chosen at last the plan, which, in relation to the object in view, has seemed to us, upon the whole, the most expedient.

If, then, as I cannot but think, the arrangement of the mental phenomena, as belonging to two classes of powers, the intellectual and the active, be at once incomplete, and not accurate, even to the extent to which it reaches, it may be worthwhile to try, at least, some other division, even though there should not be any very great hope of success. Though we should fail in our endeavour to obtain some more precise and comprehensive principle of arrangement, there is always some advantage gained, by viewing objects, according to new circumstances of agreement or analogy. We see, in this case, what had long passed before us unobserved, while we were accustomed only to the order and nomenclature of a former method; for, when the mind has been habituated to certain classifications, it is apt, in considering objects, to give its attention only to those properties which are essential to the classification, and to overlook, or at least comparatively to neglect, other properties equally important and essential to the very nature of the separate substances that are classed, but not included in the system as characters of generic resemblance. The individual object, indeed, when its place in any system has been long fixed and familiar to us, is probably conceived by us less as an individual, than as one of a class of individuals that agree in certain respects, and the frequent consideration of it, as one of a class, must fix the peculiar relations of the class more strongly in the mind, and weaken proportionally the impression of every other quality that is not so included. A new classification, therefore, which includes, in its generic characters, those neglected qualities, will, of course, draw to them attention which they could not otherwise have obtained; and, the more various the views are, which we take of the objects of any science, the juster consequently, because the more equal, will be the estimate which we form of them. So truly is this the case, that I am convinced that no one has ever read over the mere terms of a new division, in a science, however familiar the science may have been to him, without learning more than this new division itself, without being struck with some property or relation, the importance of which he now perceives most clearly, and which he is quite astonished that he should have overlooked so long before.

I surely need not warn you, after the observations which I made in my Introductory Lectures, on the Laws and Objects of Physical Inquiry in General, that every classification has reference only to our mode of considering objects; and that, amid all the varieties of systems which our love of novelty and our love of distinction, or our pure love of truth and order may introduce, the phenomena themselves, whether accurately or inaccurately classed, continue unaltered. The mind is formed susceptible of certain affections. These states or affections, we may generalize more or less; and, according to our generalization, may give them more or fewer names. But whatever may be the extent of our vocabulary, the mind itself – as independent of these transient designations as He who fixed its constitution – still continues to exhibit the same unaltered susceptibilities which it originally received; as the flowers, which the same divine Author formed, spring up in the same manner, observing the same seasons, and spreading to the sun the same foliage and blossoms, whatever be the system and the corresponding nomenclature according to which botanists may have agreed to rank and name their tribes. The great Preserver of nature has not trusted us with the dangerous power of altering a single physical law which He has established, though He has given us unlimited power over the language which is of our own creation. It is still with us, as it was with our common sire in the original birthplace of our race. The Almighty presents to us all the objects that surround us, wherever we turn our view; but He presents them to us only that we may give them names. Their powers and susceptibilities they already possess, and we cannot alter these, even as they exist in a single atom.

It may, perhaps, seem absurd, even to suppose, that we should think ourselves able to change, by a few generic words, the properties of the substances which we have classed; and if the question were put to us, as to this effect of our language in any particular case, there can be no doubt that we should answer in the negative, and express astonishment that such a question should have been put. But the illusion is not the less certain, because we are not aware of its influence; and indeed it could no longer be an illusion, if we were completely aware of it. It requires, however, only a very little reflection on what has passed in our own minds, to discover, that when we have given a name to any quality, that quality acquires immediately, in our imagination, a comparative importance, very different from what it had before; and though nature in itself be truly unchanged, it is, ever after, relatively to our conception, different. A difference of words is, in this case, more than a mere verbal difference. Though it be not the expression of a difference of doctrine, it very speedily becomes so. Hence it is, that the same warfare, which the rivalries of individual ambition, or the opposite interests, or supposed opposite interests, of nations have produced in the great theatre of civil history, have been produced, in the small but tumultuous field of science, by the supposed incompatibility of a few abstract terms; and, indeed, as has been truly said, the sects of philosophers have combated, with more persevering violence, to settle what they mean by the constitution of the world, than all the conquerors of the world have done to render themselves its masters.

Still less, I trust, is it necessary to repeat the warning already so often repeated, that you are not to conceive that any classification of the states or affections of the mind, as referable to certain powers or susceptibilities, makes these powers any thing different and separate from the mind itself, as originally and essentially susceptible of the various modifications, of which these powers are only a shorter name. And yet what innumerable controversies in philosophy have arisen, and are still frequently arising, from this very mistake, strange and absurd as the mistake may seem. No sooner, for example, were certain affections of the mind classed together, as belonging to the will, and certain others, as belonging to the understanding —that is to say, no sooner was the mind, existing in certain states, denominated the understanding, and in certain other states denominated the will—than the understanding and the will ceased to be considered as the same individual substance, and became immediately, as it were, two opposite and contending powers, in the empire of mind, as distinct as any two sovereigns, with their separate nations under their control; and it became an object of as fierce contention to determine, whether certain affections of the mind belonged to the understanding, or to the will, as in the management of political affairs, to determine, whether a disputed province belonged to one potentate, or to another. Every new division of the faculties of the mind, indeed, converted each faculty into a little independent mind —as if the original mind were like that wonderful animal, of which naturalists tell us, that may be cut into an almost infinite number of parts, each of which becomes a polypus, as perfect as that from which it was separated. The only difference is, that those who make us acquainted with this wonderful property of the polypus, acknowledge the divisibility of the parent animal; while those, who assert the spiritual multiplicity, are at the same time assertors of the absolute indivisibility of that which they divide.

After these warnings, then, which, I trust, have been almost superfluous, let us now endeavour to form some classification of the mental phenomena, without considering, whether our arrangement be similar or dissimilar to that of others. In short, let us forget, as much as possible, that any prior arrangements have been made, and think of the phenomena only. It would, indeed, require more than human vision to comprehend all these phenomena of the mind, in our gaze, at once,

> To survey,
> Stretch'd out beneath *us,* all the mazy tracts
> Of passion and opinion — like a waste
> Of sands, and flowery lawns, and tangling woods,
> Where mortals roam bewilder'd.[8]

But there is a mode of bringing all this multitude of objects within the sphere of our narrow sight, in the same manner as the expanse of landscape, over which the eye would be long in wandering — the plains, and hills, and woods, and waterfalls — may be brought by human art within the compass of a mirror, far less than the smallest of the innumerable objects which it represents.

The process of gradual generalization, by which this reduction is performed, I have already explained to you. Let us now proceed to avail ourselves of it.

All the feelings and thoughts of the mind, I have already frequently repeated, are only the mind itself existing in certain states. To these successive states our knowledge of the mind, and consequently our arrangements, which can comprehend only what we know, are necessarily limited. With this simple word *state,* I use the phrase *affection of mind* as synonymous, to express the momentary feeling whatever it may be — with this difference only, that the word affection seems to me better suited for expressing that momentary feeling, when considered as an effect — the feeling itself as a state of

---

[8] [Mark Akenside,] *The Pleasures of Imagination*, Book IV. pp 9-13.

the mind, and the relation which any particular state of mind may bear to the preceding circumstances, whatever they may be, that have induced it.

Our states of mind, however, or our affections of mind, are the simplest terms which I can use for expressing the whole series of phenomena of the mind in all their diversity, as existing phenomena, without any mixture of hypothesis as to the particular mode in which the successive changes maybe supposed to arise.

When we consider, then, the various states or affections of the mind, which form this series, one circumstance of difference must strike us, that some of them arise immediately, in consequence of the presence of external objects — and some, as immediately, in consequence of certain preceding affections of the mind itself. The one set, therefore, are obviously the result of the laws both of matter and of mind — implying, in external objects, a power of affecting the mind, as well as, in the mind, a susceptibility of being affected by them. The other set result from the susceptibilities of the mind itself, which has been formed by its divine Author to exist in certain states, and to exist in these in a certain relative order of succession. The affections of the one class arise, because some external object is present; the affections of the other class arise, because some previous change in the states of the mind has taken place.

To illustrate this distinction by example, let us suppose ourselves, in walking across a lawn, to turn our eyes to a particular point, and to perceive there an oak. That is to say, the presence of the oak, or rather of the light reflected from it, occasions a certain new state of the mind, which we call a sensation of vision; an affection which belongs to the mind alone, indeed, but of which we have every reason to suppose, that the mind, of itself, without the presence of light, would not have been the subject. The peculiar sensation, therefore, is the result of the presence of the light reflected from the oak; and we perceive it, because the mind is capable of being affected by external things. But this affection of the mind, which has an external object for its immediate cause, is not the only mental change which takes place. Other changes succeed it, without any other external impression. We compare the oak with some other tree which we have seen before, and we are struck with its superior magnificence and beauty — we imagine how some scene more familiar to us would appear, if it were adorned with this tree, and how the scene before us would appear, if it were stripped of it — we think of the number of years, which must have passed, since the oak was an acorn; and we moralize, perhaps, on the changes which have taken place in the little history of ourselves and our friends, and, still more, on the revolutions of kingdoms, and the birth and decay of a whole generation of mankind; while it has been silently and regularly advancing to maturity, through the sunshine and the storm.

Of all the variety of states of the mind, which these processes of thought involve, the only one which can be ascribed to an external object as its direct cause, is the primary perception of the oak: the rest have been the result, not immediately of any thing external, but of preceding states of the mind—that particular mental state, which constituted the perception of the oak, being followed immediately by that different state which constituted the remembrance of some tree observed before, and this by that different state which constituted the comparison of the two; and so successively, through all the different processes of thought enumerated. The mind, indeed, could not, without the presence of the oak—that is to say, without the presence of the light which the oak reflects—have existed in the state which constituted the perception of the oak. But as little could any external object, without this primary mental affection, have produced, immediately, any of those other states of the mind which followed the perception. There is, thus, one obvious distinction of the mental phenomena; as, in relation to their causes external or internal; and, whatever other terms of subdivision it may be necessary to employ, we have, at least, one boundary, and know what it is we mean, when we speak of the external and internal affections of the mind.

The first stage of our generalization, then, has been the reduction of all the mental phenomena to two definite classes, according as the causes, or immediate antecedents, of our feelings are themselves mental or material. Our next stage must be the still further reduction of these, by some new generalizations of the phenomena of each class.

The former of these classes—that of our external affections of the mind—is indeed so very simple, as to require but little subdivision. The other class, however—that of the internal affections or states of the mind—comprehends so large a proportion of the mental phenomena, and these so various, that, without many subdivisions, it would be itself of little aid to us in our arrangement.

The first great subdivision, then, which I would form, of the internal class, is into our intellectual states of mind, and our emotions. The latter of these classes comprehends all, or nearly all, the mental states, which have been classed, by others, under the head of active powers. I prefer, however, the term *emotions,* partly because I wish to avoid the phrase, *active powers*; which, I own, appears to me awkward and ambiguous, as opposed to other powers, which ore not said to be passive, and partly, for reasons before mentioned, because our intellectual states or energies — far from being opposed to our active powers — are, as we have seen, essential elements of their activity; so essential, that, without them, these never could have had the name of active; and because I wish to comprehend, under the term, various states of the mind which cannot, with propriety, in any sense, be termed active — such as grief, joy, astonishment — and others which have been commonly, though, I think, inaccurately, ascribed to the intellectual faculties — such as the feelings of beauty and sublimity — feelings which are certainly much more analogous to our other emotions — to our feelings of love or awe, for example — than to our mere remembrances or reasonings, or to any other states of mind which can strictly be called intellectual. I speak at present, it must be remembered, of the mere feelings produced by the contemplation of beautiful or sublime objects; not of the judgment, which we form of objects, as more or less fit to excite these feelings; the judgment being truly intellectual, like all our other judgments; but being, at the same time, as distinct from the feelings which it measures, as any other judgment from the external or internal objects which it compares.

The exact meaning of the term *emotion,* it is difficult to state in any form of words — for the same reason which makes it difficult, or rather impossible, to explain, what we mean by the term thought, or the terms sweetness or bitterness. What can be more opposite than pleasure and pain! the real distinction of which is evidently familiar, not to man only, but to every thing that lives; and yet if we were to attempt to show, in what their difference consists, or to give a verbal definition of either, we should find the task to be no easy one. Every person understands what is meant by an emotion, at least as well as he understands what is meant by any intellectual power; or, if he do not, it can be explained to him only, by stating the number of feelings to which we give the name, or the circumstances which induce them. All of them, indeed, agree in this respect, that they imply peculiar vividness of feeling, with this important circumstance, to distinguish them from the vivid pleasures and pains of sense: that they do not arise immediately from the presence of external objects, but subsequently to the primary feelings, which we term sensations or perceptions. Perhaps, if any definition of them be possible, they may be defined to be vivid feelings, arising immediately from the consideration of objects, perceived, or remembered, or imagined, or from other prior emotions. In some cases — as in that of the emotion which beauty excites – they may succeed so rapidly to the primary perception, as almost to form a part of it. Yet we find no great difficulty of analysis, in separating the pleasing effect of *beauty* from the perception of the mere form and colour, and can very readily imagine the same accurate perception of these, without the feeling of beauty, as we can imagine the same feeling of beauty to accompany the perception of forms and colours very different.

> Sure the rising sun,
> O'er the cerulean convex of the sea,
> With equal brightness, and with equal warmth,
> Might roll his fiery orb; nor yet the soul
> Thus feel her frame expanded, and her powers
> Exulting in the splendour she beholds,
> Like a young conqueror moving through the pomp.
> Of some triumphal day. When, joined at eve,
> Soft murmuring streams, and gales of gentlest breath.
> Melodious Philomela's wakeful strain
> Attemper, could not man's discerning ear,
> Through all its tones, the sympathy pursue;
> Nor yet this breath divine of nameless joy
> Seal through his veins, and fan the awaken'd heart
> Mild as the breeze yet rapturous as the song.[9]

Our emotions, then, even in the cases in which they seem most directly to coexist with perception, are still easily distinguishable from it; and, in like manner, when they arise from the intellectual states of memory, imagination, comparison, they are equally distinguishable from what we remember, or imagine, or compare. They form truly a separate order of the internal affections of the mind; as distinct from the intellectual phenomena, as the class, to which they both belong, is distinguishable from the class of external affections that arise immediately from the presence of objects without.

[9] [Mark Akenside,] *The Pleasures of Imagination*, Book III. V. 464-478

SELECTION 19

Emotions[10]

Gentlemen, after the attention which we have paid to the class of external affections of the mind, and to that great order of its internal affections, which I have denominated intellectual, the only remaining phenomena which, according to our original division, remain to be considered by us, are our emotions.

This order of our internal feelings is distinguished from the external class, by the circumstances which I have already pointed out, as the basis of the arrangement: that they are not the immediate consequence of the presence of external objects, but, when excited by objects without, are excited only indirectly, through the medium of those direct feelings, which are commonly termed sensations or perceptions. They differ from the other order of the same internal class— from the intellectual states of mind, which constitute our simple or relative suggestions of memory or judgment—by that peculiar vividness of feeling which every one understands, but which it is impossible to express by any verbal definition; as truly impossible, as to define sweetness, or bitterness, a sound, or a smell, in any other way, than by a statement of the circumstances in which they arise. There is no reason to fear, however, from this impossibility of verbal definition, that any one, who has tasted what is sweet or bitter, or enjoyed the pleasures of melody and fragrance, will be at all in danger of confounding these terms; and, as little reason is there to fear, that our emotions will be confounded with our intellectual states of mind, by those who have simply remembered and compared, and have also loved or hated, desired or feared.

Before we proceed to consider the order of emotions, it may be interesting to cast a short glance over the other orders of the phenomena of the mind, before considered by us.

In the view which we have taken of the external or sensitive affections of the mind, we have traced those laws, so simple and so efficacious, which give to the humblest individual, by the medium of his corporeal organs, the possession of that almost celestial scene, in which he is placed, till he arrive at that nobler abode which awaits him; connecting him not merely with the earth which he treads, but

---

[10] [Extracted from *Lectures on the Philosophy of the Human Mind*, London: William Tegg, 1860, Lecture LII, pp. 338-340]

indirectly also with those other minds which are journeying with him in the same career, and that enjoy at once, by the same medium of the senses, the same beauties and glories that are shed around them, with a profusion so divine, as almost to indicate, of themselves, that a path so magnificent is the path to heaven. A few rays of light thus reveal to us, not forms and colours only, which are obviously visible, but latent thoughts, which no eye can see; a few particles of vibrating air enable mind to communicate to mind, its most spiritual feelings, to awake and be awakened mutually to science and benevolent exertion, as if truths, and generous wishes, and happiness itself, could be diffused in the very voice that scarcely floats upon the ear.

Such are our mere sensitive feelings, resulting from the influence of external things, on our corresponding organs, which are themselves external. The view of the intellectual states of the mind, to which we next proceeded, laid open to us phenomena still more astonishing: those capacities, by which we are enabled to discover in nature more than the causes of those brief separate sensations which follow the affections of our nerves; to perceive in it proportion and design, and all those relations of parts to parts, by which it becomes to us a demonstration of the wisdom that formed it; capacities, by which, in a single moment, we pass again over all the busiest adventures of all the years of our life, or, with a still more unlimited range of thought, are present, as it were, in that remote infinity of space, where no earthly form has ever been, or, in the still more mysterious infinity of time—in ages, when the universe was not, nor any being, but that Eternal One, whose immutable existence is all which we conceive of eternity.

Such are the wonders, of which we acquire the knowledge, in those phenomena of the mind which have been already reviewed by us. The order of feelings, which we are next to consider, are not less important, not important only in themselves, but also in their relation to those other phenomena which have been the subjects of our inquiry; since they comprehend all the higher delights which attend the exercise of our sensitive and intellectual functions. The mere pleasures of sense, indeed, as direct and simple pleasures, we do not owe to them; but we owe to them every thing which confers on those pleasures a more ennobling value, by the enjoyments of social affection which are mingled with them, or the gratitude which, in the enjoyment of them, looks to their divine author. We might perhaps, in like manner, have been so constituted with respect to our intellectual states of mind, as to have had all the varieties of these, our remembrances, judgments, and creations of fancy, without one emotion. But without the emotions which accompany them, of how little value would the mere intellectual functions hare been! It is to our vivid feelings of this class we must look for those tender regards which make our remembrances sacred; for that love of truth and glory, and mankind, without which, to animate and reward us, in our discovery and diffusion of knowledge, the continued exercise of judgement would be a fatigue rather than a satisfaction; and for all that delightful wonder which we feel, when we contemplate the admirable creations of fancy, or the still more admirable beauties of their unfading model; that model which is ever before us, and the imitation of which, as it has been truly said, is the only imitation that is itself originality.

By our other mental functions, we are mere spectators of the machinery of the universe, living and inanimate; by our emotions, we are admirers of nature, lovers of man, adorers of God. The earth, without them, would be only a field of colours, inhabited by beings who may contribute, indeed, more permanently, to our means of physical comfort, than any one of the inanimate forms which we behold, but who, beyond the moment in which they are capable of affecting us with pain or pleasure, would be only like the other forms and colours, which would meet us wherever we turned our weary and listless eye; and God himself, the source of all good, and the object of all worship, would be only the Being by whom the world was made.

In the picture which I have now given of our emotions, however, I have presented them to you in their fairest aspects: there are aspects, which they assume, as terrible as these are attractive; but even, terrible as they are, they are not the less interesting objects of our contemplation. They are the enemies with which our moral combat, in the warfare of life, is to be carried on; and, if there be enemies that are to assail us, it is good for us to know all the arms and all the arts with which we are to be assailed; as it is good for us to know all the misery which would await our defeat, as much as all the happiness which would crown our success, that our conflict may be the stronger, and our victory, therefore, the more sure.

In the list of our emotions of this formidable class, is to be found every passion which can render life guilty and miserable; a single hour of which, if that hour be an hour of uncontrolled dominion, may destroy happiness for ever, and leave little more of virtue than is necessary for giving all its horror to remorse. There are feelings, as blasting to every desire of good, that may still linger in the heart of the frail victim who is not yet wholly corrupted, as those poisonous gales of the desert, which not merely lift in whirlwinds the sands that have often been tossed before, but wither even the few fresh leaves which, on some spot of scanty verdure, have still been flourishing amid the general sterility.

When we consider the pure and generous, as well as the selfish and malignant desires of man, in the effects to which they have led — that is to say, when we consider the varieties of some of our mental affections of this class — we may be said to consider every thing which man has done and suffered, because we consider every thing from which his actions and his very sufferings have flowed. All civil history is nothing more than the record of the passions of a few leaders of mankind. "Happy, therefore," it has been said, "the people whose history is the most wearisome to read."[11] Whatever the Caesars, and Alexanders, and the other disturbers of the peace of nations, have perpetrated, may have been planned with relation to the particular circumstances of the time; but this very plan, even when accommodated to temporary circumstances, was the work of some human emotion which is not of a month, or year, or age, but of every time. In perusing the narratives of what they did, we feel that we are reading not so much, the history of the individuals, as the history of our common nature; of those passions by which we are agitated, and which, while the race of mankind continue to subsist, will always, but for the securer restraints which political wisdom and the general state of society may have imposed, be sufficiently ready to repeat the same project of personal advancement, at the same expense of individual virtue and public happiness. The study of the mental phenomena, in their general aspect, as it is the study of the sources of human action, is thus, in one sense, a sort of compendious history of the civil affairs of the world, a history not merely of the past and the present, but of the future also. It resembles, in this respect, what we are told of the hero of a metaphysical romance: that in physiognomy his penetration was such, that "from the picture of

---

[11] [A variant of this frequently quoted but rarely sourced aphorism is attributed to Montesquieu in Thomas Carlyle's *History of Frederick the Great*, XVI.1.]

any person he could write his life, and from the features of the parents, draw the features of any child that was to be born."[12] Such, in some measure, though certainly far less exact, is that future history of the world, which a speculator on the state and prospects of civil society draws from a knowledge of the nature of man. He may err, indeed, in his picture of unexisting things; but every political regulation, must, in part at least, proceed on views of events that do not yet exist, as thus prophetically imaged in the very nature of the mind, or it scarcely can deserve the name of an act of legislative wisdom; and he is truly the wisest politician, who is, in this sense, the most accurate historian of the future.

In now entering on the consideration of that order of our feelings, which I have comprehended under the name of Emotions, it may seem doubtful whether it would be more expedient to treat of them simply as elementary feelings, or in those complex forms in which they usually exist, and have received certain definite characteristic names that are familiar to you. This latter mode appears to me, on the whole, more advisable, as affording many advantages, direct and indirect, and allowing equally the necessary analysis in each particular case. If I were to treat of them only as elementary feelings, they might be classed under a very few heads; the whole, as I conceive, or certainly, at least, the greater number of them, under the following: joy, grief, desire, astonishment, respect, contempt, and the two opposite species of vivid feelings, which distinguish to us the actions that are denominated vicious or virtuous. But, though the vivid feelings, to which we give these names, may, from their general analogy, admit of being comprehended in this brief arrangement, it must be remembered, that, brief as the vocabulary is, it comprehends feelings, which, though analogous, are still not precisely the same; that the single word joy, for example, expresses many varieties of delightful feelings, the single word desire, many feelings, which, in combination with their particular objects, are so modified by these, as to appear to us, in their complex forms, almost as different as any other feelings of our mind which we class under different names. It is in their complex state that they impress themselves most strongly on our observation in others, and form, in ourselves, all that renders most interesting to us the present and the future, and all that is most

---

[12] [This is a slightly modified quotation from *The Memoirs of Martinus Scriblerus,* Part I, Ch. 14.]

vivid in our remembrances of the past. Considered, therefore, in this aspect, they admit of much illustration from the whole field of human life, and afford opportunities for many practical references to conduct, and many analyses of the motives that secretly influence it; for which there would scarcely be a place, if they were to be considered simply as elementary feelings. I repeat, therefore, that the order in which, I intend to treat of them, will regard them in their ordinary state of complication with particular conceptions or other emotions, though I shall be careful, at the same time, to state to you, in every case, as minutely as may be in my power, the elements of which the complex whole is composed.

In treating of them in this view, the most obvious principle of general arrangement seems to me to be one of which I have already more than once availed myself: their relation to time; as immediate, or involving no notion of time whatever; as retrospective, in relation to the past; or as prospective, in relation to the future. Admiration, remorse, hope, may serve as particular instances, to illustrate my meaning in this distinction which I would make. We admire what is before us, we feel remorse for some past crime, we hope some future good.

In conformity with this arrangement of our emotions, as immediate, retrospective, prospective, the first set which we have to consider are those which arise without involving necessarily any notion of time.

These immediate emotions, as I have termed them, may be subdivided, according to the most interesting of their relations — as they do not involve any feeling that can be termed moral, or as they do involve some moral affection.

Of the former kind, which do not involve necessarily any moral affection, are cheerfulness, melancholy, our wonder at what is new and unexpected, our mental weariness of what is long continued without interest, our feeling of beauty, and that opposite emotion — which has no corresponding and equal name, since ugliness can scarcely be regarded as coextensive with it — our feelings of sublimity and ludicrousness.

To the latter subdivision may be referred the vivid feelings, that constitute to our heart what we distinguish by the names of vice and virtue — if these vivid feelings be considered simply as emotions, distinct from the judgments, which may at the same time measure actions, in reference to some particular standard of morality, or to the amount of particular or general good, which they may have tended to produce, and which might so measure them, without any moral emotion, as a mathematician measures the proportion of one figure to another — our emotions of love and hate, of sympathy with the happy and with the miserable, of pride and humility, in the various forms which these assume.

These, if not all, are at least the most important of our immediate emotions.

SELECTION 20

Sympathy[13]

The emotions to which I am next to direct your attention, are those by which, instantly, as if by a sort of contagion, we become partakers of the vivid feelings of others, whether pleasing or painful. They are general affections of sympathy; a term which expresses this participation of both species of feelings, though, in common language, it is usually applied more particularly to the interest which we take in sorrow. By some philosophers, indeed, we have been said to be incapable of this participation, except of feelings of that sadder kind; though the denial of this sympathy with happiness — a denial so unfavourable and so false to the social nature of man — is surely the result only of narrow views and imperfect analysis. Nor is it difficult to discover the circumstances which may have tended to mislead them. The state of happiness is a state which we are so desirous of feeling, and so readily affect to feel, even when we truly feel it not, that our participation of it becomes less remarkable, being expressed merely in the same way as the common courtesies of society require us to express ourselves, even when we are feeling no peculiar satisfaction. If the face must, at any rate, be dressed in smiles at meeting, and retain a certain number of these smiles, with an occasional smile more or less, according to the turn of the conversation, during the whole of a long interview, the real complacency which is felt in the pleasures of others is not marked, because the air of complacency had been assumed before. All this is so well understood, in that state of strange simulation and dissimulation, which constitutes artificial

---

[13] [Extracted from *Lectures on the Philosophy of the Human Mind*, London: William Tegg, 1860, Lecture LXI, pp. 406-411]

politeness, that a smile of welcome is as little considered to be a certain evidence of gratification at heart, as the common forms of humility, which close a letter of business, are understood to signify truly, that the writer is the very humble and most obedient servant of him to whom the letter is addressed.

Joy, then – that is to say, the appearance of joy — may be regarded as the common dress of society, and real complacency is thus as little remarkable as a well-fashioned coat in a drawing-room. Let us conceive a single ragged coat to appear in the brilliant circle, and all eyes will be instantly fixed on it. Even Beauty itself, till the buzz of astonishment is over, will for the moment scarcely attract a single gaze, or Wit a single listener. Such, with respect to the general dress of the social mind, is grief. It is something, for the very appearance of which we are not prepared. A face of smiles is what we meet contstantly; a face of sorrow, the fixed and serious look, the low or faltering tone, the very silence, the tear, are foreign, as it were, to the outward scene of things in which we exist. We see evidence, in this case, that something has happened to change the general aspect; while the look, and the voice of gaiety, as they are the look and the voice of every hour, indicate to us only the presence of the individual, and not any peculiar affection of his mind. It is not wonderful, therefore that the appearance of grief, as the more unusual of the two, should absorb to itself, in common language, a name which may have been originally significant alike of the participation of grief and joy. It must be remembered, too, that joy, though delighting in sympathy, does not stand in need of this sympathy so much as sorrow.

In diffusing cheerfulness, we seem rather to give to others than to receive; while, in the sympathy of grief which we excite, we feel every look and tone of kindred sorrow as so much given to us. It is as if we were lightened of a part of our burden; and we cannot feel the relief without feeling gratitude to the compassionate heart that has lessened our affliction, by dividing it with us. It is not merely, therefore, because the appearance of grief is more unusual, that we have affixed to this appearance a peculiar language, or at apply to it more readily the terms that are significant also of other appearances; but to some degree also because the sympathy of those who sorrow with us, is of far more value than the sympathy of those who merely share our rejoicing, and therefore dwells more readily and lastingly in our remembrance. ...

Whatever may be the comparative tendencies of our nature, however, to the participation of the gay and sad emotions of those around us, there can be no doubt as to the double tendency. We rejoice with those who rejoice, merely because they are rejoicing; and, without any misfortune of our own, we feel a sadness at the very aspect of affliction in those around us, and shrink and shudder on the application to them of any cause of pain which we know cannot reach ourselves.

Many of the phenomena of sympathy, I have little doubt, are referable to the same laws to which we have traced the common phenomena of suggestion or association. It may be considered as a necessary consequence of these very laws, that the sight of any of the common symbols of internal feeling should recall to us the feeling itself, in the same way as a portrait, or rather as the alphabetic name of our friends recalls to us the conception of our friend himself. Some faint and shadowy sadness we undoubtedly should feel, therefore, when the external signs of sadness were before us, some greater cheerfulness on the appearance of cheerfulness in others, even though we had no peculiar susceptibility of sympathizing emotion, distinct from the mere general tendencies of suggestion. To these general tendencies I am inclined, particularly, to refer the external involuntary signs of our sympathy; the shrinking of our own limbs, for example, when we see the knife in any surgical operation about to be applied to the limb of another; the contortions of body with which the mob regard the feats of a rope-dancer, when they throw themselves into the postures that would be necessary for counteracting their own tendency to fall, if they were in the situation observed by them. Whatever state of mind, in the direction of our muscular movements, may be necessary for producing these instant postures, is associated with the feeling of peril which the mind would have in the situation observed; and this feeling is suggested by the attitude in others, that may be considered as an external sign of the feeling.

That the mere conception is sufficient for producing these muscular movements, without the actual presence of any one with whose movements our own may be thought to accord, by some mysterious harmony, is shown by cases, in which ethereal communications, and vibrations, and every foreign cause of sympathy that can be imagined by the most extravagant lover of hypothesis, must be allowed to be absent, because there is no foreign object of sympathy whatever; in which we may be said, almost without absurdity, to sympathize with ourselves; when we shudder, indeed, as if sympathizing, but shudder at a mere thought. Thus, in looking down from a precipice, we shrink back as we gaze on the dreadful abyss which would receive us if we were to make a single false step, or if the crumbling soil on which we tread were to betray our footing. The notion of our fall is readily suggested by the aspect of the abyss, and of the narrow spot which separates us from it; this notion of our fall, of course, suggests the feelings which would arise at such a dreadful moment; and these again produce, in the same manner, that consecutive state of mind, whatever it may be, on which the bodily movements of shrinking depend. We first have the simple conception of the fall; we then have, in some degree, the feelings that would attend the beginning fall; we then, having this lively image of peril, shrink back to save ourselves from that which seems to us more real, because, in harmony with the whole scene of terror before us, which presents to us the tame aspect that would be present to us, if what we merely imagine were actually at that very moment taking place. Such is the series of phenomena that produce one of the most uneasy states in which the mind can exist; a state which I may suppose you all have experienced in some degree, before the frequent repetition of these giddy views, with impunity, has counteracted the giddiness itself, by rendering the feeling of security so habitual, as to rise instantly, and be a constant part of the whole complex state of mind.

But, though I conceive that a great part of what is called sympathy, is truly referable to the common laws of suggestion, that, by producing certain conceptions, produce also, indirectly, the emotions that are consequent on these; and, though it is possible that not the chief part only, but the whole may flow from these simple laws, I am far from asserting that all its phenomena depend on these alone. On the contrary, I am inclined to think that there is a peculiar susceptibility of this reflex emotion in certain minds, by which, even when the laws of suggestion, and the consequent images which rise to the mind, are similar, the sympathy, as a subsequent emotion, is more or less vivid; since there is no particular law of suggestion, unless we form one for this particular case, the force of which, in any greater degree, seems to accompany with equal and corresponding proportion the more lively compassion; but our sympathies are stronger and weaker, with all possible varieties of suggestion, in every other respect. It would be vain, however, if there truly be such a peculiar susceptibility, to attempt any nicer inquiry, in the hope of discovering original elements, which are obviously beyond the power of our analysis, or of fixing the precise point at which the influence of ordinary suggestion ceases, and the influence of what is peculiar in the tendency to sympathy, if there be any peculiar influence, begins.

One most important distinction, however, it is necessary to make, to save you from an error into which the use of a single term for two successive feelings, and, I may add, the general imperfect analysis of philosophers might otherwise lead you.

What is commonly termed pity, or compassion, or sympathy, even when the circumstances which merely lead to the sympathy are deducted from the emotion itself, is not one simple state, but two successive states of the mind; the feeling of the sorrow of others, and the desire of relieving it. The former of these is that which leads me to rank pity as an immediate emotion; the latter, which is a separate affection of the mind, subsequent to the other, and easily distinguished from it, we should rank, if it were to be considered alone, with our other desires, which, in like manner, arise from some view of good to be attained, or of evil to be removed.

After this analysis of the emotion of pity into its constituent elements, a lively feeling participant of the sorrow of others, and the desire of relief to that sorrow, a desire which, in the same circumstances, may be greater or less, as the mind is more benevolent, it can scarcely fail to occur to you, that the first of these elements is, as mere grief, an emotion of the same species with the primary grief with which we are said to sympathize, or with any other grief which we are capable of feeling — a form, in short, of that general sadness which has been already considered by us. And, as a mere state or affection of the mind, considered without regard to the circumstances which produce it, or the circumstances which follow it, I confess that there does not seem to me any thing peculiar in the grief itself of pity, when separated, by such an analysis, from all thought of the primary sufferer, whose sorrow we feel to have been reflected on us, and from the consequent desire of affording him aid. But, though the elementary feeling itself may be similar, the circumstances in which it arises, and the circumstances which accompany it, when, without any direct cause of pain, we yet catch pain, as it were, by a sort of contagious sensibility, from the mere violence of another's anguish, are of so very peculiar a kind, that I have not hesitated to give to this susceptibility of sympathetic feeling a distinct place in our arrangement; for the same reason, as in our systems of physics, we refer to different physical powers; and, therefore, to different parts of our system, the same apparent motions of bodies, when these motions, though in themselves apparently the same which might be produced by other causes, are the results of causes that are in their own nature strikingly different. Pity, however complex the state of mind may be which it expresses, is one of the most interesting of all the states in which the mind can exist, and affords itself an example of the advantage of treating our emotions as complex rather than elementary; an advantage which led me to form that particular arrangement of our emotions, in the order of which they have been submitted to your consideration; when, if the mere elements had been all that were submitted to you, you would perhaps have been little able to distinguish in them the familiar complex states of mind, which alone you have been accustomed to distinguish as emotions.

Even that primary feeling of sympathy, which is a mere participation of the sufferings of another, it may perhaps be thought, is only a form of the affection of love before considered by us, since there can be no love without a participation of the sorrows and joys of the object beloved. But these sympathies are emotions arising from love, not the mere regard itself. We must not forget that the word love is often employed very vaguely to signify, not the mere affections of mind which constitute the vivid feelings of regard, but every affection of mind that has any reference to the object of this regard. We give the name of love, in this way, to the whole successive states of mind of the lover, as if love were something diffused in them all; but this, though a convenient expression, is still a very vague one; and the emotions are not the less different in themselves, for being comprehended in a single word. The emotion of sympathy is still different from the simple feeling of affection, even when the object of our sympathy is truly the object of our love. It may have arisen from it, indeed, but it is not the same as that feeling of warm regard from which, in such a case, it arose.

So different is the mere sympathy from simple love, that it takes place when there is no actual love whatever, but, on the contrary, positive dislike or abhorrence. Let us imagine, not one atrocious crime only, but many crimes the most atrocious, to have been committed by any individual; and let us then suppose him stretched upon the rack, every limb torn, and every fibre quivering. Let us imagine, that we hear the heavy fall of that instrument, by which bone after bone is slowly broken, dividing, with dreadful intervals, the groans of the victim, that cease at the moment at which the new stroke is expected, and afterwards rise again instantly in more dreadful anguish, to cease only when another more agonizing stroke is again on the point of falling, or when the milder agony of death overwhelms at once the suffering and the sufferer. Does our hatred of the criminal save us even from the slightest uneasiness at what we see and hear? Do we feel no cold shuddering at the sound of the worse than deadly blow; no terror, increasing into agony at the moment when it pauses, as we expected it to fall again? It is enough for us that there is agony before our eyes. Without loving the sufferer — for though the feelings that oppress us may not allow us to think of his atrocities at the moment, they certainly do not invest him with any amiable qualities, except that of being miserable — we feel for him what it is impossible for us not to feel for any living thing that is in equal anguish. We should feel this — if the anguish be of a kind that forces itself upon our senses in all its dreadful reality — though his crimes were whispered to us every moment; and, when he lies mangled and groaning before us, if we were forced to inflict another stroke with our own hands, that was to break the last unbroken limb, or to receive the blow ourselves, it is not easy to say from which alternative we should shrink with a more frightful and sickly loathing.

In all this, Nature has consulted well. If our sympathy had been made to depend on our moral approbation, it would rise in many cases too late to be of profit. We are men; and nothing which man can feel is foreign to us. The friend of the Self-tormenter in Terence's comedy, when he uttered these memorable words which have been so often quoted, "Homo sum; humani nihil a me alienum puto,"[14] expressed only what the Author of our being has fixed, in some degree, in every heart, and which is as much a part of the mental constitution of the virtuous, as their powers of memory and reason.

If compassion were to arise only after we had ascertained the moral character of the sufferer, and weighed all the consequences of good and evil which might result to society from the relief which it is in our power to offer, who would rush to the preservation of the drowning mariner, to the succour of the wounded, to the aid of him who calls for help against the ruffians who are assailing him? Our

---

[14] ["I am human: nothing human is foreign to me." Terence, *The Self-Torturer*, Act 1, Scene 1, v. 25.]

powers of giving assistance have been better accommodated to the necessities which may be relieved by them. By the principle of compassion within us, we are benefactors almost without willing it; we have already done the deed, when, if deliberation had been necessary as a previous step, we should not have proceeded far in the calculation which was to determine by a due equipoise of opposite circumstances, the propriety of the relief.

Even in the case of our happier feelings, it is not a slight advantage, that nature has made the sight of joy productive of joy to him who merely beholds it. Men are to mingle in society; and they bring into society affections of mind that are almost infinitely various: hopes and fears, joy and sadness, projects and passions, far more contrasted than their mere external varieties of form and colour. If these internal diversities of feeling were to continue as they are, what delight could society afford? The opposition would render the company of each a burthen to the other. The gay would fly from the sullen gloom of the melancholy; the melancholy would shrink from the mirth which they could not partake, and which would throw them back upon their own sorrows with a deeper intensity of grief. Such is the confusion which society of itself would present. But the same Power which formed this beautiful system of the universe out of chaos, reduces to equal regularity and beauty this and every other confusion of the moral world. By the mere principle of sympathy, all the discord in the social feelings becomes accordant. The sad unconsciously become gay; the gay are softened into a joy, that has less perhaps of mirth, but not less of delight; and though there is still a diversity of cheerfulness, all is cheerfulness; as in a concert of many instruments, in which, though we are still able to distinguish each instrument from the others, and though the simple tones of each may be various, there is still one universal harmony that seems to animate the whole, like the presence, and the voice or inspiration of the celestial power of Music herself.

But if the bounty of our Creator be shown, in the provision which he has made for diffusing to many the joy which is felt by one, how much more admirable is the providence of his bounty, in that instant diffusion to others of the grief which is felt only by one, that makes the relief of this suffering not a duty merely, which we coldly perform, but a want, which is almost like the necessity of some moral appetite! Every individual has thus the aid of all the powers of every other individual. When some wretch is found lying bleeding on the common street, all who see him run to his assistance, as if their own immediate ease depended on their speed. The aged, the infirm, mix in the mob, with an interest as eager as if they were able to join in the common aid; the very child stops as he passes, and cannot resume his sport, till he has followed with the crowd the half-insensible object of so many cares to a place where surer relief may be procured. When, in a storm, some human being is seen, in the distant surf, clinging to a plank, that is sometimes driven nearer the shore, and sometimes carried farther off, sometimes buried in the surge, and then rising again, as if itself struggling, like the half-hopeless wretch whom it supports, that looks sadly to the shore as he rises from every wave. Has nature abandoned the sufferer without aid ? Is he to find no one who will make at least one effort to save a human being that is on the point of perishing? He is not so abandoned. Nature has provided a deliverance for him in the bosom of every spectator. There are courageous hearts and strong hands, that, in the very peril of an equal fate, will rush to his succour, and that, in laying him in safety on that soil which he despaired of treading again, will feel only the joy of having delivered a human being, whose name and whose very existence were unknown to them before.

SELECTION 21

Ethics[15]

We have reviewed, then, all the principal phenomena of the mind; and I flatter myself, that now, after this review, you will see better the reasons which have led me, in so many instances, to deviate from the order of former arrangements; since every former arrangement of the phenomena would have been absolutely inconsistent with the results of the minuter analysis into which we have been led. With the views of other philosophers, as to the nature and composition of our feelings, I might, indeed, have easily adhered to their plan; but I must then have presented to you views which appear to myself defective; and however eminent the names of those from whom I may have differed, it appeared to me my duty, in every instance in which I believed their opinions to be erroneous, to express to you my

---

[15] [Extracted from *Lectures on the Philosophy of the Human Mind*, London: William Tegg, 1860, Lecture LXXIII, pp. 485-488]

dissent firmly, though, I hope, always with that candour, which not the eminent only deserve, but even the humblest of those who have contributed their wish at least, and their effort to enlighten us.

In reducing to two generic powers or susceptibilities of the mind, the whole extensive tribe of its intellectual states, in all their variety, I was aware that I could not fail at first to be considered by you as retrenching too largely that long list of intellectual faculties to which they have been commonly referred. But I flatter myself you have now seen that this reference to so long a list of powers has arisen only from an inaccurate view of the phenomena referred to them, and particularly from inattention to the different aspects of the phenomena, according as they are combined or not combined with desire, in the different processes of thought, that have thence been termed inventive, or creative, or deliberative.

In like manner, when I formed one great comprehensive class of our emotions, to supersede what appeared to me to have been misnamed, by a very obvious abuse of nomenclature, the active powers of the mind, as if the mind were more active in these than in its intellectual functions, I may have seemed to you at the time to make too bold a deviation from established arrangement. But I venture to hope, that the deviation now does not seem to you without reason. It is only now, indeed, after our comprehensive survey of the whole phenomena themselves has been completed, that you can truly judge of the of the principles which have directed our arrangement of them in their different classes. I know well the nature and the force of that universal self-illusion, by which analyses and classifications that have been made by ourselves, seem always to us the most accurate classifications and analyses which could be made; but if all the various phenomena of the mind admit of being readily reduced to the classes under which I would arrange them, the arrangement itself, I cannot but think, is at least more simple and definite than any other previous arrangement which I could have borrowed and adopted....

I now, however, proceed to that part of my course which is more strictly ethical.

The science of ethics, as you know, has relation to our affections of mind, not simply as phenomena, but as virtuous or vicious, right or wrong. ...

What then is the virtue which it is the practical object of this science to recommend?

That the natural state of man is a state of society, I proved in a former lecture, when, in treating of our desires in general, in their order as emotions, I considered the desire of society as one of these.

That man, so existing in society, is capable of receiving from others benefit or injury, and, in his turn, of benefiting or injuring them by his actions, is a mere physical fact, as to which there cannot be any dispute.

But though the physical fact of benefit or injury is all which we consider in the action of inanimate things, it is far from being all of which we think in the case of voluntary agents, when there is not merely benefit or injury produced, but a previous intention of producing it. In every case of this kind in which we regard the agent as willing that particular good or evil which he may have produced, there arise certain distinctive emotions of moral approbation or disapprobation, those immediate emotions, of which, as mere states or affections of the mind, I before treated, when I considered the order of our emotions in general. We regard the action in every such case, when the benefit or injury is believed by us to have entered into the intention of him who performed the action, not as advantageous or hurtful only, but as right or wrong; or, in other words, the person who performed the particular action, seems to us to have moral merit or demerit in that particular action.

To say that any action which we are considering is right or wrong, and to say that the person who performed it has moral merit or demerit, are to say precisely the same thing; though writers on the theory of morals have endeavoured to make these different questions, and have even multiplied the question still more by other divisions, which seem to me to be only varieties of tautological expression, or at least to be, as we shall find, only the reference to different objects of one simple feeling of the mind.

When certain actions are witnessed by us, or described to us, they excite instantly certain vivid feelings, distinctive to us of the agent, as virtuous or vicious, worthy or unworthy of esteem. His action, we say, is right, himself meritorious. But are these moral estimates of the action and of the agent founded on different feelings, or do we not mean simply, that he, performing this action, excites in us a feeling of moral approbation or disapprobation, and that all others, in similar circumstances, performing the same action, that is to say, willing, in relations exactly similar, a similar amount of benefit or injury, for the sake of that very benefit or injury, will excite in us a similar feeling of approbation in the one case, and of disapprobation in the other case? The action cannot truly have any quality which the agent has not, because the action is truly nothing, unless as significant of the agent whom we know, or of some other agent whom we imagine. Virtue, as distinct from the virtuous person, is a mere name, as is vice distinct from the vicious. The action, if it be any thing more than a mere insignificant word, is a certain agent in certain circumstances, willing and producing a certain effect; and the emotion, whatever it may be, excited by the action is, in truth, and must always be the emotion excited by an agent real or supposed. We may speak of the fulfilment of duty, virtue, propriety, merit, and we may ascribe these variously to the action, and to him who performed it; but whether we speak of the action or of the agent, we mean nothing more, than that a certain feeling of moral approbation has been excited in our mind by the contemplation of a certain intentional production, in certain circumstances, of a certain amount of benefit or injury. When we think within ourselves, "is this what we ought to do?" we do not make two inquiries, first, whether the action be right, and then, whether we should not have merit in doing what is wrong, or demerit in doing what is right for us to do; we only consider whether doing it, we shall excite in others approbation or disapprobation, and in ourselves a corresponding emotion of complacency or remorse. According to the answer which we give to our own heart, in this respect, an answer which relates to the single feeling of moral approbation or disapprobation, we shall conceive that we are doing what we ought to do, or what we ought not to do; and knowing this, we can have no further moral inquiry to make as to the merit or demerit of doing what is previously felt by us to be right or wrong.

Much of the perplexity which has attended inquiries into the theory of morals, has arisen, I have little doubt, from distinctions which seemed to those who made them to be the result of nice and accurate analysis, but in which the analysis was verbal only, not real, or at least related to the varying circumstances of the action, not to the moral sentiment which the particular action in certain particular circumstances excited. What is it which constitutes an action virtuous? What is it which constitutes the moral obligation to perform certain actions? What is it which constitutes the merit of him who performs certain actions? These have been considered as questions essentially distinct; and because philosophers have been perplexed in attempting to give different answers to all these questions, and have still thought that different answers were necessary, they have wondered at difficulties which themselves created, and struggling to discover what could not be discovered, have often, from this very circumstance, been led into a scepticism which otherwise they might have avoided, or have stated so many unmeaning distinctions as to furnish occasion of ridicule and scepticism to others. One simple proposition has been converted into an endless circle of propositions, each proving and proved by that which precedes or follows it. Why has any one merit in a particular action ? Because he has done an action that was virtuous. And why was it virtuous? Because it was an action which it was his duty, in such circumstances, to do. And why was it his duty to do it in such circumstances? Because there was a moral obligation to perform it. And why do we say that there was a moral obligation to perform it? Because if he had not performed it he would have violated his duty, and been unworthy of our approbation.

In this circle we might proceed for ever, with the semblance of reasoning, indeed, but only with the semblance; our answers, though verbally different, being merely the same proposition repeated in different forms, and requiring, therefore, in all its forms to be proved, or not requiring proof in any. To have merit, to be virtuous, to have done our duty, to have acted in conformity with obligation; all have reference to one feeling of the mind, that feeling of approbation which attends the consideration of virtuous actions. They are merely, as I have said, different modes of stating one simple truth; that the contemplation of any one, acting as we have done in a particular case, excites a feeling of moral approval.

SELECTION 22

Virtue and Moral Emotion[16]

That virtue is nothing in itself, but is only a general name for certain actions, which agree in exciting, when contemplated, a certain emotion of the mind, I trust I have already sufficiently shown. There is no virtue, no vice, but there are virtuous agents, vicious agents; that is to say, persons whose actions we cannot contemplate without a certain

---

[16] [Extracted from *Lectures on the Philosophy of the Human Mind*, London: William Tegg, 1860, Lecture LXXIV, pp. 494-499]

instant emotion; and what we term the law of nature, in its relation to certain actions, is nothing more than the general agreement of this sentiment in relation to those actions. In thinking of virtue, therefore, it is evident that we are not to look for anything self-existing, like the universal essences of the schools, and eternal like the Platonic ideas; but a felt relation, and nothing more. We are to consider only agents, and the emotions which these agents excite; and all which we mean by the moral differences of actions, is their tendency to excite one emotion rather than another.

Virtue, then, being a term expressive only of the relation of certain actions, as contemplated, to certain emotions in the minds of those who contemplate them, cannot, it is evident, have any universality beyond that of the minds in which these emotions arise. We speak always, therefore, relatively to the constitution of our minds, not to what we might have been constituted to admire if we had been created by a different Being, but to what we are constituted to admire, and what, in our present circumstances, approving or disapproving with instant love or abhorrence, it is impossible for us not to believe to be, in like manner, the objects of approbation or disapprobation to him who has endowed us with feelings so admirably accordant with all those other gracious purposes which we discover in the economy of nature.

Virtue, however, is still, in strictness of philosophic precision, a term expressive only of the relation of certain emotions of our mind to certain actions that are contemplated by us: its universality is coextensive with the minds in which the emotions arise, and this is all which we can mean by the essential distinctions of morality, even though all mankind were supposed by us, at every moment, to feel precisely the same emotions on contemplating the same actions.

But it must be admitted, also, that all mankind do not feel at every moment precisely the same emotions on contemplating actions that are precisely the same; and it is necessary, therefore, to make some limitations even of this relative universality.

In the first place, it must be admitted that there are moments in which the mind is wholly incapable of perceiving moral differences; that is to say, in which the emotions that constitute the feeling of these moral differences do not arise. Such are all the moments of very violent passion. When the impetuosity of the passion is abated, indeed, we perceive that we have done what we now look upon with horror, but when our passion was most violent, we were truly blinded by it, or at least saw only what it permitted us to see. The moral emotion has not arisen, because the whole soul was occupied with a different species of feeling. The moral distinctions, however, or general tendencies of actions to excite this emotion, are not on this account less certain; or we must say, that the truths of arithmetic, and all other truths, are uncertain, since the mind, in a state of passion, would be equally incapable of distinguishing these. He who has lived for years in the hope of revenge, and who has at length laid his foe at his feet, may, indeed, while he pulls out his dagger from the heart that is quivering beneath it, be incapable of feeling the crime which he has committed; but would he at that moment be abler to tell the square of four, or the cube of two? All in his mind, at that moment, is one wild state of agitation, which allows nothing to be felt but the agitation itself.

"While the human heart is thus agitated," it has been said, "by the flux and reflux of a thousand passions, that sometimes unite and sometimes oppose each other, to engrave laws on it, is to engrave them not on sand, but on a wave that is never at rest. What eyes are piercing enough to read the sacred characters?"

"Vain declamation!" answers the writer from whom I quote. "If we do not read the characters, it is not because our sight is too weak to discern them, it is because we do not fix our eyes on them; or if they be indistinguishable, it is only for a moment."

"The heart of man," he continues,

> may be considered, allegorically, as an island almost level with the water which bathes it. On the pure white marble of the island are engraved the holy precepts of the law of nature. Near these characters is one who bends his eyes respectfully on the inscription, and reads it aloud. He is the lover of Virtue, the Genius of the island. The water around is in continual agitation; The slightest zephyr raises it into billows. It then covers the inscription. We no longer see the characters. We no longer hear the Genius read. But the calm soon rises from the bosom of the storm. The island reappears white as before, and the Genius resumes his employment.[17]

That passion has a momentary influence in blinding us to moral distinctions, or, which is the same thing, an influence to prevent the rise of certain emotions, that, but for the stronger feeling of the passion

---

[17] [Translated from the French of François-Vincent Toussaint, *Les Moeurs* (1748), 'Discours Preliminaire', pp. xxiii-xxv.]

itself, would arise, may then be admitted; but the influence is momentary, or little more than momentary, and extends, as we have seen, even to those truths which are commonly considered as best entitled to the appellation of universal. The moral truths, it must he allowed — if I may apply the name of truths to the felt moral differences of actions — are, to the impassioned mind, as little universal as the truths of geometry.

Another still more important limitation of the universality for which we contend, relates to actions which are so complex as to have various opposite results of good and evil, or of which it is not easy to trace the consequences. An action, when it is the object of our moral approbation or disapprobation, is, as I have already said, the agent himself acting with certain views. These views, that is to say the intention of the agent, are necessary to be taken into account, or, rather, are the great moral circumstances to be considered; and the intention is not visible to us like the external changes produced by it, but is, in many cases, to be inferred from the apparent results. When these results, therefore, are too obscure or too complicated to furnish clear and immediate evidence of the intention, we may pause in estimating actions which we should not fail to have approved instantly, or disapproved instantly, if we had known the intention of the agent, or could have inferred it more easily from a simpler result; or by fixing our attention chiefly on one part of the complex result, that was perhaps not the part which the agent had in view, we may condemn what was praiseworthy, or applaud what deserved our condemnation. If the same individual may thus have different moral sentiments, according to the different parts of the complex result on which his attention may have been fixed, it is surely not wonderful that different individuals, in regarding the same action, should sometimes approve in like manner, and disapprove variously, not because the principle of moral emotion, as an original tendency of the mind, is absolutely capricious, but because the action considered, though apparently the same, is really different as an object of conception in different minds, according to the parts of the mixed result which attract the chief attention. ...

To these two limitations it is necessary to add a third, that operates very powerfully and widely on our moral estimates: the influence of the principle of association. We are not to suppose, that because man is formed with the capacity of certain moral emotions, he is therefore to be exempt from the influence of every other principle of his constitution. The influence of association, indeed, does not destroy his moral capacity, but it gives it new objects, or at least varies the object in which it is to exercise itself, by suggesting with peculiar vividness certain accessory circumstances, which may variously modify the general sentiment that results from the contemplation of particular actions.

One very extensive form of the influence of association on our moral sentiments, is that which consists in the application to particular cases of feelings that belong to a class. In nature there are no classes. There are only particular actions, more or less beneficial or injurious. But we cannot consider these particular actions long, without discovering in them, as in any other number of objects that may be considered by us at the same time, certain relations of analogy or resemblance of some sort, in consequence of which we class them together, and form for the whole class one comprehensive name. Such are the generic words justice, injustice, malevolence, benevolence. To these generic words, which, if distinguished from the number of separate actions denoted by them, are mere words, invented by ourselves, we gradually, from the influence of association in the feelings that have attended the particular cases to which the same name has been applied, attach one mixed notion, a sort of compound, or modified whole, of the various feelings which the actions separately would have excited, more vivid, therefore, than what would have arisen on the contemplation of some of these actions, less vivid than what others might have excited.

It is enough that an action is one of a class which we term unjust; we feel instantly not the mere emotion which the action of itself would originally have excited, but we feel also that emotion which has been associated with the class of actions to which the particular action belongs; and though the action may be of a kind which, if we had formed no general arrangement, would have excited but slight emotion, as implying no very great injury produced or intended, it thus excites a far more vivid feeling, by borrowing, as it were, from other analogous and more atrocious actions, that are comprehended under the same general term, the feeling which they would originally have excited. It is quite evident, for example, that in a civilized country, in which property is largely possessed, and complicated in its tenure, and as in the various modes in which it may be transferred, the infringement of property must be an object of peculiar importance, and what is commonly termed justice, in regard to it, be a virtue of essential value, and injustice a crime against which it is necessary to prepare many checks, and which is thence regarded as of no slight delinquency. The offence of the transgressor is estimated, in such a case, not by the little evil which, in any particular case, he may intentionally have occasioned to another individual, but in a great degree also by the amount of evil which would arise in a system of society constituted as that of the great nations of Europe is constituted, if all men were to be equally regardless of the right of property in others.

When we read, therefore, of the tendency to theft, in many barbarous islanders of whom navigators tell us, and of the very little shame which they seemed to feel on detection of their petty larcenies, we carry along with us our own classes of actions and the emotions to which our own general rules, resulting from our own complicated social state, have given rise. We forget, that to those who consider an action simply as it is, the guilt of an action is an object that is measured by the mere amount of evil intentionally produced in the particular case; and that the theft which they contemplate is not, therefore, in its moral aspect, the same offence that is contemplated by us. I need not trace out, in other cases, the influence of general rules, which you must be able to trace with sufficient precision for yourselves.

Such, then, is one of the modes in which association operates. But it is not in general rules alone that the influence of the associating principle is to be traced. It extends in some degree to all our moral feelings. There is no education, indeed, which can make the pure benevolence of others hateful to us, unless by that very feeling of our own inferiority which implies in envy itself our reverence, and consequently our moral approbation of what we hate; no education which can make pure deliberate malice in others an object of our esteem. But if there be any circumstances accompanying the benevolence and malice, which tend to the disparagement of the one and the elevation of the other, the influence of association may be excited powerfully, in this way, by fixing our attention more vividly on these slight accompanying circumstances. The fearlessness which often attends vice, may be raised into an importance beyond its merit, in savage ages, in which fearlessness is more important for the security of the state, and in which power and glory seem to wait on it; the yielding gentleness of benevolence may, in such circumstances, appear timidity, or at least a degree of softness unworthy of the perfect man. In like manner, when a vice is the vice of those whom we love—of a friend, a brother, a parent—the influence of association may lessen and overcome our moral disapprobation, not by rendering the vice in itself an object of our esteem, but by rendering it impossible for us to feel a vivid disapprobation of those whom we love, and mingling, therefore, some portion of this very regard in our contemplation of all their actions.

It is because we have the virtue of loving our benefactor, or friend, or parent, that we seem not to feel in so lively a manner the unworthiness of that vice which is partly lost to our notice, in the general emotion of our gratitude. But when we strip away these illusions, or when the vice is pure intentional malice, which no circumstance of association can embellish, it is equally impossible for us to look upon it with esteem, as it is impossible for us to turn away with loathing from him whose whole existence seems to be devoted to the happiness of others, and to rejoice, as we look upon him, that we are not what he is.

SELECTION 23

William Paley and Adam Smith[18]

Gentlemen, in the close of my last Lecture, after examining different modifications of the selfish system, I proceeded to consider one form of it which has not usually been ranked with the others, but which is not less absolutely selfish; since it supposes the sole motive to virtue to be the view of our own personal advantage; the only difference being, that instead of fixing its desires on the quantity of pleasure which can be enjoyed in this life, it extends them to the greater quantity of pleasure which may be enjoyed by us in the everlasting life that awaits us; having still, however, no other motive than the desire of this personal enjoyment, and the corresponding fear of pain, in the actions which may seem, but only seem, to arise from a disinterested love of God, or a disinterested love of those whom God has committed to our affection.

The greater or less quantity of pleasure, however, which is coveted by us, either in intensity or duration, does not alter the nature of

---

[18] [Extracted from *Lectures on the Philosophy of the Human Mind*, London: William Tegg, 1860, Lecture LXXX, pp. 535-539]

the principle which covets it; if the perception of the means of gratifying our own individual appetite for enjoyment, whether the pleasure be great or slight, near or remote, brief or everlasting, be all which constitutes what is in that case strangely termed moral obligation: and the system of Paley, therefore, to which I particularly alluded—a system which defines virtue to be "the doing good to mankind, in obedience to the will of God, for the sake of everlasting happiness," and which makes, not the love of God, nor the love of mankind, but this love of everlasting happiness the motive and sole obligation to the good which otherwise we should have had as little moral desire of producing or promoting, as of producing an equal or greater amount of evil, must be allowed to be, in its very essence, as truly selfish, as if it had defined virtue to be the pursuit of mere wealth, or fame, or of the brief dignities, or still briefer pleasures of this mortal existence.

> There is always understood to be a difference between an act of prudence and an act of duty. Thus, if I distrusted a man who owed me money, I should reckon it an act of prudence to get another bound with him; but I should hardly call it an act of duty. On the other hand, it would be thought a very unusual and loose kind of language to say, that, as I had made such a promise, it was prudent to perform it; or that, as my friend, when he went abroad, placed a box of jewels in my hands, it would be prudent in me to preserve it for him till he returned.[19]

If the most prudent labourer after his own selfish interest, without the slightest regard for the happiness of others, unless as that happiness may be instrumental to his own, be constantly actuated by the same moral motive which influences the most generous lovers of mankind, how strange an illusion is all moral sentiment, which views with such different feelings objects that are in every moral respect precisely the same. But it is in our emotions alone that our notions of morality have their rise: and how illusive, therefore, and radically false I should rather say, must be that system which is founded on the absolute similarity of feelings that are recognized by every bosom as absolutely dissimilar. ...

But for the principle of moral approbation which the divine being has fixed in our nature, the expression of his will would itself have no moral power, whatever physical pain or pleasure it might hold

---

[19] Paley's *Moral Philosophy*, book ii. chapter iii

out to our prudent choice. It may be asked, why should we obey the divine command, with as much reason as it may be asked, why should we love our parents or our country; and our only answer to both questions, as far as morality can be said to be concerned, or any feeling different from that of a mere calculation of physical loss or gain, is, that such is our nature; that, in considering the command of God, our greatest of benefactors, or in considering the happiness of our parents, our country, mankind, which it is in our power to promote, we feel that to act in conformity with these, will be followed by our moral approbation; as to act in opposition to them will be followed by inevitable self-reproach. There is a principle of moral discrimination already existing in us, that, even when we conform our conduct to the divine will, is the very principle by which we have felt the duty of this delightful conformity; and if there be no such principle in our nature, by which we discover the duty of the conformity, it is surely very evident that there can be no such duty to be felt, any more than there can be colour to the blind, or melody to the deaf.

God may be loved by us, or feared by us. He may be loved by us as the source of all our blessings, conferred or promised. He may be feared by us as a being who has the power of inflicting on us eternal anguish. In one of these views, we may, when we obey him, act from gratitude; in the other, from a sense of the evils which we have to dread in offending him. But if it be a duty of gratitude to obey God, we must previously have been capable of knowing that gratitude is a virtue, as much as we must have been capable of knowing the power of God, before we could have known to fear his awful dominion. We consider the Deity as possessing the highest moral perfection: but in that theological view of morality which acknowledges no mode of estimating excellence beyond that divine command itself, whatever it might have been, these words are absolutely meaningless; since if, instead of what we now term virtue, he had commanded only what we now term vice, his command must still have been equally holy. If indeed the system of Paley, and of other theological moralists, were just, what excellence beyond the excellence of mere power, could we discover in that divine being whom we adore as the supreme goodness, still more than we fear him as the omnipotent.

God has, indeed, commanded certain actions, and it is our virtue to conform our actions to his will; but if the virtue depend exclusively on obedience to the command, and if there be no peculiar moral excellence in the actions commanded, he must have been equally adorable, though nature had exhibited only appearances of unceasing malevolence in its author; and every command which he had delivered to his creatures had been only to add new voluntary miseries to the physical miseries which already surrounded them. In the system of Hobbes, which considers law itself as constituent of moral right, a tyrant, if his power of enacting law be sufficiently established, is not to be distinguished, in his very tyranny, from the generous sovereign of the free; because the measure of right is to be found in his will alone. In the system of Paley, in like manner, if virtue be conformity to the will of God, whatever that will may be, and there be no moral measure of the excellence of that will itself, God and the most malignant demon have no moral difference to our heart, but as the one and not the other is the irresistible sovereign of the universe.

The will of God, then, though it is unquestionably the source of virtue, in the most important sense — as it was his will that formed all the principles of our constitution, of which the principle of moral approbation is one — is not the source of virtue in the sense in which that phrase is understood by some theological writers as limited to the mere declaration of his will, sanctioned by punishment and reward. There is an earlier law of God, which he has written in our hearts; and the desire of our mere personal happiness or misery, in this or in another world, is truly an object of our approbation, not the source of it, since the love of mere selfish enjoyment is at least as powerfully the motive to vice, in some cases, as it is in other cases the motive to virtue. We do not merely submit to the will of God as we submit to any power which it is impossible for us to resist. We feel that it would be not imprudence only, but guilt, to wish to disobey it. We seek, in the constitution of our nature, the reason which leads us to approve morally of the duty of this conformity of our will to his beneficent and supreme will; and we find, in one of the essential principles of our nature, the moral reason which we seek.

After this examination of the various systems, which may be considered as more or less directly opposed to the belief of that principle of moral feeling — the original susceptibility of moral emotion on the contemplation of certain actions — for which I have contended, there is still one system which deserves to be considered by us, in relation to this belief, not as being subversive of morality, in any one of its essential distinctions, but as appearing to fix morality on a basis that is not sufficiently firm; with the discovery of the instability of which, therefore, the virtues that are represented as supported on it, might be considered as themselves unstable; as the statue, though it be the image of a god, or the column, though it be a part of a sacred temple, may fall, not because it is not sufficiently cohesive and firm in itself, but because it is too massy for the feeble pedestal on which it has been placed.

The system to which I allude, is that which is delivered by Dr Smith, in his Theory of Moral Sentiments — a work unquestionably of the first rank in a science which I cannot but regard, as to man, the most interesting of sciences. Profound in thought, it exhibits, even when it is most profound, an example of the graces with which a sage imagination knows how to adorn the simple and majestic form of science, that is severe and cold, only to those who are themselves cold and severe, as in those very graces it exhibits, in like manner, an example of the reciprocal embellishment which imagination receives from the sober dignity of truth. In its minor details and illustrations, indeed, it may be considered as presenting a model of philosophic beauty, of which all must acknowledge the power, who are not disqualified by their very nature for the admiration and enjoyment of intellectual excellence; so dull of understanding as to shrink with a painful consciousness of incapacity at the very appearance of refined analysis, or so dull and cold of heart, as to feel no charm in the delightful varieties of an eloquence that, in the illustration and embellishment of the noblest truths, seems itself to live and harmonize with those noble sentiments which it adorns.

It is chiefly in its minor analyses, however, that I conceive the excellence of this admirable work to consist. Its leading doctrine I am far from admitting. Indeed it seems to me as manifestly false, as the greater number of its secondary and minute delineations appear to me faithful, to the fine lights, and faint and flying shades, of that moral nature which they represent.

According to Dr Smith, we do not immediately approve of certain actions, or disapprove of certain other actions, when we have become acquainted with the intention of the agent, and the consequences, beneficial or injurious, of what he has done. All these we might know thoroughly, without a feeling of the slightest approbation or disapprobation. It is necessary, before any moral sentiment arise, that the mind should go through another process, that by which we seem for the time to enter into the feelings of the agent, and of those to whom his action has relation in its consequences, or intended consequences, beneficial or injurious. If, by a process of this kind, on considering all the circumstances in which the agent was placed, we feel a complete sympathy with the passions or calmer emotions that actuated him, and with the gratitude of him who was the object of the action, we approve of the action itself as right, and feel the merit of the agent; our sense of the propriety of the action depending on our sympathy with the agent, our sense of the merit of the agent on our sympathy with the object of the action. If our sympathies be of an opposite kind, we disapprove of the action itself as improper, that is to say, unsuitable to the circumstances, and ascribe not merit but demerit to the agent. In sympathizing with the gratitude of others, we should have regarded the agent as worthy of reward; in sympathizing with the resentment of others, we regard him as worthy of punishment.

Such is the supposed process in estimating the actions of others. When we regard our own conduct we in some measure reverse this process; or rather, by a process still more refined, we imagine others sympathizing with us, and sympathize with their sympathy. We consider how our conduct would appear to an impartial spectator. We approve of it, if it be that of which we feel that he would approve; we disapprove of it if it be that which we feel by the experience of our own former emotions, when we have ourselves, in similar circumstances, estimated the actions of others, would excite his disapprobation. We are able to form a judgment as to our own conduct, therefore, because we have previously judged of the moral conduct of others, that is to say, have previously sympathized with the feelings of others; and but for the presence, or supposed presence, of some impartial spectator, as a mirror to represent to us ourselves, we should as little have known the beauty or deformity of our own moral character, as we should have known the beauty or ugliness of our external features without some mirror to reflect them to our eye.

In this brief outline of Dr Smith's system, I have of course confined myself to the leading doctrine, of which his theory is the development. If this doctrine of the necessary antecedence of sympathy to our moral approbation or disapprobation be just, the system may be admitted, even though many of his minor illustrations should appear to be false. If this primary doctrine be not just, the system, however ingenious and just in its explanation of many phenomena of the mind, must fail as a theory of our moral sentiments.

To derive our moral sentiments, which are as universal as the actions of mankind that come under our review, from the occasional sympathies, that warm or sadden us with joys and griefs and resentments which are not our own, seems to me, I confess, very nearly the same sort of error as it would be to derive the waters of an ever-flowing stream from the sunshine or shade which may occasionally gleam over it. That we have a principle of social feeling, which, in its rapid participation of the vivid emotions of others, seems to identify us in many cases with the happy or the sorrowful, the grateful or the indignant, it is impossible to deny. But this sympathy, quick as it truly is to arise, in cases in which the primary feelings are vivid and strongly marked, is not a perpetual accompaniment of every action of every one around us. There must be some vividness of feeling in others, or the display of vividness of feeling, or at least such a situation as usually excites vivid feeling, of some sort, in those who are placed in it, to call the sympathy itself into action. In the number of petty affairs which are hourly before our eyes, what sympathy is felt either with those who are actively or those who are passively concerned, when the agent himself performs his little offices with emotions as slight as those which the objects of his actions reciprocally feel? Yet, in these cases, we are as capable of judging, and approve or disapprove, not with the same liveliness of emotion indeed, but with as accurate estimation of merit or demerit, as when we consider the most heroic sacrifices which the virtuous can make, or the most atrocious crimes of which the sordid and the cruel can be guilty.

It is not the absolute vividness of our emotion, however, but its mere correspondence in degree with the emotion of others, which affects our estimates of the propriety of their actions; and it must be remembered, that it is not any greater or less vividness of our sympathetic feeling, but the accuracy of our estimation of merit and demerit, whether great or slight, by the sympathetic feelings supposed, which is the only point in question. There is no theory of our moral distinctions, which supposes that we are to approve equally of all actions that are right, and to disapprove equally of all actions which are wrong; but it is essential to one theory — that theory which we are considering — that there should be no feeling of right or wrong, merit or demerit, and consequently no moral estimation whatever, where there is no previous sympathy in that particular case. The humblest action, therefore, which we denominate "right," must have awakened our sympathy as much as those glorious actions which we are never weary of extolling, in the very commendation of which we think not of the individual only with thankfulness, but with a sort of proud delight of ourselves, of our country, of the common nature of man, as ennobled by the virtue, that, instead of receiving dignity from the homage of our praises, confers dignity on the very gratitude and reverence which offer them. If we were to think only those actions right in which our sympathy is excited, the class of indifferent actions would comprehend the whole life, or nearly the whole life, of almost all the multitude of those around us, and indeed of almost all mankind. A few great virtues and great iniquities would still remain in our system of practical ethics, to be applauded or censured; but the morality of the common transactions of life, which, though less important in each particular case, is, upon the whole, more important from its extensive diffusion, would disappear altogether as morality, as that which it is right to observe, and wrong to omit, and though it might still be counted useful, would admit of no higher denomination of praise. The supposed necessary universality then, in our moral sentiments, of that which, however frequent, is surely far from universal, would of itself seem to me a sufficient objection to the theory of Dr Smith.

Even if the sympathy for which he contends were as universal as it is absolutely necessary for the truth of his theory that it should be, it must still be admitted that our sympathy is, in degree at least, one of the most irregular and seemingly capricious of principles in the constitution of the mind; and on this very account, therefore, not very likely to be the commensurable test or standard of feelings so regular, upon the whole, as our general estimates of right and wrong. But though it would be very easy to show the force of this objection, I hasten from it, and from all objections of this kind to that which seems to me to be the essential error of the system.

This essential error, the greatest of all possible systematic errors, is no less than the assumption, in every case, of those very moral feelings which are supposed to flow from sympathy, the assumption of them as necessarily existing before that very sympathy in which they are said to originate.

SELECTION 24

Moral Sense and Moral Emotion[20]

In tracing to an original susceptibility of the mind our moral feelings of obligation in the conception of certain actions as future, of virtue, in the present performance or wish to perform certain actions, and of merit, in the past performance or past resolution to perform certain actions, we may be considered as arriving at a principle like that which Dr Hutcheson, after Lord Shaftesbury, has distinguished by the name of the Moral Sense, and of which, as an essential principle of our constitution, he has defended the reality with so much power of argument, in his various works on morals. In our moral feelings, however, I discover no peculiar analogy to perceptions or sensations, in the philosophic meaning of those terms, and the phrase moral sense, therefore, I consider as having had a very unfortunate influence on the controversy as to the original moral differences of actions, from the false analogies which it cannot fail to suggest. Were I to speak of a moral sense at present, you would understand me as speaking rather metaphorically, than according to the real place which we should be inclined to give in our arrangement, to the original principle of our nature, on which the moral emotions depend. But by Hutcheson it was asserted to be truly and strictly a sense, as much a sense as any of those which are the source of our direct external perceptions; and though this difference of nomenclature and of arrangement on his part, evidently arose from a misconception, or, at least, a very loose meaning of the word sense, different from that in which it is commonly understood, as limited to the feelings which we acquire directly from affections of our bodily organs, still this loose meaning of the term which he intended it to convey, was, in some measure, mingled and confused in the minds of others, with the stricter meaning commonly assigned to it, and the assertion of a moral sense has been regarded almost as the assertion of the existence of some primary medium of perception, which conveys to us directly moral knowledge, as the eye enables us to distinguish directly the varieties of colours, or the ear the varieties of sounds; and the scepticism, which would have been just with respect to such an organ of exclusive moral feeling, has been unfortunately

---

[20] [Extracted from *Lectures on the Philosophy of the Human Mind*, London: William Tegg, 1860, Lecture LXXXII, pp. 551-556]

extended to the certain moral principle itself, as an original principle of our nature. Of the impropriety of ascribing the moral feelings to a sense, I am fully aware then, and the place which I have assigned to them among the moral phenomena is, therefore, very different. In the emotions, which the contemplation of the voluntary actions of those around us produces, there is nothing that seems to demand, for the production of such emotions, a peculiar sense, more than is to be found in any of our other emotions. Certain actions excite in us, when contemplated, the vivid feelings which we express too coldly when, from the poverty of language, we term them approbation or disapprobation, and which are not estimates formed, by an approving or disapproving judgment, but emotions that accompany and give warmth to such estimates. Certain other objects of thought excite in us other vivid feelings that are in like manner classed as emotions—hope, jealousy, resentment; and, therefore, if all emotions, excited by the contemplation of objects, were to be referred to a peculiar sense, we might as well speak of a sense of those emotions or of a sense of covetousness or despair as of a sense of moral regard. If sense, indeed, were understood in this case to be synonymous with mere susceptibility, so that, when we speak of a moral sense, we were to be understood to mean only a susceptibility of moral feeling of some sort, we might be allowed to have a sense of morals, because we have, unquestionably, a susceptibility of moral emotion; but, in this very wide extension of the term, we might be said, in like manner, to have as many senses as we have feelings of any sort; since, in whatever manner the mind may have been affected, it must have had a previous susceptibility of being so affected, as much as in the peculiar affections that are denominated moral.

The great error of Dr Hutcheson, and of other writers who treat of the susceptibility of moral emotion, under the name of the moral sense, appears to me to consist in their belief of certain moral qualities in actions, which excite in us what they consider as ideas of these qualities, in the same manner as external things give us, not merely pain or pleasure, but notions or ideas of hardness, form, colour. Indeed, it is on this account that the great champion of this doctrine professes to regard the moral principle as a sense; from its agreement, as he says, with this definition, which he conceives to be the accurate definition of a sense, "a determination of the mind to receive any idea from the presence of an object which occurs to us independent on our will."[21] What he terms an idea, in this case, is nothing more than an emotion considered in its relation to the action which has excited it. A certain action is considered by us — a certain emotion arises. There is no idea in the philosophic meaning of that term, but of the agent himself and of the circumstances in which he was placed, and the physical changes produced by him; and our ideas or notions of these we owe to other sources. To the moral principle, the only principle of which Hutcheson could mean to speak as a moral sense, we owe the emotion itself, and nothing but the emotion.

In one use of the word, indeed, we may be said to owe to our susceptibility of moral emotion, ideas, because we owe to it, as the primary source, the emotions of this species which we remember; and remembrances of past feelings are often termed ideas of those feelings; but in this application of the word, as synonymous with a mere remembrance, every feeling, as capable of being remembered, may be a source of ideas independently of the will, and therefore, according to the definition which is given by Hutcheson, equally a sense.

There is yet another meaning of the word, however, and a still more important one, in relation to our present inquiry, in which our susceptibility of moral emotion is productive of what, in the general loose language of metaphysical writers, have been termed ideas; and it is by his defective analysis, of what is truly meant in the phrase, moral ideas, and of the process which evolves them, that I conceive Hutcheson to have been chiefly misled, in supposing us to be endowed with a sense of moral qualities of actions. The process to which I allude, is the common process of generalization, to which alone we owe the general notions of virtue, vice, right, and wrong, which he ascribes to a particular sense that affords us these ideas. If we had never contemplated more than a single virtuous or vicious action, we should have had only the particular emotion which followed that particular contemplation, and should as little have formed the general notions of virtue and vice, as we should have formed the notion which is expressed by the word quadruped, if we had seen only a single animal with four legs. It is not by one action only of one definite kind, however, that is to say, by an agent placed only in one set of circumstances, and producing only one particular effect, that our moral emotion is excited; nor is there only one

---

[21] [Hutcheson, *Inquiry into the Original of our Ideas of Beauty and Virtue*, II.i.]

unvarying feeling of the mind, of one exact degree of intensity which we denominate a moral emotion, as excited by various moral actions. There are various analogous actions which excite various analogous moral feelings of approbation or disapprobation, and it is in consequence of the feeling of the similarity of these emotions, that we learn to class together the different actions that excite these similar emotions under a single word, virtuous or right, or proper, or vicious, wrong, improper. The ideas, of which Hutcheson speaks, are these general notions only. ...

You are not to conceive, as Dr Hutcheson's view of our moral feelings might lead you to imagine, that we discover a certain idea of right or wrong, virtue or vice, from the contemplation of any one particular action, as if there were a sense for the reception of such ideas, that flow from them like light from the sun, or fragrant particles from a rose. There is no right or wrong, virtue or vice, but there are agents whose actions cannot be contemplated by us without an emotion of approbation or disapprobation; and all actions, that is to say, all agents, that agree in exciting moral feelings which are thus analogous, we class together as virtuous or vicious, from this circumstance of felt agreement alone. The similarity of the emotions which we feel, in these particular cases, is thus all to which we owe the notions, or, as Dr Hutcheson calls them, the ideas, of right and wrong, virtue and vice; and it is not more wonderful that we should form these general notions, than that we should form any other general notions whatever.

The error of Dr Hutcheson with respect to qualities, in objects that excite in us what he terms moral ideas, is similar to that which led many ethical writers — as we saw in reviewing their different systems — to refer our moral sentiments to reason or judgment, as the principle which measures the fitnesses of certain actions for producing certain ends; and which approves or disapproves accordingly, as different actions seem more or less adapted for producing the desired end. The truth is, that moral approbation or disapprobation, though, from the common use of those terms, and the poverty of our language, I have been obliged to employ them in our past discussions, are terms that are very inadequate to express the liveliness of the moral feelings to which we give those names. The moral emotions are more akin to love or hate, than to perception or judgment. What we call our approbation of an action, inasmuch as the moral principle is concerned, is a sort of moral love when the action is the action of another, or moral complacency when the action is our own, and nothing more.

It is no exercise of reason, discovering congruities, and determining one action to be better fitted than another action, for affording happiness or relieving misery. This logical or physical approbation may precede, indeed, the moral emotion, and may mingle with it, and continue to render it more and more lively while we are under its influence; but even when such approbation precedes it, it is distinct from the emotion itself; and we might judge and approve of the fitness, or disapprove of the unfitness, of certain actions to produce happiness, with the same precision as we now judge and approve, or disapprove, though we had not been, as we are, moral beings, desirous of the happiness of others, and feeling a vivid delightful emotion, on the contemplation of such actions as tend to produce that happiness. However our judgment, as mere judgment, may have been exercised before, in discerning the various relations of actions to the happiness of the world, the moral principle is the source only of the emotion which follows the discovery of such fitness; and not in the slightest degree of the judgment which measures and calculates the fitness, any more than it is a source of the fitness itself. When we speak of our moral approbation of an action, we may indeed, from the convenience of such brief expressions, have some regard to both feelings, to our judgment of the fitness of an action to produce good to an individual or to the world, and to our moral love of the beneficial action which follows this discovery. But still, it is not be forgotten, that it is the latter part only, the distinctive moral regard, that belongs to the principle which we have been considering; the discovery of the fitness is a common exercise of judgment, that differs no more from the other exercises of it than these differ from each other. It is in the order of our emotions, accordingly, that I have assigned a place to our moral feelings, in my arrangement of the phenomena of the mind; because, though we are accustomed to speak of moral approbation, moral judgments, or moral estimates of actions, the feelings which we thus comprehend under a single term are not the simple vivid feeling, which is all that truly constitutes the moral emotion, but a combination of this vivid feeling with the judgment as to the fitness or tendency of the action, which, as a mere judgment, preceded and gave rise to the emotion. What is strictly the moral part of the compound is, however, as I have already said, the emotion, and the emotion only. ...

The reference of our moral love of certain actions and moral abhorrence of other actions to a peculiar sense, termed the moral sense, has arisen, then, we may conclude, from a defective analysis, or at least from a misconception of the nature of those moral ideas of which the defenders of this sense speak, and which seem to them falsely to indicate the necessity of such a sense for affording them. The ideas of which they speak are truly complex feelings of the mind. We have only to perform the necessary analysis, and all which we discover is a certain emotion of moral love, that, according to circumstances, is more or less lively, and the notion of certain actions, that is to say, of agents real or supposed, willing and producing certain effects. We may, for the sake of brevity, invent the general words virtue, right, propriety, as significant of all the actions which are followed in us by this emotion. But these are mere generalizations, like other generalizations; and there is no virtue in nature, more than there is quadruped or substance.

But, though Dr Hutcheson may have erred in not analyzing with sufficient minuteness the moral ideas of which he speaks, and in giving the name of a moral sense to the susceptibility of a mere emotion akin to our other emotions, this error is of little consequence as to the moral distinctions themselves. Whether the feeling that attends the contemplation of certain actions admit of being more justly classed with our sensations or perceptions, or with our emotions, there is still a susceptibility of this feeling or set of feelings, original in the mind, and as essential to its very nature as any other of the principles or functions, which we regard as universally belonging to our mental constitution; as truly essential to the mind, indeed, as any of those senses among which Dr Hutcheson would fix its place.

The sceptical conclusions which some writers have conceived to be deducible from the doctrine of a moral sense, might, if they could be justly drawn from that doctrine, be equally deducible from the doctrine of moral emotions for which I have contended; since the emotions may be regarded as almost the same feelings under a different name. A very slight notice, however, of the objection which these conclusions are supposed to furnish, will be sufficient for showing the radical error in which the objection has its source. You will find it stated and illustrated at great length in Dr Price's elaborate, but very tedious, and not very clear, Review of the principal questions of morals. It is more briefly stated by Mr Stewart in his Outlines.

> From the hypothesis of a moral sense various sceptical conclusions have been deduced by later writers. The words Right and Wrong, it has been alleged, signify nothing in the objects themselves to which they are applied, any more than the words sweet and bitter, pleasant and painful; but only certain effects in the mind of the spectator. As it is improper, therefore, (according to the doctrines of modern philosophy) to say of an object of taste, that it is sweet; or of heat, that it is in the fire; so it is equally improper to say of actions, that they are right or wrong. It is absurd to speak of morality as a thing independent and unchangeable: inasmuch as it arises from an arbitrary relation between our constitution and particular objects.
>
> In order to avoid these supposed consequences of Dr Hutcheson's philosophy, an attempt has been made by some later writers, in particular by Dr Price, to revive the doctrines of Dr Cudworth, and to prove, that moral distinctions, being perceived by reason or the understanding, are equally immutable with all other kinds of truth.[22]

That right and wrong signify nothing in the objects themselves, is indeed most true. They are words expressive only of relation, and relations are not existing parts of objects, or things, to be added to objects, or taken from them. There is no right nor wrong, virtue nor vice, merit nor demerit, existing independently of the agents who are virtuous or vicious; and, in like manner, if there had been no moral emotions to arise on the contemplation of certain actions, there would have been no virtue, vice, merit, or demerit, which express only relations to these emotions. But though there be no right nor wrong in an agent, the virtuous agent is not the same as the vicious agent—I do not say merely to those whom he benefits or injures, but to the most remote individual who contemplates that intentional production of benefit or injury. All are affected, on the contemplation of these, with different emotions; and it is only by the difference of these moral emotions that these actions are recognized as morally different. We feel that it will be impossible, while the constitution of nature remains as it is—and we may say, even from the traces of the divine benevolence which the universe displays, impossible, while God himself, the framer of our constitution, and adapter of it to purposes of happiness, exists—that the lover and intentional producer of misery, as misery, should ever be viewed with tender esteem; or that he whose only ambition has been to diffuse happiness more widely than it could have flowed without his aid, should

---

[22] *Qualities of Moral Philosophy*, 4th ed., p. 132.

be regarded with the detestation, on that account, which we now feel for the murderer of a single helpless individual, or for the oppressor of as many sufferers as a nation can contain in its whole wide orb of calamity; and a distinction which is to exist while God himself exists, or at least which has been, and as we cannot but believe will be, coeval with the race of man, cannot surely be regarded as very precarious.

It is not to moral distinctions only that this objection, if it had any force, would be applicable. Equality, proportion, it might be said, in like manner, signify nothing in the objects themselves to which they are applied, more than vice or virtue. They are as truly mere relations, as the relations of morality. Though the three sides of a right angled triangle exist in the triangle itself, and constitute it what it is, what we term the properties of such a triangle do not exist in it, but are results of a peculiar capacity of the comparing mind. It is man, or some thinking being like man, whose comparison gives birth to the very feeling that is termed by us a discovery of the equality of the squares of one of the sides to the squares of the other two; that is to say — for the discovery of this truth is nothing more — it is man who, contemplating such a triangle, is impressed with this relation, and who feels afterwards that it would be impossible for him to contemplate it without such an impression.

If this feeling of the relation never had arisen, and never were to arise in any mind, though the squares themselves might still exist as separate figures, their equality would be nothing — exactly as justice and injustice would be nothing, where no relation of moral emotion had ever been felt; for equality, like justice, is a relation, not a thing; and, if strictly analyzed, exists only, and can exist only, in the mind, which, on the contemplation of certain objects, is impressed with certain feelings of relation — in the same manner as right and wrong, virtue, vice, relate to emotions excited in some mind that has contemplated certain actions — without whose contemplations of the actions, it will readily be confessed, there could be no right nor wrong, virtue nor vice, as there could be no other relation without a mind that contemplates the objects said to be related. Certain geometrical figures cannot be contemplated by us without exciting certain feelings of the contemplating mind — which are notions of equality or proportion. Is it necessary that the equality should be itself something existing in the separate figures themselves, without reference to any mind that contemplates them, before we put any confidence in geometry? Or is it not enough that every mind which does contemplate them together, is impressed with that particular feeling, in consequence of which they are ranked as equal? And, if it be not necessary, in the case of a science which we regard as the surest of all sciences, that the proportions of figures should be any thing inherent in the figures, why should it be required, before we put confidence in morality, that right and wrong should be something existing in the individual agents? It is not easy, indeed, to understand what is meant by such an inherence as is required in this postulate; or what other relations actions can be supposed to have as right or wrong, than to the minds which are impressed by them with certain feelings.

Of this, at least, we may be sure, that, if any doubt can truly exist as to relations which we and all mankind have felt, since the creation of the very race of man—because, though, with our present constitution, we feel it impossible to consider cruelty as amiable, and greater cruelty as more amiable, we might, if the frame of our mind were altered, love the ferocity which we now detest, and fly from freedom and general benevolence, to take shelter in some more delightful waste, where there might be the least possible desire of good, and the least possible enjoyment of it, among plunderers whom we loved much, and murderers whom we loved and honoured more – if any doubt of this kind could truly be felt, the reference which Dr Price would make, of our moral sentiments to reason, would leave the difficulty and the doubt exactly where they were before; since reason is but a principle of our mental frame, like the principle which is the source of moral emotion, and has no peculiar claim to remain unaltered in the supposed general alteration of our mental constitution. What we term reason, is only a brief expression of a number of separate feelings of relation, of which the mind might or might not have been formed to be susceptible. If the mind of man remain as it is, our moral feelings, in relation to their particular objects, are as stable as our feelings of any other class; and if the mind of man be altered in all its functions, it is absurd for us to make distinctions of classes of feelings in the general dissolution of every thing which we at present know – absurd even to guess at the nature of a state which arises from a change that is imaginary only, and that by our very supposition is to render us essentially different in every respect from the state with which we are at present acquainted.

It is a very powerless scepticism, indeed, which begins by supposing a total change of our nature. We might, perhaps, have been formed to admire only the cruel, and to hate only the benevolent; as in spite of an axiom, that now seems to us self-evident, we might all have been formed to think with the lunatic, that the cell in which he is confined is larger than the whole earth, of which it is a part. What the mind of a single madman is, the minds of all men might certainly be; and we might no longer feel the same moral relations, as we might no longer feel the same geometrical relations of space. But if the moral distinctions be as regular as the whole system of laws which carry on in unbroken harmony the motions of the universe, this regularity is sufficient for us while we exist on earth; and when we leave this earth, we carry with us a conscience which can have little fear, that the virtues which Heaven has made it so delightful for us to practice below, and which have been the chief instruments of producing a happiness which, when the universe was formed with such innumerable adaptations to the enjoyment of all who live, was surely not foreign to the intention of its Author, will, in that immortality, which is only a prolongation of this mortal life, be regarded with abhorrence by that great Being, whose perfections, however faintly, we have endeavoured to image, and who has here been so lavish to us of a love as constant in its approbation of moral good as the moral excellence which it has made happy.

Index

Abercrombie, John 21
Adamson, Robert 3
Akenside, Mark 142, 146
Aristotle 116
Atherstone, Edwin 3

Bacon, Francis 10
Bain, Alexander 5, 22
Belsham, Thomas 10
Berkeley, George 19, 20, 35, 55, 84, 109-10, 117
Blakey, Robert 20
Brougham, Henry 7
Buckle, Henry 12, 16

Campbell, George 62
Carlyle, Thomas 4, 5, 150
Chalmers, Thomas 5, 17, 21, 22-3
Cockburn, Henry 2, 11
Comte, Auguste 15-16
Condillac, Etienne de 1, 19-21, 123-4
Cousin, Victor 6
Cowper, William 56
Crousaz, Jean-Pierre de 119-20
Cudworth, Ralph 185

Darwin, Erasmus 6-10, 17, 20, 31-41
Descartes, René 117-18
Destutt de Tracy, Antoine 20

Erskine, William 7, 12, 17

Fraser, Alexander Campbell 12

Gilman, Samuel 4
Grant, Anne Macvicar 4
Gregory, James 6, 11, 16

Hamilton, William 4, 5-6, 11, 19-20
Hartley, David 17
Hobbes, Thomas 118, 174
Horner, Francis 7, 16
Hume, David 1, 2, 3, 6, 12-16, 17, 18, 19, 24, 43-88, 120, 122-3
Hutcheson, Francis 24, 179-85

James, William 5
Jeffrey, Francis 7, 11

Kant, Immanuel 10-11

Leslie, John 11-13, 16
Leyden, John 7
Locke, John 20, 118, 124
Lockhart, John Gibson 3
Lyall, William 21-2

Mackintosh, James 1, 7
Malebranche, Nicolas 117
March, Francis 4, 5
McCosh, James 2-3, 10, 20, 22
Mill, James 5, 16, 21
Mill, John Stuart 1, 4, 5, 9, 15-16, 21
Montesquieu, Baron de 150
Morell, J. D. 3, 20

Newton, Isaac 10, 32, 137

Paley, William 24, 171-4
Payne, George 21
Plato 166
Pope, Alexander 119
Porter, Noah 4
Price, Richard 184-8
Psillos, Stathis 13-14

Ramsay, George 21
Reid, Thomas 1, 3, 5, 11, 13, 15, 17-22, 35, 71, 73-82, 87, 111-26, 127, 131-2
Réthoré, François 5-6
Rollin, Bernard 14

Schneewind, Jerome 24
Scott, Walter 3, 11
Seneca 137
Shaftesbury, Earl of 179
Shepherd, Mary 13
Smith, Adam 175-8
Smith, Norman Kemp 15
Spencer, Herbert 5, 22

Stephen, Leslie 1, 16
Stewart, Dugald 6, 10, 12, 16-17, 19, 21, 23, 184

Terence 159
Toussaint, François-Vincent 167

Upham, Thomas 21

Villers, Charles 10

Wellek, René 10
Welsh, David 5, 8, 11, 21, 22
Whewell, William 4
Wright, John P. 16